People Skills for Managers

PEOPLE SKILLS FOR MANAGERS

Samuel A. Malone

The Liffey Press

Published by
The Liffey Press
Ashbrook House, 10 Main Street
Raheny, Dublin 5, Ireland
www.theliffeypress.com

A catalogue record of this book is
available from the British Library.

ISBN 978-1-905785-43-8

Printed in the Republic of Ireland by Colour Books

Contents

PREFACE

Managers spend most of their time interacting with staff. As people advance up the management hierarchy people skills become more critical than technical skills. People are often promoted into management positions because they were very technically competent in their previous role. However, this does not mean that they will have the skills to manage staff effectively. This book is aimed at managers who need to acquire the vital people skills needed for success in a management career. The book is divided into fourteen chapters, each one dealing with an essential people skill. To facilitate the learning process each chapter has a summary, a Memory Map overview, a people skills quotient and five practical things you can do to improve your skills in that specific area. Acronyms and inspirational quotations are sprinkled throughout the text.

After reading this book you will be able to:

❖ Improve your interpersonal relationships with others

❖ Deal with personality clashes

❖ Deal with difficult employees

❖ Use your communication skills to deal more successfully with employees

❖ Interpret and use non-verbal signals

❖ Identify your own and others' passive, aggressive and assertive behaviours

❖ Know when it is most useful to be assertive

❖ Say no without feeling guilty

❖ Resolve conflicts in the workplace

❖ Run effective performance appraisal interviews

❖ Coach employees to work more efficiently and effectively

❖ Delegate in appropriate circumstances

❖ Lead people successfully

❖ Deal effectively with discipline, grievance and counselling situations

❖ Motivate staff to achieve superior performance

❖ Build and lead teams including using facilitation skills to encourage dialogue and discussion

❖ Negotiate successfully

❖ Run effective meetings

❖ Conduct selection interviews in a professional manner.

Practising good **interpersonal skills** is the hallmark of a good manager. Good managers earn the trust of their staff by keeping their word and staying loyal to them. They expect their staff to stay loyal to them in return. Managers should understand the importance of emotional intelligence and practise the skills of empathy. They build rapport with staff by remembering their names and taking an interest in their welfare. Managers need to be good at managing upwards (i.e. their boss) as well as downwards (i.e. their staff).

A manager gets things done through people. To do this effectively the manager must practise the art of good **communication**. The higher up you go in the management hierarchy the greater the need for good interpersonal relationships and communication skills. We don't need to learn how to hear, as it is an innate capacity. However, we do need to learn how to listen. Most people feel that listening comes naturally. This is not true. Active listening must be learned and includes restating, summarising, paraphrasing and clarifying to check understanding. People like people who listen attentively to them. Listening is probably the easiest and best way to win friends, and influence people.

A good manager knows the difference between passive, aggressive and **assertive** behaviour. Passive people are submissive and taken for granted. Aggressive people get angry and upset at the least provocation. Assertive people assert their rights while respecting the rights of others. They seek win-win solutions to conflicts. The advantages of assertiveness are many and include expressing yourself confidently without hurting the feelings of others. Knowing when to be assertive is a vital skill for a manager.

Conflict is a natural part of life. Managers should know how to handle **conflict** situations in a satisfactory manner. Conflict can be interpersonal, group or organisational. Interpersonal conflict can be caused by different perceptions of roles. Group conflict can be caused by a lack of common goals. Organisational conflict can be caused by poor organisation structure or office politics. Minor disputes if not resolved at source may fester into major conflicts. Personality clashes can lead to needless arguments and disputes, and can result in a lack of co-operation between departments and employees.

Performance appraisal is part of a manager's job and is used to evaluate an employee with the objective of improving job competence. It can also be used to improve job satisfaction, career planning, management succession, manpower planning and as a basis for deciding levels of pay. The performance appraisal process should be continuous rather than just once a year. Managers need a variety of skills for the appraisal interview including communication, counselling, conflict resolution and problem solving.

Managers need the skills to handle **discipline, grievance and counselling** situations. A disciplinary situation arises if an employee breaches a rule or consistently fails to reach the required level of job performance. Disciplinary problems include breaking health and safety rules, unacceptable behaviour and insubordination. The disciplinary action steps include informal talk, oral warning, written warning and dismissal. The principles of natural justice include the right to question, defence and to consistency and fairness of treatment. When an employee alleges that the manager has acted unfairly against them you are dealing with a grievance. Counselling is the process of helping employees recognise their feelings about issues, define personal problems accurately and find solutions, or learn to accept a difficult situation.

A good manager will **coach** their employees to reach their full potential. There are similarities and differences between coaching, mentoring and training. All of these approaches can be used to improve the productivity of managers and staff. Coaching is just-in-time and is skills-

and performance-related. Mentoring is usually done by an internal manager other than the line manager and is development- and growth-oriented. Training is usually generic and just-in-case and more short term.

The modern manager needs to develop **leadership skills**. Leaders create an inspirational vision to gain the trust and commitment of staff to achieve goals. There are differences between managers and leaders. Managers implement policy and direct activities. Leaders create and enunciate policy and lead people. The sources of power and influence include physical, resource, personal, position and expert. The dark side of leadership includes withholding information and emotional immaturity. The best practices of leadership include creating a no-blame culture by encouraging employees to learn from their mistakes.

Since it is impossible to do everything oneself it pays to use the skills and expertise of others by **delegating** to them. Managers thus free themselves up to concentrate on the tasks of management. Managers might be reluctant to delegate because they fear that their staff will do a better job and they will be shown up as less competent. Employees may be reluctant to accept delegated tasks because they are already overworked and they fear criticism if they make mistakes. There are certain things a manager should not delegate including appraisal, discipline and hiring and firing. You can delegate authority but you can't delegate responsibility. The manager is ultimately responsible for the work of their section. You should delegate and not abdicate. If you delegate work to your staff you should give them sufficient authority and support to carry it out.

Managers need to be able to **motivate** themselves and others. Different things motivate people. What motivates one person will not necessarily motivate another. There are numerous ways of motivating staff. People feel more motivated if their views are valued and if they are consulted and involved in decision-making. A good way of motivating oneself is to become a lifelong learner and seek out ways of continually improving performance. Office politics and poor systems are some things staff find de-motivating. The power of expectation is a great motivator, as staff like to live up to their manager's expectations.

Managers need **team-building** skills as most employees now work in teams. It's critical that a manager knows how to build teams. Team development goes through five stages: forming, storming, norming, performing and adjourning. People adopt different roles within teams to make them run more effectively. In modern business the manager is moving from a directive to a facilitative style of management. **Facilitation** skills are needed to get teams to accept responsibility, develop team spirit and encourage collaboration. Group think can prevent a team from functioning successfully. Group think occurs when teams become arrogant and feel invulnerable to outside threats. To run an effective team, leaders need to inspire commitment and be supportive, visible and available when needed by the other team members. Team members need good interpersonal relationship skills and have expertise in problem-solving and creativity techniques such as brainstorming. To build an effective team, foster morale and develop trust, confidence and respect. Teams should be congruent with the culture of the company, meaning that they should be collaborative rather than competitive.

Managers spend a significant proportion of their time **negotiating** with employees, other managers, customers and suppliers. They thus need to know how to negotiate effectively. The basic skills of negotiation can be recalled by the acronym POCKET. This stands for **p**lan, have an **o**pening position, **c**ommunicate, **k**now your opponent, **e**xplore options and **t**erminate or conclude. There are numerous negotiation strategies for different situations. Persuasion skills will help you get others to do willingly what you want them to do. Support your case by relying on precedent, quoting an impartial eminent source or claiming that it has been conceded to others in the past in similar circumstances.

Managers spend a good deal of their time either running **meetings** or attending them. They therefore need to know how an effective meeting is organised. Before the meeting you should plan and prepare and circulate an agenda. At the meeting start promptly, finish on time, and during the meeting encourage participation. After the meeting you should write up the minutes and circulate action plans. Some of the pitfalls include allowing interruptions, tolerating talkative people to dominate proceedings, and allowing people to get off the point. The chairman should ensure that the rules of the meeting are adhered to and give participants an equal chance of contributing. A good meeting will have clear objectives and stick to the agenda. The main role of participants at a meeting is to come prepared, obey the rules and make a contribution.

As a manager you will conduct interviews from time to time. A **selection interview** is held to assess the suitability of a candidate for a particular job. Before the interview it's important to prepare thoroughly and do a checklist of questions to ask. Study the CV, application form, job description and person specification. During the interview put the candidate at ease and let them do most of the talking. When closing the interview inform the candidate when they will hear from you. Common mistakes of interviewing include talking too much, not identifying the key success factors for the job and relying too much on hunch rather than objective judgement.

Samuel A. Malone
March 2008

1

INTERPERSONAL RELATIONSHIPS

☑ What are influencing skills?

☑ What is the Johari Window?

☑ How can you build up rapport?

☑ What are the attributes of a good manager?

☑ How can you manage upwards?

INTRODUCTION

Managers need good interpersonal skills to do their jobs effectively. They need to create a vision of the future and get their employees' commitment behind it. Good managers generate trust by keeping their promises and being loyal to their staff. You need to understand yourself if you are to understand others. The Johari Window will help you acquire self-knowledge and the life positions matrix will help you understand the perspectives of others. Build rapport with others by being pleasant and adopting positive body language. Practise the skills of empathy by being aware of the importance of emotional intelligence. Remembering people's names and taking an interest in their lives is an important aspect of building rapport. Good managers need to be able to handle difficult employees and be flexible and creative as well as being logical. As a manager, you will need to acquire the skills of managing your boss effectively as well as being able to manage your staff.

INFLUENCING SKILLS

Influencing means getting others to do willingly what you want them to do in an unobtrusive manner. Influencing issues can be categorised under three headings: managerial, relationship and staff management.

Managerial Issues

❖ Create a vision of the future and share it with employees. They will only feel that they own the vision if they helped formulate it. This will give them a sense of ownership and a commitment to see it through to fruition. The vision must be backed up by realistic and measurable goals so that progress towards its achievement can be measured. Get the staff to commit, verbally or in writing, to the vision because then they are more likely to honour that commitment.

❖ Set challenging goals. Buckingham (2005) found research showing that managers with self-assurance set high goals, persist in the face of obstacles and have the resilience to bounce back when setbacks occur.

❖ Aristotle identified three types of influence: logos, pathos, and ethos. *Logos* is the logic of an argument supported by proof to make a case. This approach would be very successful if everybody was a logical, linear thinker. *Pathos* is an appeal to the emotions. People are emotional in nature and are strongly influenced by their emotions. *Ethos* is an appeal based on the speaker's perceived character. For Aristotle, ethos is the most important source of influence. If the listener does not trust or believe the speaker, logic or emotion will have little effect. Thus a manager with demonstrated ethical values will command a high level of respect and influence. Espoused values are not the same as enacted ones. The manager must walk the talk to gain employees' trust and credibility.

❖ Generate trust by doing what you say you will do and by being loyal to your staff. Mutual trust means that staff can rely on you and you can rely on them. Trust is won by having a high sense of integrity, being honest, telling the truth and doing what is ethically right. Trust is like a bank account: hard to fill but easy to empty. Managers who tell the truth are trusted more by their staff even if at times they find the truth hard to swallow. Those who are guarded in what they say and put on a false front are unlikely to be trusted by their staff.

❖ Be credible. Authentic managers are honest with themselves as well as being honest with others. This is the opposite of being phoney as in pretending to be something that you are not.

❖ Double check information that you receive. This will ensure that decisions are objective and based on sound advice and information. If you are unsure about the likely reception to a change of policy use the grapevine to test the reaction you will get. Discuss issues with as many interested parties as possible so that you can gauge the reaction to important decisions beforehand. This will help to anticipate problems and take corrective action before it is too late.

❖ Be imaginative. Develop your creative as well as analytical abilities. Foster the ability to cut through convoluted arguments and complex problems to reveal the basic issues underneath.

"Today the most useful person in the world is the man or woman who knows how to get along with other people. Human relations is the most important science in the broad curriculum of living." — Stanley C. Allen

---

Relationship Issues

❖ Influence others by maintaining good relationships. Be human and keep your feet on the ground by staying on friendly terms with employees, customers and suppliers. Show that you value and appreciate them by being courteous at all times, as good manners cost nothing but will win you the respect of all you come in contact with. Rudeness and arrogance are never acceptable.

❖ Always acknowledge mistakes, as you are not infallible. Apologise when you make a mistake or do something inappropriate. This is not a sign of weakness. President Kennedy accepted full responsibility for the disastrous Bay of Pigs operation and afterwards his popularity in the polls soared higher than ever.

❖ Develop a positive assertive attitude and encourage staff to do likewise. Ask employees directly, clearly and confidently what you want them to do. See staff strengths rather than weaknesses. Focus on solutions rather than problems. Banish the fear of failure from your employees. Get them to learn from their mistakes and accept responsibility. Create a no-blame culture by seeing mistakes as learning opportunities.

❖ Scarcity affects the value not only of goods but of information as well. Goods become more desirable as they become scarce and less available. Likewise, information considered exclusive or that confers unique benefits is more persuasive. Give the impression that the information given is exclusive and confidential to staff. This will increase the strength of its influence and the desirability of its acquisition.

"The deepest principle in human nature is the craving to be appreciated." — William James

---

Staff Management Issues

❖ Use your staff as colleagues and advisers, not mere employees. Share relevant information with staff by being approachable and accessible. Employees prefer to be kept informed by their manager about company performance and developments, particularly those that have an impact on their immediate jobs or future employment prospects. However, the grapevine is the main source of information for employees despite the fact that it is inaccurate much of the time. The grapevine has its uses but should not be relied on exclusively. Unfounded rumours can do untold damage to a business and so managers should ensure that the grapevine is fed accurate and up-to-date information.

❖ Treat people equally. Employees like their managers to be fair and consistent in their dealings with them. A manager should not have favourites among staff. Always act impartially and respect the human dignity of staff and never undermine their sense of self-worth.

❖ Get to know staff as well as you know the company you work for. Take a genuine interest in their welfare. Do this by active listening to find out their wishes, concerns, ambitions and needs. The best way of doing this is by being available to staff when they need you. Social gatherings for employees and their families provide the opportunity to get to know people better in an informal context and creates a sense of belonging that will transfer to the work place.

❖ Demonstrate that you care about staff by empowering them to make decisions and to take responsibility for results. Make people feel powerful and capable by delegating authority and encouraging them to accept challenges. The art of delegation is dealt with in Chapter 9. Exploit the differences between people by using and developing their unique abilities. Fine tune jobs to match their individual needs and abilities. Find ways for individuals to grow and develop on the job. Be conscious that knowledge workers may need more scope to use their initiative than others do.

❖ Make your expectations known so that staff are aware of exactly what they need to do to achieve desired results. Tell them how they are doing so that they are in a position to improve their performance if necessary.

❖ Reward employees as appropriate with money, praise and recognition. Catch people doing things right and praise them. Praise should be given as near to the event as possible for greatest effect. Always qualify the praise with the reason for giving it as undeserved praise will only arouse cynicism and is counterproductive. There is nothing more meaningful than a simple sincere "thank you" for a job well done.

❖ Encourage staff development by acting as a role model. Demonstrate that you are a lifelong learner and encourage staff to be likewise. Coach and mentor them to develop their skills. Book them on appropriate courses to broaden their horizons. Get to know the learning styles of staff so that you can match them with appropriate on-the-job and off-the-job learning opportunities.

"Recognition for a job well done is high on the list of motivating influences for all people; more important in many instances than compensation itself. When someone is promoted, a promotion that everyone could see coming because of an excellent record, the entire department is stimulated. For it is clear, then, that promotion is based on merit. A promotion that seems to come out of the blue, which is always the case when no one knows what the next fellow is doing, causes nothing but resentment and a further weakening of the will to work." – John M. Wilson

---

AMICABLE MODEL

There are many different influencing styles that can be practised by a manager. What suits you and the context in which they are used will be deciding factors. Practising the ideas contained in this model will win you the respect of your staff. AMICABLE is an acronym that will help you do this:

❖ **A**uthority. People admire and look up to authority figures. In the modern world we routinely look to legal, financial, medical or technical experts for advice and so we are more likely to defer to managers with authority, knowledge and expertise. Keep up to date in your specialist field so that you know what your are talking about and win the respect of your staff. Relying too much on positional authority may backfire. Thus the autocratic style of management is not recommended and may breed resentment and can often turn into intimidation.

❖ **M**arketing. Selling ideas to staff is often effective, particularly if the topic is new to them. Another technique of marketing is influencing people to buy by giving them free gifts. This is the principle of reciprocation, meaning that people feel obliged to return a favour. Give and take is a normal part of everyday life. If you are obliging, supportive and helpful to staff they are likely to act likewise with you. Provide evidence that other employees are doing what you suggest. Most of us are influenced to behave in a particular way if we believe other people like ourselves are doing the same. If you can convince people that they have control over the situation then they are more likely to be persuaded to do it.

"Leadership is based on inspiration, not domination; on cooperation, not intimidation." – William Arthur Ward

---

❖ **I**mpassive. People who are calm under pressure earn the respect of their staff. Managers who lose their temper will be seen as irrational, volatile and emotionally unpredictable. Impassive managers quietly, calmly and patiently demonstrate the validity of their case to staff to win them over.

❖ **C**ollaborative. Managers who are friendly and collaborative are liked by their staff and thus likely to win their trust, respect and co-operation. The good manager knows how to complement the styles of other team members, coordinate team efforts without managing them, get members involved in decision making and build consensus.

❖ **A**ssertive. Assertive male managers tend to be seen as self-assured and having greater credibility, while assertive female managers are sometimes perceived as "pushy" and "masculine". The more women in higher management the less likely this attitude will pre-vail, however. Employees admire assertive traits in managers such as decisiveness, confidence and persistence.

❖ **B**argaining. The good manager aims for win-win solutions rather than win-lose. By making concessions on both sides you will reach a mutually acceptable agreement. This wins the respect of employees rather than their resentment because they see they are not being exploited.

❖ **L**ogical. Managers who solve problems in a logical way and build conclusions on the basis of factual evidence rather than hearsay will win the respect of employees. However, don't go overboard on the logic as you will need to connect emotionally with your staff as well.

❖ **E**motional intelligence. Managers who are emotionally intelligent by being sensitive to the moods and concerns of their employees win their respect. The sensitive manager knows how to listen without judging or giving unwanted advice. Commenting diplomatically that an employee seems to be a bit down is often taken as a sign of car-ing rather than prying. Judge staff by their actions rather than their words as an employee will often say one thing but do another.

"There is nothing which we receive with so much reluctance as ad-vice." – Joseph Addison

---

SELF-KNOWLEDGE

As a manager the more you know about yourself the better. Understand your flaws and weaknesses because these are the shortcomings that will get you into trouble. The more accurate feedback you get from others the more self-knowledgeable you will be about your own behaviour and how it affects others. Undertake a 360 degree feedback if you feel you have the maturity to accept its findings and the courage to take corrective action.

The Johari Window

The Johari Window will help you become more self-assured and transparent in your dealings with others. It was designed to help people understand how they interact with others and how disclosing personal information can improve rapport. Johari is named after the creators of the model, Joe Luft and Harry Ingram. The Johari Window as illustrated in Figure 1 is a two-by-two table that contrasts areas of public and private information.

The first box of the window is known as the public or open area. This represents information known to both yourself and others, including your experience, skills and expressed views. A person's idiosyncrasies, manner of speech, mode of dress, marital status and favourite pastimes will be in the public area. Other people's perceptions about your behaviour, views, attitude, feelings, emotions, knowledge, skills and experience may be known. This is the type of information that facilitates communication, rapport and interaction with others. According to the model, the more information that is in the public area the greater the co-operation and the less mistrust, confusion, conflict and misunderstanding. Good managers build trust by sharing information. Where information is lacking it is human nature to fill the void by rumour and gossip. Gossip reflects the culture of an organisation. Malicious gossip suggests an organisation that is secretive and vindictive. Self-disclosure requires a great deal of self-confidence and trust. The size of the public area can be increased horizontally into the blind area, by giving and getting feedback, and can be increased vertically into the closed area by self-disclosure. Top performing organisations encourage the expansion of the public area by policies of open communication and transparency.

"Knowledge of the self is the mother of all knowledge. So it is incumbent on me to know my self, to know it completely, to know its minutiae, its characteristics, its subtleties, and its very atoms."
– Kahlil Gibran

The second box of the window is the blind area and occurs when others know information about you that you do not know yourself. For example, staff might know that you are usually in a bad mood early in the morning but by the afternoon your mood improves for the better. So if they want to get approval for something from you the best time to look for it is in the afternoon. Thus managers with large blind areas can be difficult to deal with and are often insensitive and inaccessible to others without being conscious of it. They are totally unaware what people think about them and may not realise that they are arrogant, patronising or talk too much, or at times that they are rude. They may lack sensitivity about particular mannerisms they have that are annoying, irritating or distracting to others. Managers should promote a climate of non-judgemental feedback. This reduces fear and encourages disclosure on all sides. Feedback will help managers eliminate their weaknesses and help them become more self-aware and self-actualised.

Figure 1: The Johari Window

Your View of Yourself

		Known	Unknown
Others' View of You	*Known*	Public Area	Blind Area
	Unknown	Closed Area	Unknown Area

The third box of the window is the closed or hidden area. It represents information known to you but not shared with others. This area may include personal feelings about others, your opinion about the boss, views on sensitive issues and information about one's personal life. It may also include fears, hidden agendas, secrets and manipulative intentions. People keep information in the closed area because they feel that disclosure would damage their reputation, undermine their position in the hierarchy, or hinder their chances of promotion. Where trust in an organisation is low, then the closed area will be large, and the public area will be small. On the other hand, where trust is high in the organisation, the closed area will be small and the public area will be large. Managers will differ to the extent that they are prepared to disclose personal information. It is natural and often wise to keep private information relating to one's personal life hidden, and ultimately the amount of disclosure will be at the manager's discretion. A small closed area reduces the potential for confusion, misunderstanding and poor communication. The culture of the organisation will have a major influence on a manager's willingness to disclose information. A bureaucratic culture tends to be cautious and secretive and encourages cumbersome paper procedures.

The fourth box of the window is called the unknown area so that information in this box is unknown to oneself and others. It includes unconscious motivations, repressed feelings and past memories. One may also be unaware of latent abilities, aptitudes, subconscious feelings, repressed desires and certain attitudes and motivations. Most of us have acquired conditioned behaviour and attitudes from childhood. Some psychologists believe that information from the unknown area has an important impact on the way people behave in all areas. One would expect young people, and people who lack experience or self-belief, to have large unknown areas. Providing staff with the opportunity to develop new experiences and skills is often a useful way to discover unknown abilities, and thereby reduce the unknown area.

Conclusions on Johari

As a manager, create a work environment that encourages two-way feedback, self-discovery and self-development. Help staff to reach their potential and become self-actualised by discovering and developing their talents. It is a well-known fact that most employees in organisations are working well below their potential.

Obviously, the Johari Window can be very useful as a personal development tool. When we meet people for the first time we tend to be reserved and are reluctant to disclose much about ourselves. The open window is thus very small. As trust and familiarity develop we become less inhibited and disclose more and more about ourselves. Our background, history, beliefs, attitudes, needs and ambitions become known. Thus the open window becomes larger and the closed window becomes smaller.

To increase the open window further it is necessary to reduce the blind area. This can be achieved by being more open and honest and by seeking and accepting feedback from other people. As the open area grows and the hidden and blind areas diminish, it is likely that the unknown area will reduce as well. This will lead to greater self-awareness, self-confidence, transparency and rapport with others.

Unfortunately, most organisations encourage the expansion rather than the contraction of the closed area. Companies tend to hire hands rather than hearts and minds and show only superficial interest in people's personal and domestic lives. Dealing with personal issues is viewed as a minefield exposing managers to problems demanding their valuable time and attention.

UNDERSTANDING OTHERS

Harris (1969) describes four fundamental life positions that will help you understand the behaviour of others.

1. **I'm okay – You're okay**: People who hold this position see themselves as interdependent with others and their environment. They are self-confident, happy and comfortable with themselves and view others as likewise. They are more likely to seek social support and network with others and have no difficulty being assertive, open and discussing their problems. Because they see others as okay, other people will reciprocate in a similar fashion. This is a position of mutual recognition and self-respect.

2. **I'm okay – You're not okay**: People who adopt this position are angry and consider that they can only rely on themselves. They consider other people as worthless and potential enemies and so they may try to dominate and bully them. They are suspicious and blame everybody else for their problems and so consider it pointless to speak out, as they believe nobody will do anything to help them.

3. **I'm not okay – You're okay**: People who adapt this life position feel helpless and have an inferiority complex. They compare themselves unfavourably with others and lack self-confidence and have low self-esteem. If they have problems, they blame themselves because they are incompetent or lack sufficient influence to change events.

4. **I'm not okay – You're not okay:** People with this life position feel hopeless and consider themselves and others equally worthless and are consumed with negative feelings. They feel disconnected from

others and from their environment and tend to be introverted and obsessed with their own problems and concerns. Consequently, they are likely to be depressed and lack motivation and interest in life.

Figure 2: Life Positions

I'm OK You're OK *Happy*	I'm OK You're not OK *Angry*
I'm not OK You're OK *Helpless*	I'm not OK You're not OK *Hopeless*

From a manager's perspective, adopting the first position means you are positive about yourself, self-confident, assertive and willing to delegate. These skills are particularly appropriate if you want to avoid work overload and burnout by asserting yourself and delegating appropriately. The other three life positions do not make an effective manager. Feeling angry, helpless or hopeless is not a recipe for success.

BUILDING RAPPORT

The following are some behaviours you can practise to build rapport with your staff. They can be divided into non-verbal and verbal approaches.

Non-Verbal Communication (NVC)

❖ Smile sincerely. A smile lights up your face and encourages others to smile back, however a false smile will be seen as insincere. Even forcing a smile may put you in a better mood. Try smiling at yourself in the mirror early in the morning to start the day on a positive note.

> "The most effective way to achieve right relations with any living thing is to look for the best in it, and then help that best into the fullest expression."— Allen J. Boone

❖ Keep a relaxed open stance. Show that you are friendly, open and welcoming rather than closed, distant and unapproachable.

❖ Lean slightly towards the other person to show you're engaged, but do not invade their personal space.

❖ Maintain eye contact, however don't stare! Occasionally break eye contact when you feel it is appropriate to do so.

❖ Occasionally touch the other person on the elbow or shoulder in a friendly non-invasive way. Personal contact should be done very sensitively, however, as it has the potential for creating difficulties. It may be misunderstood as an invasion of privacy or even sexual harassment.

❖ Mirror the other person's behaviour such as their breathing, rate of speech, tone of voice, hand movements and posture. If a person is sitting, you should sit too. People like people who are like themselves. As Aristotle first pointed out, birds of a feather stick together.

Verbal Communication

❖ Use the other person's name during the conversation. If you are likely to meet the person again be sure to remember their name as the sweetest sound to another person's ears is the sound of their own name.

❖ Use humour as appropriate. In this politically correct world, however, sexist and racist jokes are unacceptable and should be avoided.

❖ Emphasise the things on which you agree such as shared beliefs and values. This forms the basis for all good relationships.

❖ Build goodwill by meeting the needs of your staff and helping them solve personal issues. Move quickly to resolve interpersonal conflicts.

❖ Practise the skills of empathy. Make staff feel valued as individuals by tuning into their feelings and understand where they are coming from.

❖ Know the importance of emotional intelligence. Understand yourself and be able to express yourself in a friendly and tactful way, having regard to the sensitivities and needs of others. Control your anger, impulses and desires so that you do not upset others.

❖ Develop political awareness, which is often described as political savvy. It is the ability to read hidden agendas, to work the formal and informal decision making processes in the company and to decipher the subtext of what is said or not said. It also means the ability to get things done informally without relying on formal status and authority.

"The tragedy of life is in what dies inside a man while he lives — the death of genuine feeling, the death of inspired response, the death of the awareness that makes it possible to feel the pain or the glory of other men in yourself." — Norman Cousins

---

Rapport Breakers

The following are behaviours to be avoided because they prevent rapport from developing. The acronym DAFT TIP will help you remember the points:

❖ **D**ogmatic. The more dogmatic you are in your approach to people, the more likely they are to resist. People are very reluctant to give up their own beliefs, values and attitudes, especially when they feel pressurised or intimidated.

❖ **A**rguing. If you argue with people they are likely to argue back, but are more likely to agree with you if you show consideration and try to understand their point of view.

❖ **F**ormal language. Build up rapport with people by talking to them in a friendly conversational way. Formal language is a barrier to understanding.

❖ **T**alkative. People like people who actively listen to them. They get defensive if talked down to, or have to deal with someone who wants to dominate the conversation. We all prefer dialogue to monologue.

❖ **T**hinking for others. Doing other people's thinking for them is patronising. A phrase like "what you don't seem to realise is ..." can be insulting.

❖ **I**rritators. Phrases such as "with respect", "let's be realistic", and "I'm perfectly reasonable" annoy people and should be avoided.

❖ **P**arental language. When talking to children parents often use words such as "can't", "must", "should" and, "ought". Delivered to an adult these create resistance rather than rapport.

REMEMBERING NAMES

As a manager you should do everything you can to develop the skill of remembering names. Employees respect managers who take the trouble to get to know their names and something about their backgrounds. The acronym MEMORY will help you develop the skill of remembering names:

❖ **M**inutes not seconds. When you meet an employee for the first time take the opportunity to absorb their name rather than being preoccupied with your own thoughts. This takes concentrated attention, reflection and practice. Most people are so conscious of themselves, and what they are going to say next, that they fail to hear and register the other person's name. Ask them to repeat their name, if necessary, as people usually don't mind this as they appreciate the interest you are taking in them. If their name is strange ask them to spell it for you. Imagine their name printed in large capital letters emblazoned on their forehead.

❖ **E**valuate. Ask questions about the name, as curiosity is the key to a good memory. Inquire about the name's origin and the person's background. Family names have a unique history and meaning attached to them. What county or country does the name originate from? What does it mean? Can you name any famous people with the same name? Then link the person's name you want to remember with the famous name. Use the power of visualisation by painting word pictures to remember names. For example, to remember Walker you could visualise the person with a rucksack or a walking frame. Your ability to paint word pictures is only limited by your imagination. All these questions will help you to imprint the name on your mind.

"The secret of a good memory is attention, and attention to a subject depends upon our interest in it. We rarely forget that which has made a deep impression on our minds." — Tryon Edwards

---

❖ **M**ake an effort. Use the name frequently but naturally during the conversation. Link the face to the name in a memorable fashion, for example, to a prominent feature of the face. Also, you can link the name to a person you know already. Imagine in your mind's eye the two people shaking hands with each other, or make it more memorable by seeing them argue or fighting over some dispute or in some slapstick situation. Lastly, make sure you address the person by name when saying your goodbyes.

❖ **O**rganise. Do this by exchanging business cards if these are available. Otherwise, write the name into your diary with a few points about the individual to help you place them in context for the future, for example, where they come from, what they do for a living and where they currently reside. Background family information will help you put the name in a stronger context.

❖ **R**epeat and review. Repetition is the secret of a good memory. Constantly review information to imprint it on your long-term memory. Occasionally look up your diary and bring the person to mind so that if you meet them again you will remember their name. Similarly, review the business cards you have collected. Use your powers of imagination and visualisation to recall their face and general appearance. When going to a meeting or conference review the names of the participants before you go.

❖ **Y**our curiosity. Exercise curiosity about the person and build up a dossier by inquiring with others who may know something about their background. Look up the telephone number in the directory and see if they are listed. If they are members of a professional body looking up a membership directory will reinforce the name.

HANDLING DIFFICULT PEOPLE

Most of us come in contact with difficult people from time to time. In everyday life you may be able to avoid or ignore such people. However, as a manager you have to work with these people and you should know how to successfully manage them. There are different types of difficult people. Some are aggressive, others are complainers and procrastinators. Some have a negative attitude to life and others are indecisive. Some are argumentative while others are moody and silent. Some are perfectionists while others love to work to a deadline. Some are sycophants and others are know-it-all experts. Some make impractical suggestions or question every instruction. Some are rude and say harsh things behind your back about you.

Irrespective of what is said you should not take it personally or react in a confrontational way. As a manager your job is to create a pleasant working environment for staff by encouraging collaboration and maintaining morale and productivity. To do this you must have the flexibility to adapt your style to different situations and personalities. Below are some suggestions on how to deal with difficult people:

❖ Establish the facts. Don't jump to conclusions. Maybe it's not the person's fault and you may be partly to blame. It takes self-knowledge and courage to admit you are part of the problem and should take the initiative to improve someone else's behaviour by changing your own. Ask questions to ascertain how the employee sees the situation from their perspective and listen carefully to what they say. Acknowledge their feelings while controlling the natural urge to interrupt or argue. Enquire if you can do anything differently to improve or rectify the situation. For example, you may be giving instructions in a cursory way without adequate explanation or without giving the employee an opportunity to raise questions and explore issues.

"Eventually we will find (mostly in retrospect, of course) that we can be very grateful to those people who have made life most difficult for us." — Ayya Khema

---

❖ Do not make the mistake of responding in public to sarcastic or rude remarks, personal attacks or other inappropriate behaviour by a difficult employee. Instead, inform the employee that you will discuss the matter later in private. Public criticism is always demotivational for the employee and nobody wants to lose face in front of colleagues. In private, praise the employee's good points but tell them that certain behaviours are unacceptable in the workplace. Behave in a cool, polite and professional manner. Make it clear what your expectations are regarding acceptable behaviour for the future. It is your duty to help employees understand when their actions are perceived as disrespectful and suggest to them alternative ways of behaving.

❖ Out of character behaviour. If employees have become argumentative and difficult to deal with it may because they are having personal problems. They may have a parent who is sick or their marriage may be breaking up. The manager should discreetly enquire with other employees to find out the reason for the sudden change in behaviour. If this is not successful they should raise the issue in a diplomatic and sensitive way with the employee concerned.

❖ The energies of chronic complainers may be productively directed elsewhere. Their talents might be used to spot mistakes, flaws in design, or inconsistencies in planning. Their ability to critique may help you eradicate mistakes that otherwise could spell disaster. They may help you identify the reasons for customer complaints and service problems. In this way the chronic complainer's talents may be directed in a more constructive way.

❖ Directly challenge the person with the problem behaviour. Tell them the detrimental effect their behaviour is having on you, fellow workers and the work situation. Sometimes being confrontational can stop the negative behaviour on track and clear the air. Care must be taken to criticise the behaviour and not the person, however.

**"Arrogance and rudeness are training wheels on the bicycle of life — for weak people who cannot keep their balance without them."
— Laura Teresa Marquez**

❖ Micromanaging staff. Most people like to get on with the job without too much interference. You may be creating a difficult employee by looking over their shoulder all the time. When you delegate work to your staff you should tell them what to do but not how to do it. Let them exercise their own initiative on developing the methodology of doing the job. This will prevent arguments about how the job should be done.

❖ Leave the situation alone if the benefits of doing something are not worth the risks involved. Some problems tend to disappear or get forgotten with the passage of time. Another option is to decide to be neutral in your reaction to the problem behaviour and behave as if it doesn't bother you. If the difficult person provides you with what you want when you need it then you may be willing to over-look the problem behaviour.

❖ Redesign the job. Some people may be difficult because they are bored with the job they have. Improve the situation by job simplifi-cation, job rotation, job enlargement or job enrichment. Cumber-some procedures can be rationalised by reducing the number of forms involved and by improving the methods and reducing the op-erations needed to do the work. Moving people around between different jobs can relieve boredom as they will learn new things, be confronted with new challenges and meet new people. When peo-ple are removed from what they perceive to be an unpleasant work environment, their perspectives change and the problem behaviour may go away.

❖ When everything else fails you may need to avail of mediation ser-vices or in more extreme cases take disciplinary action such as transfer, demotion or dismissal to sort out the situation. Discipline, grievance and counselling are discussed in Chapter 6.

PERSONAL ATTRIBUTES OF A GOOD MANAGER

Personality plays a big part in the success of any manager. The acronym PEACE will help you remember some of the desired traits of a good manager:

❖ **P**ersonally imaginative. A combination of creativity and logical think-ing will help generate alternatives and solve problems. In these times of lifelong learning and continuous improvement a creative approach to solving problems is necessary. Creative people tend to be intellectually curious and enjoy new experiences such as getting involved in training and development opportunities and new learn-ing situations.

❖ **E**xtroversion. Management is about working with and through other people. Managers need to be sociable, gregarious and assertive. Interpersonal relationship and good communication skills are a requisite to doing the job effectively. Introverts are more suited to research and specialist type jobs and people who are reserved, quiet and shy are unlikely to make successful managers.

❖ **A**greeableness. Ideally, managers should be empathic, good-natured and cooperative. Managers spend a lot of their time in the company of others so it is important that they can get on with other people and be sensitive to their needs. To be a successful manager you need to be politically astute.

❖ **C**onscientious. Managers need to have a good work ethic if they are to be successful at their jobs. They should be dependable, reliable, careful and thorough. Managers are hired to achieve desired results.

❖ **E**motional maturity. Good managers are positive, optimistic, confident and resilient and are sensitive to their own needs and to the needs of others. They are able to handle stressful situations without getting agitated and solve interpersonal conflicts satisfactorily. They know how to control their own emotions and pacify the emotions of others. They have a strong sense of self-belief and have the resilience to bounce back from difficult situations.

"One of the great undiscovered joys of life comes from doing everything one attempts to the best of one's ability. There is a special sense of satisfaction, a pride in surveying such a work, a work which is rounded, full, exact, complete in its parts, which the superficial person who leaves his or her work in a slovenly, slipshod, half-finished condition, can never know. It is this conscientious completeness which turns any work into art. The smallest task well done, becomes a miracle of achievement." — Og Mandino

---

UNDERSTANDING PERSONALITY TYPES

An understanding of personality will help us become more effective managers as we become aware that different personalities require different approaches. Psychologists have researched personality and have come up with various models. One of the most popular and useful is the Myers-

Briggs Type Indicator (MBTI). A brief overview of this model will help the manager to become aware of the importance of personality when dealing with people. The model presents four categories: Extraversion–Introversion, Sensing–Intuition, Thinking–Feeling, and Judging–Perceiving. These preferences result in 16 personality types. We all exhibit these behaviours in different combinations and to different degrees. The MBTI is an instrument requiring a professional to administer and evaluate it.

1. *Extraversion–Introversion*. Extraverts like to focus on the outer world of people and things and are energised by them. They like interpersonal relationships and are action-oriented. If they understand something they like to explain it to others. They enjoy working in teams. Extraverts like to respond to things quickly and tend to talk before they think things through thoroughly. They tend to be animated during a conversation and use a lot of body language. Introverts tend to look inwards at concepts, thoughts, ideas and impressions. They like theories and abstract models and tend to think things through before they speak. They like frameworks to integrate and connect information so that it becomes meaningful. They can be sociable but are usually reserved and may be shy with strangers. They prefer concentration to interaction and are more comfortable when dealing with people on a one-to-one basis. They like to reflect on issues and to plan carefully before they take any action. They don't use much body language during conversation. People are both extraverted and introverted with one type dominant over the other. The dominant one is expressed in conscious behaviour.

2. *Sensing–Intuition*. This describes what people pay attention to and their preferred way of taking in information. Sensing people use all their senses such as sight, hearing and touch and like detail and facts. They tend to focus on the here and now and on concrete information gained through their senses. They prefer organisation and structure. They like the practical and to discover things for themselves. Intuitive people tend to focus on the future with a view to seeing patterns and possibilities. They like to see relationships between facts that they have collected. They are imaginative and like new ideas and stimulating assignments. They trust their hunches and like to see the big picture. They love variety and prefer to work on several projects at the same time. Their office environment is often untidy with their desk cluttered with files, books and magazines.

3. *Thinking–Feeling*. This describes the preferred way of making decisions. Thinking people are logical and objective and like to have the facts before making a decision. They like to discover cause and effect relationships. They appreciate visions, goals and objectives, as they like to know where they are going and what they should be aiming for. Clear, precise objectives and action plans are the driving force for thinking people. They tend to be cold, detached and impersonal. This person's working environment is tidy and organised. Feeling people are value-driven and emotion plays a significant part in their lives. They value interpersonal relationships and harmony with others, and focus on human values and needs when making judgements or decisions. They like attending meetings and working in teams. Their office environment tends to be personalised with family photos, certificates and group photos of staff adorning the wall.

4. *Judging–Perceiving*. Judging people like a planned and organised approach to life and are decisive, proactive, self-organised and driven by deadlines. They like to finish jobs, only want to know the essentials, and take action quickly. They like to be led by an organised time-driven manager. Perceiving people prefer a flexible, spontaneous approach, and like to keep their options open. They are curious, adaptive and creative and tend to leave things to the last minute. They often start jobs that they find difficult to finish. They thus need to be managed and monitored to ensure that they get the job done on schedule. Deadlines keep perceptive people disciplined and on target.

MANAGING UPWARDS

Many managers are good at managing their staff but poor at managing their own boss. As a manager you will need to acquire the skills of managing your boss as well as managing staff. This is important if you have ambitions to move up the career ladder. The following are some tips to manage your boss effectively.

❖ Know the type of boss you're working for. Study their management style, temperament, likes and dislikes, strengths and weaknesses, and idiosyncrasies. Some managers like to be kept informed verbally while others prefer written reports and memoranda. Find out what the preferences, priorities and goals of your boss are.

❖ Never gossip about or bad-mouth your boss. Even if you have genuine concerns about their managerial competencies keep them to yourself. Nobody is perfect. Learn to work around your boss's shortcomings and try to compensate for them. On the other hand, your boss will appreciate open and honest feedback.

❖ Build trust by being supportive, loyal and reliable. Trust takes a long time to build up but can be destroyed instantly. Don't argue aggressively with your boss if you value your career, as it is likely to be counterproductive. Be more diplomatic in your approach if you have genuine concerns or disagreements about work issues.

❖ Match your strengths to your boss's weaknesses. Support your boss in every way and help them do their job successfully. Encourage your boss to delegate tasks to you that you're particularly competent to do.

❖ Under-promise and over-deliver. Build up your reputation by over-delivering on your promises. People are particularly impressed with people who exceed expectations.

❖ Focus on solutions rather than problems. Never bring a problem to your boss without having thought out possible solutions first. Offer suggestions on how to fix immediate problems and how to avoid likely ones in the future. This gives you an opportunity to demonstrate problem solving and creative abilities. A good boss won't steal your ideas and will give you credit for them.

❖ Take every opportunity to make a good impression on your boss. Use opportunities like presentations, chairing meetings, assignments and budgets to make your mark.

"If the boss is a jerk, get over it. First of all, don't you think there's a good chance that your boss's boss knows what's going on? If so, just keep your head down and do the work. Usually, if you put in maximum effort and produce excellent results, someone in the company is going to take notice. Either you will get promoted or your jerky boss will get the heave-ho. It happens all the time." – Suze Orman

---

❖ Compliment your boss in a genuine way on their strengths and special expertise. Likewise, don't be reluctant to accept compliments. Accept them graciously rather than downplaying them.

❖ Keep your boss informed on a management-by-exception basis, by concentrating on the important rather than the routine. Your boss will not appreciate surprises. If the problem is first heard on the management grapevine then be prepared for trouble.

❖ Get regular feedback from your boss on your performance. Don't wait until the annual performance review. Have plenty of time to put things right if need be. Find out exactly what the boss's expectations for you are. What should your goals be and what will the boss hold you accountable for? How will your performance be measured? Make your career goals known to your boss.

❖ Keep your boss informed about your successes. Unsolicited written accolades from other managers or customers about a job well done should be forwarded to your boss. If you have acquired relevant job-related qualifications, let the boss know about them. This demonstrates that you are investing time to acquire skills to further the goals and success of the company as well as your career.

❖ Build a career network with other senior managers so that you become known and respected in the organisation. Take every opportunity to help them when the opportunity arises. Your reputation for helping others and getting things done will be enhanced throughout the organisation.

❖ Find a mentor. Mentoring is accepted as a successful way of advancing your career. Mentors can couch and guide you towards the right jobs for you in the organisation. Many prominent people attribute their success to a good mentor.

SUMMARY

Practising good interpersonal skills is the hallmark of a good manager. Managers need to create and sell a vision of the future to their employees. Good managers earn the trust of their employees by keeping their word and staying totally loyal to their staff. They expect their staff to stay loyal to them in return.

The Johari Window will help you understand yourself by understanding how others perceive you. Build rapport with others by being pleasant and adopting positive body language. Understand the importance of emotional intelligence and practise the skills of empathy. Build rapport with employees by being sensitive to their needs, remembering their names and taking an interest in their welfare. Good managers need to be both creative and logical. A manager needs to know how to handle difficult people. Different personalities need to be handled in different ways.

Managing upwards the relationship with your boss is just as important as managing downwards with your staff. Treat the boss the same way, as you would like your staff to treat you. Be loyal, faithful and supportive to your boss and they are likely to do the same.

CHECK YOUR PEOPLE SKILLS QUOTIENT – 1

	Circle the appropriate response	
1. People who commit to a goal, verbally or in writing, are more likely to honour that commitment	True	False
2. You are less likely to influence people if they like you	True	False
3. Managers who tell the truth are trusted more by their staff even if at times they find the truth hard to take	True	False
4. People are less likely to accept the opinion of experts	True	False
5. The principle of reciprocation states that people feel obliged to return a favour	True	False
6. The Johari Window will help you increase your self-knowledge	True	False
7. The more dogmatic you are with people the less likely they are to resist your views	True	False
8. If you argue with people they are likely to argue back.	True	False
9. Irritators are rapport breakers	True	False
10. Managing upward is not important	True	False

Total the number of true and false responses and check Appendix 1 at the back of the book for the answers and to determine your score.

FIVE STEPS TO IMPROVE YOUR PEOPLE SKILLS

1. Generate trust by keeping your promises, supporting your staff and being impartial and loyal to your employees.

2. Be courteous and pleasant at all times. Good manners cost nothing but will win you the respect and regard of staff. Apologise when you make a mistake or do something inappropriate.

3. Actively manage relationships downward with staff as well as upwards with your boss. Take a genuine interest in the welfare of staff. Find out and try to meet their wishes, concerns, ambitions and needs. Empower staff by encouraging them to make decisions and take responsibility for results.

4. Practise influencing techniques such as reciprocation, liking, authority, assertion and win-win solutions. Memorise the acronym AMICABLE and adopt the suggested behaviours.

5. Build rapport by remembering people's names, smiling, maintaining eye contact, mirroring the other person's behaviour and empathising.

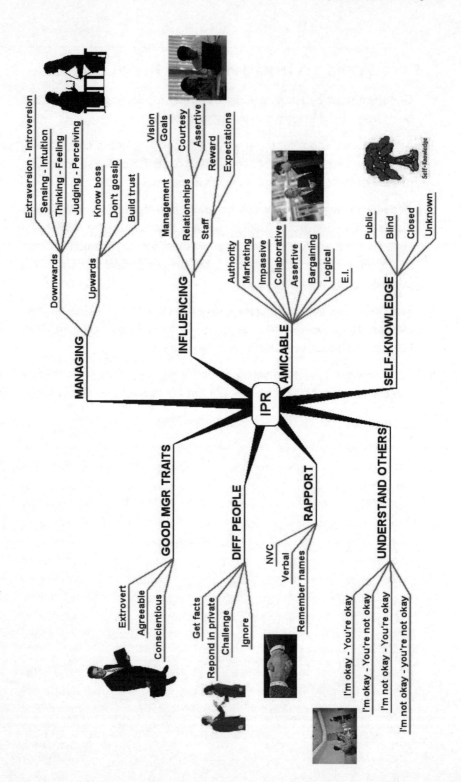

IPR

MANAGING
- Downwards
  - Extraversion - Introversion
  - Sensing - Intuition
  - Thinking - Feeling
  - Judging - Perceiving
- Upwards
  - Know boss
  - Don't gossip
  - Build trust

INFLUENCING
- Management
  - Vision
  - Goals
- Relationships
  - Courtesy
  - Assertive
- Staff
  - Reward
  - Expectations

AMICABLE
- Authority
- Marketing
- Impassive
- Collaborative
- Assertive
- Bargaining
- Logical
- E.I.

SELF-KNOWLEDGE
- Public
- Blind
- Closed
- Unknown

GOOD MGR TRAITS
- Extrovert
- Agreeable
- Conscientious

DIFF PEOPLE
- Get facts
- Repond in private
- Challenge
- Ignore

RAPPORT
- NVC
- Verbal
- Remember names

UNDERSTAND OTHERS
- I'm okay - You're okay
- I'm okay - You're not okay
- I'm not okay - You're okay
- I'm not okay - you're not okay

2

COMMUNICATION

☑ What are the features of good communication?

☑ How can you improve your listening skills?

☑ How can you ask good questions?

☑ What is body language?

☑ How can you use body language to improve communication?

INTRODUCTION

Managers need communication skills when coaching, mentoring, facilitating, counselling, negotiating, interviewing, chairing meetings and making presentations. They need these skills when interacting on a one-to-one basis and when involved in team management. To manage is to get work done through other people and to do this you need to plan, lead, organise and control, all of which require good communication skills.

The higher up the hierarchy a manager goes the greater the need for these skills. To introduce change successfully into an organisation a manager needs good influencing and persuasion skills. In very senior positions managers will need corporate communication skills such as employee relations, media relations, crisis communication and image and reputation management.

In a communication situation we have a speaker, a listener, a message and a context. The effectiveness of the communication will be adversely affected if any of these go wrong. Most people do not listen and don't realise that listening is a skill that must be practised and developed. There are various listening approaches including passive, attentive and reflective listening. The barriers to listening include mind reading, filtering and lack of attention. There are many types of questions that the manager can use including open, closed, discovery, clarification and supportive. When interpreting a message the body language of the speaker should be taken into account.

FEATURES OF COMMUNICATION

The communication process consists of a listener, a speaker, a message and a context. We will first deal with the listener. Some experts maintain that we spend about 80 per cent of our conscious hours communicating, with listening accounting for 50 per cent of this time. In other words, we spend about 40 per cent of our conscious hours listening.

Listener

Short-term memory, concentration, motivation and vocabulary range will all affect your listening skills. Our short-term memory span is between five and nine items of information. Some people have better short-term memory spans than others. Age, gender, fatigue and disposition also affect your ability to listen.

"When people talk, listen completely. Most people never listen." — Ernest Hemingway

---

Some experts maintain that we forget 50 per cent of what we hear immediately, 65 per cent within eight hours and 80 per cent within 24 hours. This shows how frail and fallible short-term memory is unless you take some action to make it more permanent and reliable. In fact, immediate memory lasts only between 20 and 60 seconds. In some situations taking notes while another person is speaking can assist memory and shows that you value what they are saying. However, though acceptable in a business context it is impracticable in most social situations. To get information into your long-term memory you need frequent recall, repetition and review.

We all have short attention spans so concentrate on key issues and prioritise them in your mind. Obviously, you must be motivated to listen.

If the speaker fails to arouse interest you are unlikely to listen attentively. The range of your vocabulary will determine the number of words understood; a limited vocabulary is a barrier to effective understanding.

The older you get the more time it takes to process information and thus to grasp issues quickly. Men prefer factual communication while women are more influenced by feelings. Obviously, if you are tired your ability to concentrate will be compromised. Personality and disposition will also affect your ability to listen so introverts are better listeners than extraverts. Some people are innate compulsive talkers with no desire to listen to what others have to say.

Speaker

The speech rate is between 125 to 175 words per minute (wpm). The thinking rate is between 400 to 800 wpm so we have plenty of spare capacity for distraction and mental doodling. Use this time constructively to summarise and prioritise key points in your mind rather than to daydream or thinking up what to say next. Speak within the normal range, as other people find it difficult to listen effectively and concentrate fully on what you are trying to say if you speak at less than 100 wpm. Slow speech creates boredom in the listener. Similarly, it is difficult to follow those who speak too quickly because we become overwhelmed with information.

Accent, tone and emotion can all affect delivery. There is nothing wrong with an accent provided you pronounce words carefully and distinctly. In fact, different accents can add colour, variety and interest to a conversation. If you speak in a monotone voice you will surely put your listener to sleep while a conversation delivered with appropriate emotion will enhance the credibility and conviction of the words spoken. An expert speaker will get more attention and carry more influence and credibility than a non-expert.

Message

The structure of your message should be clear, logical and coherent; therefore think before you speak and pick the most appropriate words to get the message across. People are different in the way they perceive the world so vary the words used to suit the needs of the listener. Remember, the most important letter in the word COMMUNICATION is U (you), i.e. the other person. Unfortunately, it is often ignored.

> "To effectively communicate, we must realise that we are all different in the way we perceive the world and use this understanding as a guide to our communication with others." — Anthony Robbins

Keep your sentences short and simple, as long-winded ambiguous sentences will challenge the concentration, patience and attention span of the listener. A slow delivery will aid understanding if the topic of conversation is complex. Arouse the interest of your listener and hold their attention by making the message relevant to their needs.

Context

The environment in which you speak will have some influence on the way the message is received. A room that is too hot or too cold will adversely affect the concentration levels of the listener. Similarly, a room that is stuffy and lacks proper ventilation will induce sleep rather than alertness. Noise will interfere with the capacity to hear. In fact, distractions of any sort will lesson the impact of the message. Uncomfortable seating is not helpful and may induce backache. Seating arrangements may also detract from the message. The positioning of seats can either discourage or encourage interaction.

SUCCESSFUL VERBAL COMMUNICATION

Verbal communication should be:

❖ Formed in the imagery, language and experience of the target audience to achieve the greatest impact.

❖ Tailored to meet the characteristics, beliefs, attitudes, concerns and values of the target audience.

❖ Understood. The structure must be logical with a start, middle and end and the language used simple. Avoid technical jargon and acronyms, or if thought necessary explain them as they are introduced. Technical jargon is a form of shorthand and in appropriate circumstances can be useful.

❖ Believed. What you say must be credible and spoken with conviction.

❖ Remembered. Short sentences are remembered better than long ones. People remember the start and end of a speech while the middle parts are less well remembered unless you make them unique and outstanding. Controversial issues are remembered better. Repeating key points help people remember them better. Psychologists maintain that you need to hear key points at least three times before they enter long-term memory. If what we say touches the emotions of the audience it is more likely to be imprinted and remembered.

❖ Acted upon. If the message is not acted upon by the recipient then it fails. Words reinforced by action are remembered better. We learn by doing and living out the words as experience.

Watch What You Say!
"In the course of your conversation each and every day,
Think twice, try to be careful of what you have to say;
Your remarks may be picked up by someone's ear,
You may be surprised at what some people think they hear.
Things that you innocently say, or try to portray,
Can be changed, and greatly exaggerated along the way;
Many stories change for the worse as they are retold,
So try to keep any questionable remarks 'on hold'.
May I give all of you some very sound advice?
When you speak of others, say something nice;
Try to say good things, regardless of who is around,
If you have nothing good to say, don't utter a sound.
You may find that an innocent remark, in the end,
May lose you a close and valued friend."
— Henry Lessor

Speaking

❖ *Before.* Establish credibility. As mentioned previously this is established by being perceived as an expert. Consider your objectives and know the outcome you want to receive and state the benefits for you and the other person.

❖ *During*. State your objectives. Vary your talk until you achieve the desired outcome. The purpose of communication lies is the response you get. If it's not working try something else. Listen to views and be prepared to change yours if necessary. Pay attention to how the other person is listening and study body language to gauge their reaction. Illustrate the points with stories, analogies and examples. Connect emotionally with the other person to build rapport.

❖ *Concluding*. Verify by getting feedback that your message has been understood. Express appreciation and acknowledge the other's contribution.

LISTENING

Meaning of Communication

We don't need to learn how to hear, as it is an innate physiological capacity, however we do need to learn how to listen because it is a psychological process. Listening is the process of interpreting and understanding what is said. Most people feel that listening comes naturally but this is not true and we must practise the art of listening to become effective listeners. In fact, some companies run courses for their managers in listening skills. Communication experts maintain that 10 per cent of communication is words, 30 per cent consists of sound and as much as 60 per cent consists of body language. Managers spend about 75 per cent of their waking hours communicating. Listening takes up about 55 per cent of this time, speaking 23 per cent, reading 13 per cent and writing 9 per cent. Thus we spend 78 per cent of our time listening or speaking to others.

> "The average person looks without seeing, listens without hearing, touches without feeling, eats without tasting, moves without physical awareness ... and talks without thinking." – Leonardo da Vinci

A person with a good vocabulary tends to be a good listener as they can understand and assimilate a greater range of concepts. They have also developed good concentration skills and can identify the key elements of a conversation and organise them into appropriate categories. A highly motivated person will remember more of the content spoken. People who are extremely tired and agitated make poor listeners. Generally, introverts are better listeners than extraverts. Some people only want to talk about themselves or about their own interests and these people make poor listeners. We tend to listen more carefully to people of high status because we perceive them as having higher credibility and thus worthy of our attention.

The EAR Model

The EAR model is a useful acronym for effective listening and succinctly summarises what we have discussed so far:

❖ **E**xplore the issue using open-ended questions such as "what", "why", "when", "how", "where" and "who". Observe body language such as head nods, facial expressions and levels of eye contact to gauge the meaning of the total message.

❖ **A**cknowledge the message by paraphrasing and summarising what you think the speaker has said and wait for confirmation. This keeps the conversation focused and on track.

❖ **R**espond. This is what you say back to the speaker after you have confirmed that you have received the message correctly. This will then encourage the speaker to continue and engage in dialogue.

When listening most people spend their time responding. Instead, spend more time exploring, observing and acknowledging for greater understanding.

Active Listening

Active listening doesn't necessarily mean agreeing to everything that is said but acknowledging the speaker's point of view even if you disagree with it. You should listen to understand not just to respond. Focus carefully on what the other person is saying while critically evaluating what they say. Active listening includes making suggestions regarding what the speaker is trying to say.

Listeners must give the speaker an opportunity to agree or disagree with their interpretation of what is being said. Active listening includes restating, summarising, paraphrasing and clarifying to check understanding. Reflect back feelings as well as the essence of the content. Also monitor body language to assess the meaning of the total message so that you take account of both the verbal and non-verbal content of the message.

"The most basic and powerful way to connect to another person is to listen. Just listen. Perhaps the most important thing we ever give each other is our attention.... A loving silence often has far more power to heal and to connect than the most well-intentioned words."
— Rachel Naomi Remen

The acronym HARNESS summarises the essentials of active listening:

❖ **H**ead nods visibly showing that you are actively listening and interested in what the speaker is saying.

❖ **A**ttention. Lean forward to demonstrate that you are actively engaged and concerned.

❖ **R**efrain from distracting mannerisms such as playing with your hair, ears, pen or watch.

❖ **N**VC (non-verbal communication). Don't interrupt the speaker but use your posture and gestures to show interest. Maintain a comfortable social distance. A distance of 2.5 to 3 feet is often suggested but this can vary in the context of culture or the relationship with the speaker.

❖ **E**ye contact. Remember that too much eye contact can be intrusive or intimidating. On the other hand, too little can be interpreted as boredom, shiftiness or lack of confidence. To maintain a balance look occasionally away or at the other person's forehead.

❖ **S**mile. A smile lights up your face and encourages the other person to smile back. A smile demonstrates that you are friendly, approachable and interested in the other person's concerns.

❖ **S**how empathy by mirroring the speaker's tone, facial expressions, posture and gestures. Reflect back the speaker's thoughts and emotions in a non-judgemental way, for example, by saying, "you sound very worried".

FACILITATIVE LISTENING

Facilitative listening like active listening is a useful skill for a manager to develop when dealing with others, especially teams. We hear with our ears but we listen with our minds and hearts so we need to listen to other's concerns and moods and react appropriately. Facilitative listening is listening attentively to speakers while being aware of how other people are listening or not listening in the group. This requires a great deal of concentration and awareness. The following are the various types of listening used in facilitation:

❖ Non-listening. This is where we are distracted with our thoughts and do not receive the message. Many people are so self-obsessed in thinking up what they are going to say next that they fail to hear what the other person is saying.

❖ Passive listening. We hear the words but not the message. The other person is doing all the talking as in a monologue so we are not engaged and may be only listening at a superficial level.

❖ Judgemental. Our prejudices and biases may affect the interpretation of the message. For example, you may have great difficulty listening to someone expressing certain political views, particularly if these are anathema to you. As a facilitator your role is to listen attentively and put your personal feelings temporarily on hold.

"Through sharing our thoughts, we inspire one another, share visions and create the future. We discover common values and build commitment. By thinking through and analysing how, we determine how we can do things together." – Ruth Hild

---

❖ Attentive. We are focused on the message by engaging with the words as well as the non-verbal signals. It can be very demanding to listen to what people are saying as well as observing their gestures, movements, posture and tone of voice simultaneously. Nevertheless, this is the way facilitators should listen. Our ability to listen attentively is constrained by the timespan of attention which is not more than 30 minutes and for most people considerably less.

❖ Visual. This is where the words are unspoken and we have only the non-verbal cues to help us interpret what is going on. The eyes are the windows of the soul and so observing the eyes of others can indicate their reactions such as interest or disinterest to what we are saying. Maintaining eye contact with the speaker also lets them know that you are actively hearing what they say.

❖ Reflective. We restate the message in our own words as feedback that the message has been received and understood. This can then be confirmed or corrected by the speaker. Reflective listening has to be done in an impartial and sensitive way so that the speaker does not feel that you are trying to manipulate words. This skill is acquired through practise.

❖ Directive. This is where the listener tries to influence or shape what the speaker is saying without being intrusive or domineering. Directive listeners may add their own interpretation and emphasis or add something that the speaker did not say. Facilitators need to be aware when this is happening and give the speaker an opportunity to clarify the situation or repeat exactly what they said.

Benefits

The benefits of listening include the following:

For managers:

❖ You become more thoughtful and observant. You can study and draw conclusions about reactions and feelings from the body language of others though it can be difficult to talk and observe at the same time.

❖ The reason we have two ears and one mouth is that we should listen twice as much as we speak. People learn more by spending more time listening than talking.

❖ Others will like you more if you listen more. It is probably the most important aspect of winning friends and influencing people – and the most neglected. Listeners are likely to show greater understanding and acceptance of the needs of others.

"Feelings of worth can flourish only in an atmosphere where individual differences are appreciated, mistakes are tolerated, communication is open, and rules are flexible ... the kind of atmosphere that is found in a nurturing family." – Virginia Satir

---

❖ Improved interpersonal relationships. Employees want to be heard, understood, respected and valued and want to be treated like unique human beings rather than automatons.

❖ Effective negotiation cannot be achieved if managers fail to listen carefully to find out what employees' really want. Industrial relations problems are often exacerbated by failure on the part of one party to listen actively to the concerns of the other.

❖ When giving advice or instruction to staff, managers who listen for feedback that their message is being received and understood prevent misunderstandings and mistakes from recurring in the future.

❖ There is a health benefit of listening. When we talk our blood pressure goes up. However, when we listen it goes down so listening is good for you.

"I need thinking time when someone asks me a searching question. I wonder why it seems to be so uncomfortable for many people to wait through the silence. People of all ages have deep feelings, and if we have patience to wait through the silence, it's often astounding what people will tell us." – Fred Rogers

---

For staff:

❖ Greater employee satisfaction. Employees who have direct and frequent communication with managers are less likely to file grievances, complain or go on strike.

❖ Employees who are listened to are flattered by the attention they receive. Listening conveys attention and interest, and encourages employees to share information, which in normal circumstances they might be hesitant to do.

BARRIERS TO LISTENING

Mental Barriers

❖ Mind reading. Some people engage in mind reading due to lack of trust. They imagine they know what others are thinking and feeling

about them and so make assumptions, anticipate what they are going to say and jump to conclusions. In fact, it is impossible to know
what other people are thinking and these misconceptions can hinder true listening. Some people assume if they know people a long
time they know what's going on in their minds. This is untrue. If you
want to find out what people are thinking, ask them!

❖ Mind set. Our perceptions are unique and are influenced by our
experiences, attitudes, values, feelings and education. We like others to confirm and support rather than to challenge our long-held
beliefs and attitudes. Perceptions are highly selective and subjective
and say as much about us as about how we feel about others.

❖ Blocking. People filter or block out what they don't want to hear
such as criticism. We all like to hear only nice things about ourselves. Some people also pre-empt a discussion by having their
minds made up in advance.

"Good communication does not mean that you have to speak perfectly
formed sentences and paragraphs. It isn't about slickness. Simple and
clear go a long way." — John Kotter

❖ Distractions. It is impossible to listen to two people at the same
time. It may be necessary to put the phone on hold so that you give
the person your complete attention. How many of us have made
presentations to managers who are continually interrupted by
phone calls and "urgent messages" from their secretaries. It is impossible to listen if attention is elsewhere!

❖ Bias. Making assumptions, jumping to conclusions and having fixed
views are all barriers to listening. Suspend judgement to open your
mind to another's point of view. We all use stereotypes to understand people, as these are useful shorthand devices, but they can in-
advertently show prejudice.

❖ If you feel very strongly about a topic or are fanatical about certain
issues then your emotions and feelings may block out the message.
For example, religious fundamentalists are not open to other viewpoints.

Personal Barriers

❖ Lack of attention. You may be preoccupied with other issues or spend time rehearsing what you're going to say next. The presence or absence of anxiety or stress will also affect the level of attention.

❖ Using complicated words and sentences will discourage people to listen to you. The content and language must be suited to the educational level and experience of the listener. The most persuasive message is one that is direct and simple and focused on one idea. Multiple ideas in the same sentence are difficult to follow.

❖ Inappropriate body language. These could include a deadpan facial expression, no eye contact and no head nods. A bored look, yawning and paying attention to other matters while the speaker is talking demonstrate disengagement and lack of interest. Body language should be congruent with the spoken word.

❖ Interrupting others when they speak by assuming that you know what they're going to say next. You can't listen and speak at the same time. Also, finishing the other person's sentences can be very irritating and patronising for the other party.

❖ Men and women communicate differently. Men tend to focus on power and status issues while women tend to focus on interpersonal relationships and emotional issues. This can lead to misunderstandings if we are unaware of these gender preferences.

❖ Monotone. It is very difficult to listen to someone who speaks in a dull monotone, or who mumbles and does not project their voice.

"One of the basic causes for all the trouble in the world today is that people talk too much and think too little. They act impulsively without thinking. I always try to think before I talk." – Margaret Chase Smith

---

DIFFERENT TYPES OF LISTENING

Being aware of these will help you practise the appropriate type of listening. The key points are recalled by the acronym DECADE:

❖ **D**iscriminate. Scan, monitor and check to differentiate between facts, opinions and assumptions. Study the person's facial expression to see if what we are saying has caused shock, surprise or acceptance.

❖ **E**valuation. To make sound judgements we need to critically weigh up the evidence supporting an argument before making up our mind. Use this type of critical listening when buying something from a salesperson, when negotiating a salary increase or when attending a meeting. We listen for the central propositions being made and the strengths and weaknesses of an argument.

❖ **C**omprehension. Here you listen for the main facts and themes to understand what is being said. This type of listening is needed when listening to new information or to a lecture or conducting a fact-finding interview. We also use this type of listening when listening to TV documentaries or news programmes on the radio.

❖ **A**ppreciation. You listen with appreciation when listening to classi-cal music for relaxation or to a good presentation by a renowned speaker on a subject that you are keenly interested in. Hold up the speaker as a role model and aspire to their style of delivery.

❖ **D**ialogue. Dialogue is a two-way conversation. The emphasis is on sharing views, giving and receiving feedback and building rapport. Dialogue is needed to arrive at a mutually acceptable position. This type of listening is essential when negotiating as the needs and goals of each side must be explored and acknowledged.

❖ **E**mpathise. You empathise when you listen sincerely with your heart to better understand thoughts, emotions, beliefs, feelings and con-cerns. In this type of listening you show unconditional positive regard for the other person, meaning that you accept them warts and all.

Four Types of Listeners

Galanes et al. (2000) report that there are four types of listener:

1. *People-oriented listeners.* They are concerned for the feelings and needs of others but can be distracted from the task owing to their focus on emotional issues. They are the people we seek out when we need emotional support and a listening ear.

2. *Task-oriented listeners.* These are mainly concerned with getting the job done and may be insensitive to the emotional needs of others. Thus they tend to be impatient with people who don't stick to the point.

3. *Content-oriented listeners.* These are logical people who enjoy analysing information and interpreting things literally. They love detail and like to hear all sides of an argument and thus make good mediators. They can be slow to make decisions, as they prefer to have gathered all the information first.

4. *Time-oriented listeners.* They like to get things done on time by practising good time management skills. They are impatient with people who are disorganised and can't seem to make up their minds. They are prone to jump to conclusions before they have heard all the information.

"He who asks is a fool for five minutes, but he who does not ask remains a fool forever." — Chinese proverb

---

ASKING QUESTIONS

Employees know things so ask them questions if you want to tap into their unique knowledge, experience and expertise. When you ask questions, communication should be purposeful and dynamic. If you are not getting the response you want you should reformulate the question or ask a different question. The answers you get are determined by the type of question you ask and the words you use. A pause before or after a question encourages maximum response.

Questioning is a skill so pay attention to the structure of your question and the pauses you use. To get the right answer you must ask the right question. Questioning involves five steps:

1. Determine the information or additional information you need

2. Select the right type of question

3. Ask the question

4. Evaluate the response

5. Take the appropriate action required.

"I keep six honest serving men
They taught me all I knew
Their names are what and why and when
And how and where and who."
— Rudyard Kipling

FACILITATION QUESTIONS

Questions can be used to involve people, create interaction and discover information. Asking provocative questions can help the team reach the right answer. There are many types of questions:

❖ *Closed.* Closed questions encourage a specific response and are used to control the conversation. They give the inquisitor control by encouraging a yes/no response or a restricted answer and are useful in fact finding, research or selection interviews. In a research situation answers will be easier to code and classify for statistical analysis. When time is limited and you need to elicit specific information the closed question is the preferred approach. Leading and direct questions are types of closed questions. Lawyers and inquisitors use leading questions to direct the accused to expected answers. Managers and interviewers use direct questions to get specific information. For example, "who was your last manager?"

❖ *Open.* Open questions encourage people to open up and explore issues. These invite self-disclosure and are used to encourage people to talk by expressing opinions, attitudes, thoughts and feelings. The respondent has greater control to shape the conversation in these situations while the questioner has more time to listen and observe. Some people use a funnel sequence, going from open to closed questions as appropriate. In other words, they start with the broader aspects of the topic and narrow down to the specifics. Less frequently they may use an inverted funnel. Here they go from a narrow perspective and then widen out to more general issues. Discovery questions are a type of open question to enable the questioner to investigate subjects.

❖ *Probing* or *clarification* questions can be used to expand on or clarify issues. A clarification question tries to make clear what the speaker has said. It may help the speaker reframe the issue so that it is clearly understood and not misinterpreted. The ability to probe is at the core of effective questioning. Clarify issues by asking the question, "what exactly do you mean?" Seek justification for issues by asking, "how did you arrive at that conclusion?" Determine relevance by asking, "how is this pertinent to the discussion?" or look for elaboration or extension by requesting more information, such as, "tell me more". Clarification questions can be either open or direct.

❖ *Confrontation.* This question is used to confront issues by trying to gain a clear understanding of what is happening by bringing it out into the open rather than sweeping it under the carpet. They tend to be direct and to the point.

❖ *Supportive.* Supportive questions boost the team's morale and self-esteem by providing them with the encouragement and confidence to continue with what they were doing.

"All new and original thought begins with a question, which leads to an exploration." — Dawna Markova

---

Advantages of Asking Questions

❖ They improve understanding by providing additional information or clarifying a situation. It is surprising how much people will tell you if you only ask the right questions at the right time and in the right way.

❖ They encourage others to communicate more concisely and clearly and keep a conversation going.

❖ They foster relationships and self-esteem through interaction. Employees will value the fact that the manager is taking the trouble to understand exactly what they mean by asking questions.

BODY LANGUAGE

Verbal communication and body language are intertwined in our everyday interactions and form a total package to help us understand others. Body language can replace, complement, modify or contradict the spoken word. It includes the look or expression on our face, the glint in our eyes, our hand gestures and the tension in our bodies. It can be considered under two headings: vocal and non-vocal. Vocal concerns aspects of speech such as volume, tone, rate and accent. Non-vocal has got to do with conveying feelings and meaning through expressions, gestures and movements.

Vocal Body Language

❖ Speech. Vary the volume for effect. A louder voice is seen as confident and assertive. A soft voice is seen as diffident and unassertive.

❖ Tone. Tone of voice is an important indicator of your emotional state and may indicate whether you are angry, sad or happy. It can also indicate your attitude towards another person such as approval or disapproval, acceptance or annoyance, friendship or antagonism.

❖ Pitch. Flat, unmodulated pitch can mean someone is sad, while a high pitch can mean that they are tense or distressed. Good speakers vary the inflexion, pitch and volume to put excitement into their voice. It's also important to control how you end your sentences. Raising the pitch of the voice at the end of a sentence makes it sound like a question while a slight lowering of pitch at the end of a sentence makes it like a statement.

❖ Rate. If you speak too fast you are less likely to be understood as you overload the mental capacity of the listener. On the other hand, if you speak too slowly you will put undue demands on their concentration abilities. Use the pause to naturally slow down your talk and collect your thoughts. A pause replaces annoying non-words like "uh", "um", "like" and "you know" and gives you an opportunity to take a relaxing breath.

❖ Accent. Accents may convey status, however an affected accent can sound insincere and undermine the credibility of the speaker. Accents can be used to identify social class or where a person comes from. However, there is nothing wrong with a local accent provided you pronounce your words clearly and can be understood.

Non-vocal Body Language

The face and eyes are the most revealing in terms of body language. Non-vocal body language may convey feelings and attitudes. However, body language can have different meanings in different cultures. Non-vocal body language includes facial expressions, gestures, movements, posture and personal appearance:

❖ Facial expressions. These display delight, liking, interest, surprise, boredom, anger, fear, sadness and disgust. The face reveals how you feel about what you're saying. A smile may indicate great happiness or pleasure. A frown may indicate great annoyance or puzzlement.

❖ Physical gestures like a head nod and touching the person's elbow or shoulder can display interest, affection, concern, warmth, friend-ship and agreement.

❖ Movement. You can use your hands to emphasise a point. Keeping your hands stiffly by the side or stuck in your pockets can create the impression that you are wooden, insecure or distant. Doodling with a pen can be a sign of boredom, but it might also indicate con-centration.

❖ Posture can display confidence or a lack thereof. Arms open can indicate a desire for engagement and involvement. Poor posture such as slouching may be interpreted as a lack of confidence or in-terest while an erect posture creates the opposite impression. A tense and rigid posture may show you are anxious and nervous and not fully in control. A casual posture at a job interview may be seen as disinterest, lack of respect or complacency and may therefore prove to be counterproductive.

"It's a mistake to think we listen only with our ears. It's much more important to listen with the mind, the eyes, the body, and the heart. Unless you truly want to understand the other person, you'll never be able to listen." – Mark Herndon

---

❖ Personal appearance. The way you dress can say a lot about you. A well-dressed manager with a relaxed commanding presence reflects confidence, credibility, competence and charisma. In a formal situa-tion a casually dressed person may be perceived as disrespectful. So dress appropriate to the situation. Being overdressed or under-dressed in comparison to others may make them feel uncomfortable.

Augmenting Communication with Body Language

The following body language augments communication:

❖ Keep arms, legs and feet uncrossed. Open your jacket as an open posture conveys the message that you are transparent, honest, approachable and willing to engage in conversation. Mirror your body language to that of the person you are talking to. This should be done naturally and unobtrusively.

❖ Face the person you are speaking to. Facing away from someone can be interpreted as indifference, ignorance or rudeness. When seated, a side-by-side position is considered co-operative, while a face-to-face position is seen as competitive. A 90-degree angle in relation to each other is perceived as non-confrontational and thus good for conversation.

❖ Maintain eye contact. This increases credibility and trust. A person who avoids eye contact is often seen as shifty and untrustworthy. A person who looks down while speaking suggests timidity and shyness and may not be taken seriously. Looking to the side as you speak may suggest avoidance and insincerity and affect your credibility. However lack of eye contact means different things to different people and in different cultures. In Latin or Asian cultures, looking down in the presence of authority is seen as a sign of respect. When you talk to people you should observe the way they use their eyes. Neuro-linguistic programming (NLP) practitioners claim than when people look to the left they are searching their memory. On the other hand, if they look to the right they are using their imagination.

❖ A handshake should not be too hard or too soft. A soft handshake may be interpreted as unfriendly or timid. A hard one may be perceived as aggressive or forceful.

Use of Body Language

Body language is useful in many situations such as:

❖ Replacing verbal communication. Deaf people, bookmakers, auctioneers, and deep-sea divers use sign language. For example, racecourse bookmakers use the ticktack system, conductors use a baton to conduct an orchestra, and policemen use hand signals for directing traffic.

❖ Complementing speech. Giving directions can be difficult using words alone. Body language such as hand movements can clarify, extend and augment what is said.

❖ Contradicting what is said. Words have one meaning while tone of voice and body language might suggest another. Sarcasm, disbelief and humour are often conveyed more forcefully through body language.

❖ Expressing emotion through facial expressions. Pupil dilation or contraction can signify surprise or interest though it is outside our control being an automatic response.

❖ Regulating conversation. Catching a person's eye indicates that you want to engage with them. Breaking eye contact may indicate that you wish to interrupt or discontinue the conversation. A drop in voice volume or change in gaze pattern may indicate that it is the other person's turn to speak or that you want to leave.

SUMMARY

A manager gets things done through people mainly through the art of good communication. The higher up you go in the management hierarchy the greater the need for communication skills and the less the need for technical skills. The ability to listen is primarily affected by the power of short-term memory, concentration, motivation and the range of your vocabulary. Age, gender, fatigue, personality and disposition also affect listening skills. In any communication situation we have a speaker, a message, a listener and a context. The effectiveness of the communication will be adversely affected if any of these go out of synchronisation.

We don't need to learn how to hear, as hearing is an innate capacity, but we do need to learn how to listen. Most people feel that listening comes naturally. This is not true and we must practise the art of active listening to become effective listeners. This includes restating, summarising, paraphrasing and clarifying to check understanding. Reflect back feelings as well as the essence of the content to create empathy.

The acronym HARNESS was used as an aid to recall the essentials for active listening. People like people who listen attentively to them. The barriers to listening include mind reading, bias, filtering, and lack of attention. Employees have expertise and knowledge so ask them questions if you want to tap into this resource. There are many types of questions that the manager can use including open, closed, discovery, clarification and supportive. The actual words used convey less than half the meaning, and so to interpret a message fully you must take the accompanying body language into account.

CHECK YOUR PEOPLE SKILLS QUOTIENT – 2

	Circle the appropriate response	
1. Immediate memory span lasts between 20 and 60 seconds	True	False
2. The older you get the less time it takes to process information	True	False
3. We think at about twice the rate that we speak	True	False
4. Listening comes naturally	True	False
5. Active listening means acknowledging the speaker's point of view even if you disagree with it	True	False
6. Managers spend about 75% of their time communicating	True	False
7. People like people who listen attentively to them	True	False
8. When we talk our blood pressure goes down.	True	False
9. Open questions discourage self-disclosure	True	False
10. If there is a lack of congruence between body language and the spoken word the body language is believed.	True	False

Total the number of true and false responses and check Appendix 1 at the back of the book for the answers and to determine your score.

FIVE STEPS TO IMPROVE
YOUR COMMUNICATION SKILLS

1. In formal situations take notes while the other person is speaking to assist your memory and show that you value what they are saying. Afterwards, frequently repeat and review the information that you wish to register in your long-term memory.

2. Use the difference between the thinking rate and speech rate productively to summarise and prioritise the key issues that the speaker is making. This will improve your listening skills.

3. Think before you speak and pick the most appropriate words to get your message across. Study body language to gauge the reaction to your words. The words used plus your interpretation of the body language used equals the total message.

4. Practise the art of facilitative listening to become an effective listener. Listen twice as much as you speak. The greatest compliment you can pay to a person is to listen to them attentively. It is the simplest and best method for winning friends and influencing people.

5. Practise the art and science of asking questions. It is the most efficient and effective way of acquiring information and keeping the conversation going.

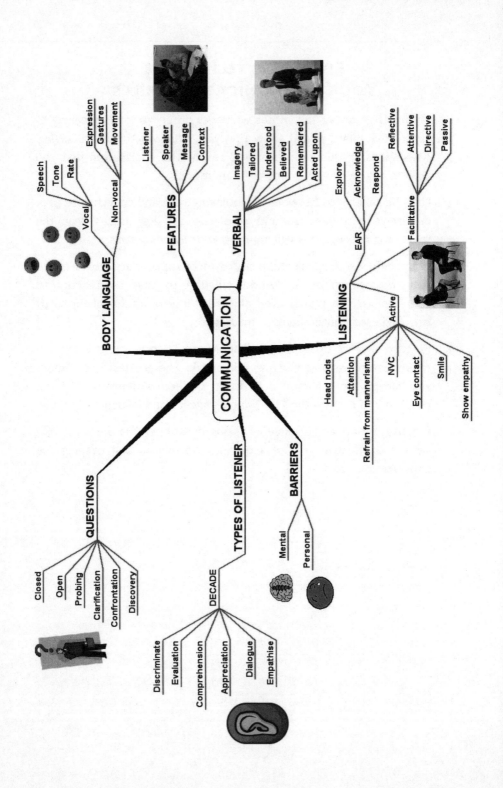

COMMUNICATION

BODY LANGUAGE

Vocal
Speech
Tone
Rate

Non-vocal
Expression
Gestures
Movement

FEATURES
Listener
Speaker
Message
Context

VERBAL
Imagery
Tailored
Understood
Believed
Remembered
Acted upon

EAR
Explore
Acknowledge
Respond

Facilitative
Reflective
Attentive
Directive
Passive

LISTENING

Active
Head nods
Attention
Refrain from mannerisms
NVC
Eye contact
Smile
Show empathy

QUESTIONS
Closed
Open
Probing
Clarification
Confrontation
Discovery

TYPES OF LISTENER

DECADE
Discriminate
Evaluation
Comprehension
Appreciation
Dialogue
Empathise

BARRIERS
Mental
Personal

3

ASSERTIVENESS

☑ What is the difference between passive, aggressive
and assertive behaviour?

☑ What does being assertive involve?

☑ What are assertive non-verbal behaviours?

☑ What are the techniques of assertion?

☑ What is the TAILOR model?

INTRODUCTION

There is a difference between passive, aggressive, passive/aggressive
and assertive behaviour. Passive people have low self-esteem and
self-confidence and can't stand up for themselves. Aggressive people
use threatening, blaming, insulting and accusing language and behaviours and tend to overreact and get agitated easily. Passive/aggressive
people use covert methods such as sabotage and backbiting to vent
their aggression on others. Assertive people know their rights and
assert them tactfully.

The advantages of assertion are many and include greater self-
confidence and feeling in control. Assertive people adopt an attitude
that everybody is of equal value. Some disadvantages are that others
may react negatively or aggressively towards you. Appropriate body
language will reinforce the assertive message. Techniques of assertion
include using "I" Statements, the Broken Record, Saying No and Fogging. TAILOR is an acronym to help you practise the assertion process.
Assertion skills are not innate but can be learned and practised.

"Tact is the ability to make a point without making an enemy." —
Anon.

PASSIVE/AGGRESSIVE/ASSERTIVE

As a continuum this is passive/assertive/aggressive. The two extremes
are passive and aggressive. Step back and consider where you fall on the
continuum in most situations. If you want to feel good about yourself
and gain the respect of others you should aim to be in the middle of this
continuum and so be assertive.

Passive

Many women are taught from an early age to be agreeable, polite and
put others' needs first. In contrast, men are often taught to be the opposite: aggressive, strong and macho. Being passive may help you avoid
conflict but at the cost of feeling inferior, helpless and out of control.
When passive you do not take responsibility for your own decisions,
and allow other people to walk all over you and make decisions for you.
When you fail to stand up for your rights people will take advantage of
you. Passive people are usually liked but not respected. Passive behaviour communicates a message of lack of confidence and inferiority.
Some organisations provide assertiveness training for women to help
them compete more effectively with men. These programmes can also
cater for the needs of unassertive male employees. The following are
some of the behaviours passive people display:

❖ Passive people may have been taught as children that their needs
   were unimportant and that putting them first was selfish. Early con-
   ditioning by parents and other significant adults taught them to be
   seen and not heard.

❖ They have a you-win-and-I-lose agenda and let other people dominate their lives, as they believe that they are inferior to others.

❖ They fail to stand up for themselves and adopt the role of victim or
   martyr. They worry incessantly about what others might think and
   are reluctant to upset people and thus avoid conflict at all costs.
   They accommodate others' views in the interests of harmony and

friendship. They allow their human rights to be violated and find it very difficult to say no. They often say yes when they mean no.

❖ They don't express their honest feelings, needs or concerns. They agree to things contrary to their own feelings and subjugate their feelings to those of others. They allow others to violate their space, deny their rights and ignore their needs. They avoid controversial issues and suppress their resentment when treated unfairly.

Aggressive

Aggressive behaviour includes arguing, blaming, accusing, name calling, using sarcasm and threats and a general disregard for the feelings and rights of others. In our culture men are taught to be strong and often equate strength with confrontation, aggression and manliness. Some women working in male-dominated workplaces adopt this kind of male persona.

Aggression often breeds counter-aggression and in extreme cases violence and may create lifelong enemies. It also creates resentment, unnecessary arguments and the desire to exact revenge. Many tolerate aggressive people because they are afraid to confront them. Aggressive people are neither liked nor respected but often secretly despised. In the work context an aggressive style by a manager may be seen as intimidation, bullying or harassment and is thus not acceptable. Indeed, aggression may lead to grievance claims, industrial relations disputes and litigation. The following are typical aggressive behaviours:

❖ Aggressive people may insist on always having the final word and try to dominate others.

❖ They almost always win an argument, speak loudly and can be abusive, rude, inconsiderate and sarcastic. They are easily aroused, annoyed and upset, becoming angry and abusive at the least provocation. They may shout or employ bully tactics to get their way.

❖ They insist that their feelings and needs are more important than those of others.

❖ They desire self-enhancement at others' expense displaying an I-win-you-lose approach. They habitually cut across and interrupt people before they finish speaking. They're so focused on themselves that they do not listen to or respond to the needs of others.

❖ They are offensive and unpleasant and thus lose the respect of others. They may openly criticise or find fault with others' ideas, opinions or behaviours.

"The basic difference between being assertive and being aggressive is how our words and behaviour affect the rights and well-being of others." — Sharon Anthony Bower

---

Assertive

You are assertive when you do not let others control you, when you stand up for your rights while respecting the rights of others and when you express your feelings honestly. The win-win approach is the assertive one. Assertive people try to achieve fair play for everyone without exploiting others. There is a high correlation between assertion and self-esteem. There is also a positive correlation between age and assertiveness, probably because older people have acquired more experience in standing up for their rights. Assertive people:

❖ Assert rights tactfully by communicating calmly, directly and honestly.

❖ Seek out win-win solutions to conflict. Thus assertive people actively listen, explain themselves clearly and invite others to jointly work towards a solution.

❖ Adopt an attitude that everybody is of equal value and thus accept the right of others to disagree with them. They give and receive in equal measure.

❖ Tackle issues promptly and focus on solutions rather than problems.

❖ Refuse to be intimidated by the aggressive actions of others.

Passive–Aggressive

This is a blend of two and is implicit rather than explicit. Passive–aggressive people feel angry with a sense of injustice when their needs are not met, but instead of speaking up or behaving aggressively they express anger or rage in an indirect or underhand way. People can use the grapevine to spread gossip in order to hurt a person's reputation. Similarly, output or work can be sabotaged in a subtle way without others being aware of what is going on.

Another type of passive–aggressive behaviour is sarcasm as in saying one thing and meaning the opposite in order to be hurtful or cutting. Passive–aggressive people may engage in manipulative behaviour to serve their own ends, by procrastinating purposefully, co-operating reluctantly, forgetting intentionally, working inefficiently and blaming others for their shortcomings. They may also sulk and use emotional blackmail to get their way. Sometimes they may act in a superficial friendly way being unwilling to confront others and cause a scene.

"Assertiveness is not what you do, it's who you are." – Cal Le Mon

---

MY BILL OF RIGHTS

These follow the principles of democracy and natural justice. You have the right to:

❖ Be firm but fair and flexible.

❖ Believe in your own self-efficacy and competence to do the job.

❖ Take responsibility for yourself but not for others on the principle that people are responsible for their own actions and their consequences.

❖ Express your views, opinions and feelings in a direct and honest way.

❖ Allow yourself to make mistakes.

❖ Look for information or help when you need to do so.

❖ Respect the dignity of yourself and others.

❖ Recognise your own and others' needs. Ask for what you want. Others have the right to refuse.

❖ Say no without feeling guilty or apologetic. Refuse unreasonable requests. Stop others from taking advantage of you.

❖ Request time to think things over. Decisions made in haste may be regretted at leisure.

❖ Have your own values, beliefs, opinions and feelings and be able express them freely.

❖ Change your mind or decide on a different course of action. Circumstances change as more information becomes available and so should viewpoints. It is silly to believe that changing your mind is always a betrayal of your principles or word.

❖ Not depend on others. In a society we do depend on others but at the same time we should always try to be as self-reliant as possible.

❖ Handle aggression with assertion. Handling aggression with aggression only adds fuel to the fire.

❖ Have your own priorities that may be expressed in the form of a mission, vision or goals.

❖ Get what you pay for. The law protects this right in many countries.

❖ Compromise as appropriate because it's the most equitable and best thing to do in certain circumstances.

❖ Object to gender stereotyping such as being asked to do something because you're a woman. For example, being asked to make the tea in the office.

"Joint undertakings stand a better chance when they benefit both sides." — Euripides

---

FAMOUS ASSERTIVE PEOPLE

Assertion is an important aspect of interpersonal relationship skills essential for success in life. Being assertive helps you stay in control and win respect. Personal credibility is enhanced if you come across as calm, rational, impartial and determined. Historical figures such as Gandhi, Dr Martin Luther King and Mrs. Rosa Parks achieved great political and social change in their lifetimes by being assertive using non-violent means.

Mahatma Gandhi, though one of the gentlest of men, used assertiveness and determination to win independence for India from Britain without striking a blow, proving that peaceful assertiveness rather than aggression can reap great results. Gandhi's life is a testament to the fact that one totally committed person can change the course of a nation's history.

On 1 December 1955, Mrs. Rosa Parks asserted her human rights under natural justice and refused to give up her bus seat to a white person, and thus helped to trigger the Civil Rights movement led by Dr. Martin Luther King. The bus driver had her arrested for violating the segregation laws. This led to a boycott of the Montgomery bus service by blacks that lasted for 382 days. It brought the bus company to its knees and changed American history forever. In December 1956, the Supreme Court ruled that bus segregation violated the constitution. The Civil Rights movement came into being and eight years later the Civil Rights Act of 1964 was passed. This gave all Americans, irrespective of colour, race, nationality or religion, the right for equal treatment under the law. Mrs. Rosa Park's life demonstrates how an ordinary person with assertiveness, extraordinary determination and resolution can achieve so much.

These people won the respect and admiration of people throughout the world because they conducted their demonstrations in an assertive, peaceful and dignified manner. They attracted large national support to pursue their aims. They refused to react in like fashion to the aggression and violence committed against them but instead continued on with their peaceful protest.

Advantages of Being Assertive

❖ It will help managers to progress in their career. If there are two managers with similar education and experience it is likely that the more assertive one will get the promotion.

❖ You can achieve your objectives in a corporate or social situation.

❖ You can negotiate a pay rise, a budget allocation, promotion or get a topic discussed at a meeting.

❖ You can deal effectively with a pushy salesperson whether on the doorstep or on the phone. Use the "thank you, but no" technique and then close the door or put down the phone.

❖ A person trained in assertion techniques will enhance their self-esteem and become more self-confident and less self-conscious.

❖ You can reduce stress by knowing how to handle difficult interpersonal relationship situations and thus have fewer arguments and conflicts with others.

❖ Assertive people give and receive criticism constructively reacting dispassionately to unfair criticism.

❖ Will help you deal confidently with situations like returning goods for a refund, or dealing with social situations like queue jumping.

❖ Reduces the number of people you will antagonise, hurt or alienate because you know how to treat people fairly and thus gain the respect, liking and friendship of those you work with.

❖ It prevents others from taking advantage of you, as you are able to express yourself with confidence and gain the respect of others.

❖ You will be able to make or refuse a request with dignity, diplomacy and self-assurance without causing offence.

"The most complete revenge is not to imitate the aggressor." – Marcus Aurelius Antoninus

---

Disadvantages of Being Assertive

❖ Inappropriate in some situations as others may not understand or accept this style of communication. If your boss is the type of person who reacts with rage to anyone questioning his orders, even when this is done in an assertive and tactful way, then it makes sense to use a different approach. If the person who jumps the queue is a big inebriated male using abusive language it may be safer, wiser and more discreet just to ignore the whole incident.

❖ Even though you put your point across in a tactful way, others may still react negatively or even aggressively. They may even harbour a desire to "get their own back". Assertion should be used wisely and sensitively.

❖ Even assertive people don't always get what they want. Others have their own agenda and rights too.

❖ It won't solve all your problems, doesn't guarantee your happiness and doesn't ensure that others will treat you fairly. However, it will make you confident about yourself and your decisions and you are less likely to be manipulated.

❖ Assertive women are often unfairly perceived as aggressive whereas assertive men are seen as confident, strong and macho.

❖ Friends may resent the newly acquired assertion and may attempt to sabotage your efforts, especially if they benefited in the past from your lack of assertion. There is no gain without some pain.

❖ In some cultures with different values assertiveness may be seen as socially unacceptable. Therefore people's values, background and identity should not be overlooked.

❖ Assertiveness assumes that everything is negotiable and that all conflicts can be resolved rationally. There are some things where there isn't scope for compromise. For instance, some people's principles, values and religious beliefs are not for negotiation. In other cases, the need for legal compliance such as health and safety means that certain issues are mandatory.

BODY LANGUAGE

There are different types of body language involved in assertive, aggressive and passive behaviours.

Assertion

Assertive people use sentences like, "This is what I think", "This is what I feel", and "This is how I see the situation". Their body language tends to be calm, controlled and smooth. The following are non-verbal assertive behaviours:

❖ Non-invasion of personal space shows respect and consideration. This means standing or sitting at a comfortable distance from the other person. Invading a person's personal space can be seen as intimidating. If a man invades the personal space of a woman it may be seen as sexual harassment. The amount of personal space depends on the situation and the culture of the person you are talking to.

❖ Receptive listening using appropriate nods and gestures. Lean slightly forward to show your interest. Look the person in the eye without staring as this demonstrates sincerity. The assertive person uses direct eye contact about 50 per cent of the time.

❖ Keep your body upright and open with your shoulders relaxed and feet firmly on the ground. Breathe naturally and normally. When seated keep an open posture with legs and arms uncrossed. This shows you are receptive and open to ideas.

❖ Smile appropriately – pleasant but at the same time serious. Match your words with your body language.

❖ A firm handshake conveys confidence and assertion. A weak handshake conveys the opposite.

❖ Speak in a clear, calm, firm but conversational tone. Speak with conviction and determination. Use co-operative phrases like, "What are your views on this?" Use emphatic statements of interest like, "I would like to…"

Aggressive

Aggressive people's attitudes could be expressed as follows, "This is what I think and you're stupid for thinking differently", "This is what I want and what you want is unimportant", and "This is what I feel and your feelings are irrelevant". Aggressive people tend to display shaky and shifty body language. The following are non-verbal aggressive behaviours and will help you anticipate problems:

❖ Using dominant eye contact with a staring, glaring, angry look.

❖ Towering posture.

❖ Being agitated and restless. Using a voice that is loud, strident, sharp, abrupt and cold.

❖ Clenched or pounding fist.

❖ Pointing or poking finger.

❖ Hands on hips or folded arms.

❖ Invading personal space.

❖ Using offensive gestures or physical aggression such as pushing.

Passive

Passive people's attitudes could be expressed as follows, "I don't matter, you can take advantage of me", "My feelings don't matter, only yours do", "My ideas are not important, only yours are significant", and

"I'm worthless and you're superior to me". The following are non-verbal passive behaviours:

❖ Lack of eye contact.

❖ Using a soft, whiny, indistinct or muffled voice.

❖ Nervously playing with hair, ear or jewellery.

❖ Shuffling feet with shoulders stooped and slumped.

❖ Nervous inappropriate smiling or laughter.

ASSERTIVENESS TECHNIQUES

There are three parts to an assertive intervention:

1. Empathy. Say something showing you understand how the other person feels while listening with empathy to the response. Ask for clarification while simultaneously acknowledging the other person's feelings and views. This shows you are conciliatory and want to conduct the conversation in a calm and constructive way without causing offence or getting personal.

2. State the problem. This highlights the difficulty you're having and why you need something to change. Take a problem solving approach to a situation. Describe the facts from your perspective and share your opinions and beliefs while seeking the opinions and beliefs of others. Avoid judgements and interpretations. Aim for a win-win outcome using collaboration and compromise.

3. State what you want and what you don't want. This is a specific request for change in the other person's behaviour. State your point of view directly and firmly without being hesitant or apologetic. Be specific about what you would like to happen in relation to the specified behaviours, describing the positive consequences resulting from the change. State what you intend to do if your wishes are not met.

The following are a variety of techniques that you can use in different situations.

Empathic Assertion

This is the most effective assertive statement you can make. Imagine, respect and acknowledge the other person's problem and feelings before you make your assertion. Then follow up with statements asserting your rights. "I know you must be feeling frustrated with the lack of deadlines on this project, but I want everything to be right before we set our targets."

"I" Statements

"You" statements are perceived as blaming and make people defensive, meaning they won't listen to you. Use "I" statements such as, "I feel", "I think", "I'd prefer". These help you to be assertive without being critical and show that you accept ownership and personal responsibility. Don't attribute blame. Focus on the other person's behaviour rather than getting personal. An "I" statement shows concern in terms of what you need, rather than in what's wrong with the other person. Telling someone they are lazy, stupid, inconsiderate or thoughtless is not assertion but rudeness. Focus on issues, not the person.

Broken Record

One of the most widely used assertiveness techniques is called the "broken record", so named because when a record gets stuck in a groove, it plays the same thing over and over again. Remain clear and calm while repeating things in a pleasant voice. Sticking to your point counteracts bullying, manipulation, baiting and irrelevant logic. If you have a legitimate complaint, continue to restate it despite opposition from the other party until you get your point across and receive satisfaction. Don't let one or two no's put you off. This technique is useful when asserting your rights for a replacement or a refund under commercial law. It will help you stand your ground when dealing with authority figures in a confident and assertive manner.

> "The most powerful assertiveness technique is to repeat your command with the confidence that the child will soon yield." — John Gray, PhD

Saying No

Most people find it extremely difficult to say no because they fear those in authority, or are afraid of an aggressive response. They may also feel that they may put a relationship in jeopardy by hurting the feelings of another. By saying no you are rejecting the request and not the person. Explain the reason for saying no and suggest an acceptable alternative to leave the other party feeling good. Saying no is preferable to agreeing to doing something that you have no intention of doing. Breaking your promise later on will show that you are unreliable and not to be trusted. In the case of another person making an offer that you do not want to pursue, express your appreciation for their kindness and then politely say no.

> "I think a compliment ought always to precede a complaint, where one is possible, because it softens resentment and insures for the complaint a courteous and gentle reception." — Mark Twain

Fogging

This is a polite way of disagreeing or deflecting negative criticism. The person accepts the negative criticism but has no intention of changing their mind or behaviour. Hear the person out and then acknowledge the criticism by saying that there might be some truth in what the person is saying. Agree in principle or part to what is said, while still retaining your point of view. For example, if a colleague says, "that was a stupid idea you put forward at the meeting", you might retort, "Yes, I can see how you think my idea has little merit". You're not agreeing with your work colleague; you're only saying that you can see that from their perspective they believe that. Fogging will help calm things down rather than using an aggressive response inflaming the situation.

The ALL Technique

Alexander (2004) reports that the ALL technique may be useful in appropriate situations. "A" stands for acknowledgement, the first "L" stands for the list of things you need to do and the second "L" stands for listing alternatives. For example, say your manager has approached you late on Thursday with a request to do an urgent and important project involving you working late. Acknowledge that the project is very important, and then make the manager aware of the other projects that you're working on. Tell him that you're on your way to an out of town meeting, and tomorrow morning you have arranged to bring your very ill mother to the hospital. Then list alternatives, offering to complete the project at a later date or by another arrangement. For example, you could say that you can attend to his request early tomorrow afternoon, and ask if that's all right.

Negative Enquiry

Negative enquiry requests further, more specific criticism. It accepts negative feedback about your behaviour at face value without feeling defensive or anxious and thus may help to defuse a situation. Accept your mistakes or faults, but do not apologise. Instead, agree with the critic's assessment of your faults and ask them for constructive criticism offering specific suggestions for improvement. For example, "Yes, you're right. I don't always listen to you. How can I listen more effectively in the future?" This retort puts the ball back in the other person's court.

Negative Assertion

This means accepting the truthful part of the criticism and restating it in positive terms, often in a humorous way. For example, a person accuses you of being aggressive and you retort, "I don't let people walk all over me, that's for sure". In response to being accused of being stupid you could reply, "I'm not the most intelligent person in the world". This dispassionate approach does not make the situation worse and ensures that the conversation can continue on an even keel.

"He who has learned to disagree without being disagreeable has discovered the most valuable secret of a diplomat." — Robert Estabrook

---

Positive Affirmations

A change in beliefs and expectations is necessary to become assertive. One way of doing this is restructuring your thoughts by positive affirmations or self-talk. Non-assertive individuals tend to engage in negative self-talk. Assertive individuals see themselves as assertive and flood their minds with assertive positive affirmations such as, "I'm entitled to ask for what I want".

THE TAILOR MODEL

This is a useful acronym to help you practise assertion:

❖ **T**hink about the outcome desired and the behaviours you want changed. Think assertiveness rather than aggressiveness or passiveness.

❖ **A**ssertive. Use assertive words such as "I" instead of "you". Say "I feel" or "I think" rather than "you always" or "you never". Be specific in what you want. Mentally rehearse affirmations to become more assertive such as, "I have the right to say no", "I have the right to be treated with respect", "I have the right to express my opinion", and "I have the right to change my mind". Visualise yourself being assertive in different situations.

❖ **I**nterrupt. Don't interrupt people when they are speaking, as this is rude and insensitive. Wait until they have made their point before responding. Listen attentively to understand what they have to say. Use silence as appropriate to encourage the other person to speak.

❖ **L**earn from experience. Reflect on situations where you have tried to be assertive. Plan to do better the next time.

❖ **O**ffer to brainstorm or solve problems together. Aim for a compromise or a win-win solution, as people are more likely to agree to something they have contributed to.

❖ **R**espect other viewpoints. Express your views and feelings honestly. Accept that others have the right to express their viewpoints too and just like you they have a right to be treated with respect.

SUMMARY

Know the difference between passive, aggressive, passive/aggressive and assertive behaviour. Passive people are submissive and taken for granted. Aggressive people get angry and upset at the least provocation. Passive/aggressive people use emotional blackmail, sabotage, and gossip surreptitiously to get back at others. Assertive people assert their rights while respecting the rights of others and seek win-win solutions to conflicts.

The advantages of assertion are many and include expressing yourself confidently without hurting the feelings of others. The disadvantages include that it may not solve all your problems. Body language can be used effectively to complement your assertion message. The techniques of assertion include, I statements, broken record, and negative enquiry. The TAILOR acronym will help you gain expertise in the process of assertion.

CHECK YOUR PEOPLE SKILLS QUOTIENT – 3

	Circle the appropriate response	
1. The passive person evokes pity or scorn rather than respect	True	False
2. The aggressive person asserts their rights in a diplomatic way	True	False
3. The assertive person asserts their rights in a tactful but firm way	True	False
4. Assertiveness should be accompanied by the appropriate body language	True	False
5. Passive/aggressive behaviour is a way of expressing anger directly	True	False
6. Assertiveness means taking responsibility for others	True	False
7. Assertiveness means saying no without feeling guilty	True	False
8. Assertiveness is appropriate in all situations.	True	False
9. The "broken record" technique means re-peating what you say	True	False
10. "Fogging" is a way of agreeing	True	False

Total the number of true and false responses and check Appendix I at the back of the book for the answers and to determine your score.

FIVE STEPS TO IMPROVE
YOUR ASSERTIVENESS SKILLS

1. Make sure you understand the difference between passive, aggressive and assertive behaviour. This will help you identify the mode you or others are in. Decide that you want to be assertive rather than passive or aggressive. Identify the situations in which you behave non-assertively. To become more assertive use assertive language such as "I feel" and "I think". Avoid aggressive language such as "You always" and "You never".

2. Adopt an attitude that everybody is of equal value. Respect the dignity and rights of others as well as your own rights. Remind yourself that you are perfectly entitled to have your own views, opinions and wishes and that you have the right to expect to be treated with respect. Get familiar with the Bill of Rights.

3. Learn to say no firmly but tactfully but without feeling guilty. If appropriate, suggest an acceptable alternative arrangement to make the negative more palatable.

4. Practise the "broken record" technique when you want to assert your point of view especially when you know that you are right or want a particular outcome.

5. Memorise the TAILOR model so that you practise the process of assertion in an effective manner. Remember that assertiveness is a skill that you can learn but it takes time and commitment to do so.

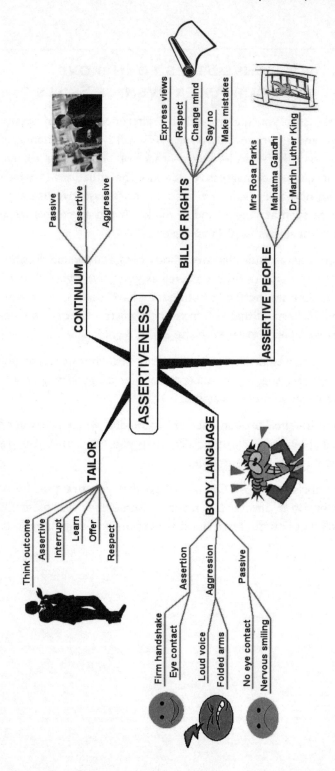

4

Conflict Management

- ☑ What are the types of conflict?
- ☑ What are the causes of conflict?
- ☑ What is conflict resolution?
- ☑ How can you manage conflict?
- ☑ What are the five steps of resolving conflicts?

Introduction

Conflict can be categorised as interpersonal, group or organisational. The causes of conflict are varied and can be due to personality clashes, power struggles, office politics or competition for scarce resources. Unresolved conflicts can cause resentment, anger and a desire for retaliation. Even minor disputes if not resolved may fester into major conflicts. A six-step process can be used to resolve conflict. There are five styles for resolving conflict: competing, accommodating, avoiding, compromising and collaborating. Ways of managing conflict include implementing suitable policies and procedures, reframing situations and thinking positively. The advantages of conflict resolution include better human relationships and better decision-making.

Types of Conflict

Interpersonal

We are programmed with a territorial instinct. Like other primates humans try to protect their space or territory and feel threatened, upset and resentful when it is invaded. Role conflict arises when our job role is not clearly defined. There may be conflict between an employee's values and sense of ethics and that of the company's culture. There may be conflict between the employer's expectations and those of the employee's family.

Most people perform several roles in their lives and, as a result, often find that the demands of one role conflict with another. A shop steward may experience conflict between their role as an employee and as a union representative. A supervisor is often put in a "no-win" situation of having to deal with the conflicting expectations of managers and workers simultaneously. A professional woman may experience conflict between the demands of her job and those of her family.

It has been found that introverts react more negatively to role conflict than extroverts; they experience more tension and poor interpersonal relations. In addition, studies have shown that anxious people are more likely to suffer role conflict than people who have a calmer and more adaptable approach to life.

Role conflict can include role incompatibility, role ambiguity, role overload and role underload. Role incompatibility arises in organisations where some roles are naturally incompatible with others because of different goals and priorities. Role ambiguity refers to a lack of clarity about how to perform one's job. It may include uncertainty about goals, how best to achieve them or how performance is evaluated. Role overload is where you have too much to do and can lead to stress and ultimately burnout, and role underload is where you have too little to do which can result in job dissatisfaction and boredom. Workers in this situation often think up things to do to fill the time available. Some of these activities may not be in the interests of the company.

Personality clashes arise when people do not get along because their temperaments are different. Competing for limited promotional opportunities may cause conflict amongst employees. Conflict may arise when employees feel they have not been kept informed about what is going on in the company.

**"All men have an instinct for conflict: at least all healthy men." —
Hilaire Belloc**

Groups

Conflict may arise within groups when members feel that they are not pursuing the same goal and are working to different agendas. The decentralisation of management means that teams are now expected to take on more responsibility and make decisions that were the prerogative of managers in the past. This causes stress and conflict. Personality clashes often arise where people work in close proximity as in teams. The convergence of different temperaments and people with different attitudes and viewpoints working closely together can cause friction.

There is inherent conflict in the business context between quality versus quantity, the demands for higher productivity versus the employees' need for compensation, the need to maintain ethical standards versus the need to compromise and short-term results versus long-term implications. Conflict may also arise if some group members fail to conform to the norms or expectations of the group. In such circumstances group members may be ostracised.

Organisational

The Iceberg Model can be used to understand conflict in organisations. In this model conflict is either overt or covert. Overt conflict sources are apparent from organisation charts, procedures and policies, plans, strategies and budgets and in job descriptions. Poor systems, policies and procedures often hinder rather than help employees from working effectively. Policies considered unfair by employees might cause resentment.

Covert conflict is hidden and arises through informal organisation, power struggles, office politics, company culture and hidden agendas. Traditionally, there is conflict between departments that have different objectives and are competing for limited resources. Marketing usually wants to carry sufficient stock to meet customer demand whilst Finance is interested in optimising stock levels to reduce costs. Research and Development might find it difficult to get Manufacturing to do a few basic tests on a prototype because they don't consider it a priority in relation to their ongoing responsibilities. Operations may see Marketing as the glamour department who take clients out dining while they get their hands dirty doing the essential work.

"A good manager doesn't try to eliminate conflict; he tries to keep it from wasting the energies of his people. If you're the boss and your people fight you openly when they think that you are wrong — that's healthy." — Robert Townsend

CAUSES OF CONFLICT

Managers

❖ Managers playing power games such as intentionally forgetting to invite someone to an important meeting. This will hurt the victim's pride and cause anger and resentment and even a desire for revenge and retaliation.

❖ Mutual suspicion and lack of trust between management and employees. Under the confrontational model of industrial relations, trade unions view management as the enemy. On the other hand, managers may view employees as untrustworthy, lazy and lacking commitment and initiative.

❖ Competition for status and power between different departments and groups within the company. Interdepartmental rivalry is a key reason for organisational conflict. Traditionally, departments such as Finance, Marketing, Human Resources and Operations do not see eye to eye as they have different priorities and objectives.

❖ Competition for scarce budgetary resources. Some managers may monopolise resources such as people, time or equipment. This creates resentment from those who feel they are not getting a fair share of the resources.

❖ Managers not treating their employees equally and fairly. Showing preference for one employee over another is a recipe for disaster. Grievances are often caused when employees feel that they are being unfairly treated. Employees may be unfairly blamed for something without being allowed to explain or defend themselves.

❖ The lack of emotional intelligence in company managers. It is now accepted that emotional intelligence is very important to good interpersonal relationships between managers and between management and staff. A manager shows a lack of emotional intelligence when unfairly criticising employees, using sarcasm and generally being insensitive to their feelings and needs.

❖ Poor communication between departmental management and employees. Information can be viewed as power with departments reluctant to share it with others. When a company has poor communication systems the grapevine will take over. Rumours are often untrue and may lead to false expectations, arguments, accusations and confrontation. The sooner a manager denounces untrue rumours the better.

❖ Some managers refuse to admit being wrong or making mistakes because of pride. This can be a source of resentment. Taking responsibility for mistakes is not a sign of weakness, submission or loss of control. It takes courage to admit a mistake, accept responsibility and apologise. There can be no learning without mistakes.

❖ Managers who fail to keep employees informed about developments in their particular work areas or about the financial and commercial prospects of the company. Some managers may withhold information or even purposefully give wrong or false data. Some operate on a need-to-know basis only providing information to employees that is essential for them to do their jobs.

Employees

❖ Personality clashes and personal antagonism between workers. People from different cultures with different beliefs, values, attitudes, philosophies and religions may experience difficulties in understanding, getting along and agreeing with each other.

❖ Employees getting involved in arguments rather than in positive communication and resolving problems.

❖ Employees having different likes and dislikes, perspectives and expectations and pursuing different goals will find it difficult to collaborate, as they may not agree on how things should be done. The job as manager is to create and sell a vision and win the commitment from employees to back and pursue it.

❖ Team members who don't pull their weight and do their fair share of the work. This will cause resentment because of the extra work burden put on the shoulders of the other workers.

❖ Rapid political, economic, social and technological change will cause
  unease and uncertainty among employees. They become fearful for
  the security of their jobs and because of this can be actively opposed to change.

"Change means movement. Movement means friction. Only in the fric-
tionless vacuum of a non-existent abstract world can movement or
change occur without that abrasive friction of conflict." — Saul Alinskey

---

❖ Thoughtless employees who do not load up the photocopier with
  paper after using it or do not clean up after they have used the break
  area for their morning coffee. They do not understand the concept of
  the internal customer and the need for good housekeeping.

Unresolved Conflicts

The effects of unresolved conflicts are many and include the following.

❖ Unresolved conflicts tend to grow into bigger ones. Small issues
  often evolve into major industrial relations problems if they are not
  attended to and solved. Don't imagine that they can be swept under
  the carpet and just disappear!

❖ Poor interpersonal relationships, jealousy and a lack of co-operation
  between employees will have an adverse effect on productivity and
  performance. It causes low morale and increases labour costs and
  the likelihood of accidents.

❖ Political and territorial conflicts between departments and groups
  results in lack of collaboration and will affect overall company performance. These power struggles are a feature of organisational life.

❖ Poor communication channels mean messages are unclear, incomplete and often not delivered. This will often give rise to unfounded
  gossip and rumour through the grapevine.

❖ Turnover and absenteeism of staff can be high, as people do not like
  working in an unhappy and conflict-ridden environment. They may
  vote with their feet and seek employment elsewhere!

❖ People may take sides so that conflict becomes institutionalised with warring factions within the company.

❖ Litigation may be resorted to if internal mediation and arbitration processes fail.

SIX STEPS TO CONFLICT RESOLUTION

1. Describe objectively the types, sources and causes of the conflict. Visualise the conflict resolution process and the positive outcome you want to achieve and the values you want to retain.

2. Ask the other parties how they see the conflict situation and the way they would like to see it resolved.

3. Respond with the appropriate style. Darling et al. (2001) reports that these styles are relater, analyser, director, or socialiser. The *relater* is likely to use empathy when solving interpersonal relationship problems. They are good at co-operating with others. Their sense of trust brings out the best in others. The *analyser* looks at issues in a systematic way. They like to have the facts before they arrive at conclusions. *Directors* tend to have a low level of emotion and a high level of assertion. They are often pragmatic, decisive, objective and competitive and tend to resist compromise in conflict situations. The *socialiser* is good at human relations while at the same time being assertive. Socialisers are outgoing, optimistic, and enthusiastic and like to be at the centre of things. The appropriate style adopted by a manager depends on the context and could be a mixture of all four.

4. Jointly agree on how to resolve the conflict.

5. Jointly commit on a solution. Agree an action plan and summarise the actions to be taken by each party.

6. Henceforth strive to resolve the conflict sooner. Reflect and learn from your conflict resolution performance.

"Nothing is given to man on earth — struggle is built into the nature of life, and conflict is possible — the hero is the man who lets no obstacle prevent him from pursuing the values he has chosen." — Andrew Bernstein

---

MANAGING CONFLICT

McGrane et al. (2005) report that there are three methods of dispute management: fight, flight and intervention. Fight results in conflict or hostility and aims to identify a winner and a loser. Employees may resolve to fight a perceived injustice by invoking an organisation's grievance, mediation or arbitration procedures to solve their dispute. They may even resort to industrial strike or to law if other means of address prove unsuccessful.

Flight is another method of dispute management and results in withdrawal or avoidance. Here managers ignore the issue hoping it will go away and the affected employee may leave the organisation in disgust. Employees respect and trust managers who confront and solve issues rather than ignoring them.

Intervention is the third method of dispute management. Employees request that their line managers intervene and solve their dispute. This presupposes that the manager has the requisite conflict resolution skills to solve the dispute to the satisfaction of both parties.

Managing conflict can be approached from two perspectives: those dealing with management and those dealing with staff.

Management Issues

❖ The manager should look, listen and learn and analyse why conflicts occur. Reflect back what you hear by asking clarifying questions. Demonstrate what you hear by validating what you agree with. Have the flexibility to adapt your behaviour as needed. Practise patience and self-control. Empathise by identifying with the feelings of the other party. Understand their values and beliefs, and respect their point of view and explain your position. Get them to explain the difficulties they are experiencing.

❖ Avoid anger. Being in control of your feelings means that reason is more likely to prevail. If the other person gets angry, don't get angry back, as losing your temper will only worsen the situation. Step back and acknowledge that both of you are upset and enquire how the other party thinks you could sort the problem out. There may be a case for postponing the meeting to allow tempers to cool and sense to prevail.

❖ Model ideal behaviour and walk the talk. Don't resort to aggressive, passive/aggressive or bullying tactics. Reward behaviour you want to encourage by positive body language responses, as behaviour that's rewarded is reinforced.

❖ Stick to facts. In the absence of factual information managers sometimes waste time in pointless debate over opinions and suppositions. Try to be non-judgemental and if you have to criticise, criticise the behaviour not the person. Focus on issues and not personalities. Respect individual differences by acknowledging that other people will have different perspectives and viewpoints. Use humour appropriately to release tension and promote collaboration.

"Difficulties are meant to rouse, not discourage. The human spirit is to grow strong by conflict." – William Ellery Channing

---

❖ The manager should aim for win-win solutions. Break the conflict resolution process into parts and put them aside as agreement is reached on each. Try to develop options for difficult parts so that you don't get bogged down.

❖ The manager should undergo a 360-degree feedback. This is based on observation and not opinion. If people become aware of their dysfunctional behaviour they are in a position to do something about it. Often managers are unaware of the way their behaviour impacts on other people. They must have the maturity to accept negative feedback and then take corrective action to put it right.

❖ Reframe situations. The manager should view conflict as a creative force and an impetus to learning. Encourage constructive conflict leading to innovation, rather than destructive conflict leading to poor relationships. Praise and reward employees for new and unusual ideas. People should be encouraged to disagree openly and challenge each other. A healthy corporate culture supports diversity of all kinds, including diversity of thought, opinion and beliefs.

❖ Facilitators. Managers with facilitation skills will help teams collaborate better and avoid conflict.

> "I loathe conflict, and I loathe not getting along well with people, so I always try very hard to be on the best terms with the people I work with." — Joan Collins

❖ Think positively. Tell yourself that issues can be resolved satisfactorily by collaborative discussion. This will enable you to respond more positively to the concerns of others. In the final analysis, if you feel that the viewpoints are irreconcilable then you could agree to differ and get on with your life.

❖ Move on when the dispute is settled by putting it behind you. It achieves no purpose reliving past resentments and experiences, such as what was said or done in the heat of the moment during the conflict resolution process.

Staff Issues

❖ Train and develop staff to be competent in doing their jobs. Provide courses in conflict resolution, interpersonal relationships, communication and problem solving.

❖ Implement suitable employee-friendly policies and procedures. Encourage the sharing of knowledge and the establishment of corporate instead of functional viewpoints. Policies and procedures should be established for conflict resolution, grievance and discipline, collective bargaining, mediation and arbitration. These should be written in booklets and made available to staff.

❖ Job satisfaction. People who are happy with their jobs are less likely to get involved in conflict. Redesign jobs to make them more challenging and rewarding.

❖ Employees will feel less threatened if change is managed incrementally. People naturally resist change and if managed inappropriately it can be a major source of conflict. Change normally puts employees under pressure because they are uncertain about their future and have to learn new things and meet new challenges. Change should be agreed with staff and introduced gradually and tactfully.

> "Conflict is the gadfly of thought. It stirs us to observation and memory. It instigates to invention. It shocks us out of sheep-like passivity, and sets us at noting and contriving." — John Dewey

STYLES

As illustrated in Figure 3 there are five styles of resolving conflicts:

1. *Competing*. This is an assertive and uncooperative style. It is a win-lose style of management. There may be a lack of common goals between the opposing sides. The manager decides that he must win at all cost or is convinced that he is right and is not prepared to entertain the views of others. Managers with this style use their formal authority, power, threats and coercion to get their way. It may be a suitable style where success is vital, and the manager is working under time pressure and possesses the knowledge and expertise to do what is required, however it is almost certain to lead to further conflict because the other party will feel resentful and seek retaliation in the future.

2. *Accommodating*. This is an unassertive but co-operative style. This is a type of appeasement, where common goals are stressed and differences played down. It is altruistic to the extent that one party puts the other party's interest first for the sake of peace and harmony in the workplace. The manager may feel the other party is right and wants to maintain good relationships or build up goodwill for the future. Also, the issues involved may not be of critical importance and the manager is prepared to concede.

3. *Avoiding*. This is an unassertive, passive and uncooperative style. This style of management tries to sweep the problem under the carpet hoping that it will go away. It is a type of withdrawal and suppression. It is merely a short-term solution, as the problem is likely to fester and raise its ugly head again in the future. At this stage it may become more urgent and difficult to resolve. This style may be effective when dealing with trivial conflicts to build relationships but otherwise it is not recommended. It may be appropriate to adopt when it is the wrong time to deal with the conflict.

4. *Compromising*. This is a middle of the road style. It is fair but does not achieve the aims of either side. If one party gives ground on a particular issue, the other yields something of equivalent value in return. Thus both parties finish up with less than they originally desired. It is often the style adopted when negotiating with trade unions on wages and conditions of employment. It suits a lot of situations such as negotiations on prices with customers and suppliers.

5. *Collaborating*. This is an assertive and co-operative style. Through a win-win approach it achieves the common goals of both sides. Both achieve what they want to achieve and the relationship is strengthened at the same time. This style of management emphasises openness, trust, spontaneity and genuineness. Differences are clarified and the full range of alternatives to resolve the issue are considered before a meeting of minds is achieved.

Figure 3: Model of Conflict Management

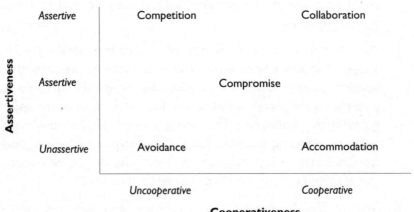

Source: Thomas–Kilman Model (1974)

This is also a useful model for influencing and negotiation. See Chapter 12, "Negotiation".

"Conflict cannot survive without your participation." — Wayne Dyer

---

ADVANTAGES OF CONFLICT RESOLUTION

❖ Constructive conflict arises when differences are valued and the parties to a conflict agree to disagree. They respect and try to see each other's point of view. They give and receive feedback in an appropriate way leading to dialogue, debate, shared ideas and creativity.

❖ Better communication and interpersonal relationships with staff, trade unions, suppliers and customers. Wise trade-offs benefit both employees and the organisation.

❖ Avoids emotional wear and tear and thus makes the workplace more stress-free. Anger is nipped in the bud and is not allowed develop into frustration and rage poisoning the atmosphere of the company. Thus industrial relations disputes and even litigation are avoided.

❖ Faster and better decision-making and improved productivity as rows and resentments are put aside and people get on with the job. Less time spent in conflict means more time to do productive work.

❖ Reduced costs through co-operation and sharing of resources.

"There are three ways of dealing with difference: domination, compromise, and integration. By domination only one side gets what it wants; by compromise neither side gets what it wants; by integration we find a way by which both sides may get what they wish." – Mary Parket Follett

---

SUMMARY

Conflict can be categorised as interpersonal, group or organisational. Role conflicts can be a source of interpersonal conflict. Group conflict can be caused by a lack of common goals. Organisational conflict can be overt or covert. Overt may be due to poor organisation structure; covert may be caused by office politics. Minor disputes if not resolved at source may fester into major conflicts. Personality clashes can lead to needless disputes and lack of co-operation between departments and employees. A six-step process can be used to resolve disputes.

There are five styles for resolving conflict: competing, accommodating, avoiding, compromising and collaborating. Ways of managing conflict include aiming for win-win solutions and implementing a fair negotiation process for the allocation of budgetary resources. The advantages of conflict resolution include better relationships with unions, staff, suppliers and customers and improved performance.

CHECK YOUR PEOPLE SKILLS QUOTIENT – 4

	Circle the appropriate response	
1. Lack of goal congruence arises when employees have different goals	True	False
2. Covert conflict arises through inadequate systems	True	False
3. Overt conflict is caused by office politics and power struggles	True	False
4. Behaviour that's rewarded is reinforced	True	False
5. Managers should focus on personalities not issues	True	False
6. Managers should model ideal behaviour	True	False
7. Collaboration is a win-win approach to conflict resolution	True	False
8. 360-degree feedback is based on opinion and not observation.	True	False
9. Change is not a significant source of conflict	True	False
10. Competing is a win-lose situation	True	False

Total the number of true and false responses and check Appendix 1 at the back of the book for the answers and to determine your score.

FIVE STEPS TO IMPROVE YOUR CONFLICT RESOLUTION SKILLS

1. Visualise the conflict resolution process and the outcome you want to achieve. Focus on common interests, beliefs, shared goals and win-win solutions rather than differences.

2. Ask the other person how they perceive the conflict situation. Ask clarifying questions and reflect back what you hear. Empathise with the other person by identifying with their feelings. Get them to explain their position and any difficulties that they might have in reaching an agreement. Explain your position and try to reach a middle ground by considering what can be done to resolve the situation. Stick to the facts by avoiding making assumptions and opinions. Depersonalise the conflict by focusing on issues not personalities.

3. Use an appropriate conflict resolution style such as collaboration. Focus on meeting your own needs as well as the needs of the other party. Study and get familiar with the conflict management model.

4. Jointly agree how to resolve the conflict. Gain people's commitment to change their attitudes and ways of communication. Use the chunking approach by breaking the conflict solution process into parts. Where you have agreement on parts, put them aside and then concentrate on the outstanding issues. This will prevent needless backtracking.

5. Jointly commit to a solution. Summarise the action that each party to the agreement is to take. Follow up to ensure that everybody is working to the agreed solution. Reflect and learn from the process so that you can apply the lessons to future conflicts.

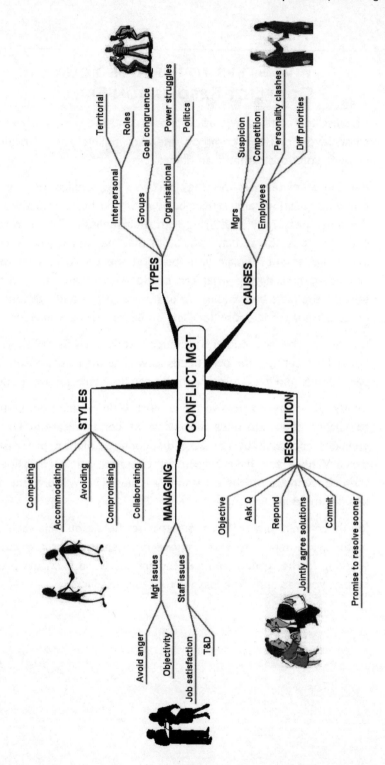

CONFLICT MGT

TYPES
- Interpersonal
  - Territorial
  - Roles
- Groups
  - Goal congruence
- Organisational
  - Power struggles
  - Politics

CAUSES
- Mgrs
  - Suspicion
  - Competition
- Employees
  - Personality clashes
  - Diff priorities

STYLES
- Competing
- Accommodating
- Avoiding
- Compromising
- Collaborating

MANAGING
- Mgt issues
  - Avoid anger
  - Objectivity
- Staff issues
  - Job satisfaction
  - T&D

RESOLUTION
- Objective
- Ask Q
- Repond
- Jointly agree solutions
- Commit
- Promise to resolve sooner

5

PERFORMANCE APPRAISAL

☑ What is performance appraisal?

☑ How is an appraisal interview conducted?

☑ How can you diagnose work performance problems?

☑ What is the Performance–Potential Model?

☑ What are the sources of bias in performance appraisal?

INTRODUCTION

Performance appraisal is about assessing employee's suitability for particular jobs or for future promotion. It may also be used to identify training and development needs and for succession planning. Each stage of the appraisal interview should be planned including before, during and after. Good job performance is determined by various factors such as motivation, knowledge, aptitude, skills and persistence.

There can be problems with the performance appraisal process, such as it being expensive and time-consuming. Many employees face the interview with fear and trepidation. Many managers are wary of the process because under employment law they could be subject to claims of discrimination if the interview is not handled fairly. Managers under time pressure may resent the demands that the appraisal process puts on them.

The Performance–Potential Model can be used to identify suitable first line managers for further development and promotion within the company. There are many potential sources of bias in appraisal interviews including the halo and horn effect and stereotyping. Inferior performance can be due to a skill deficit or a lack of motivation. To be effective, you'll need a variety of appraisal skills including communication, conflict resolution and problem solving.

Definition

Performance appraisal is where a manager examines and discusses an employee's recent successes and failures at work so that an assessment can be made of that person's suitability for a particular job or for promotion or training. In addition, employees may appraise themselves. Managers may be appraised under a management by objectives scheme. Some organisations have introduced 360-degree feedback where the appraisal is done by those who are in daily contact with the person being appraised such as other managers, employees, peers, customers and suppliers.

PURPOSE OF APPRAISAL

❖ Sets future performance goals in line with organisational and team goals. Goals should be SMART, i.e. **s**pecific, **m**easurable, **a**greed, **re**alistic and **t**ime-bound, and should stretch the employee beyond their present comfort level. Setting objectives and reviewing success or failure to achieve these is a great means of managerial control.

❖ Encourages staff to accept responsibility for their performance and seek a commitment to lifelong learning and continuous improvement. It may agree a personal development plan to meet career goals and training and development needs.

❖ Encourages those who have performed well to continue to do so in the future. Identifies any areas of unsatisfactory performance for improvement. Employees who get performance feedback are in a better position to improve their job performance substantially and contribute to organisational effectiveness and productivity.

❖ Recognises and rewards superior performance. Employees may find the interview particularly stressful, however, if it is used to determine whether they receive their next promotion, increment or bonus payment. Any increases in pay as a result of the appraisal should come as soon after the review as possible.

❖ Lets employees know where they stand about their future prospects within the company. This relieves uncertainty and sustains motivation and commitment.

❖ Facilitates succession planning to fill future managerial posts. It also identifies people who are ready for promotion or secondment.

❖ Increases employee commitment and job satisfaction and improves the climate of the organisation by improved communication.

❖ Helps managers make decisions on promotions, demotions, transfers, terminations and remuneration and rewards. Remember: a company cannot dismiss an employee without just cause and due process. Decisions on demotion or dismissal should be supported by a trend of unacceptable appraisals of poor performance.

APPRAISAL INTERVIEW

The appraisal interview can be divided into three stages: before, during and after.

Before

❖ The manager should plan and prepare thoroughly two weeks in advance to allow time to reflect on the issues that are likely to come up at the interview. Get all necessary information including previous appraisals, job descriptions, self-appraisals and personal development plans. The manager should review the list of responsibilities associated with the position and consider the key result areas. Check the company policy on appraisals, note the topics for discussion and think of questions to ask at the interview. The manager should have kept a diary of critical incidents of employee performance during the year to serve as a basis for appraisal ratings rather than relying on memory alone.

❖ The manager should have a short preliminary meeting to alert the employee to prepare for the interview. Preparing for an appraisal will help the employee focus on the key issues and examine their performance objectively. Remind them to do a self-appraisal and an assessment of their strengths and weaknesses before the interview. Get them to draw up a list of issues they want to discuss and review the performance objectives set by the manager at the previous interview. Ask them to identify barriers or constraints they encountered during the year and consider changes that could be made to help them reach their targets and improve their performance.

❖ The manager may need training to develop skills in goal setting, coaching, counselling, performance appraisal, report writing, observation, data gathering and record keeping. Similarly, the employee may need training in self-appraisal, setting objectives, keeping records, drawing up a personal development plan and communication.

❖ Give adequate notice of the appraisal interview with the time and place specified, as well as the agenda of the meeting.

During

❖ Make sure the agenda is on display and begin promptly. Create a non-threatening climate for the interview, encourage transparency and put the employee at ease. Use positive body language and establish rapport by smiling and using motivational phrases like "thank you" and "well done".

❖ Explain the nature of the interview. Use the employee's self-appraisal as the basis for discussion. Encourage dialogue by using open-ended questions to explore feelings, concerns, attitudes and opinions. The manager needs to break down barriers of fear, anxiety, suspicion and defensiveness. Intersperse the interview with closed questions as appropriate when you feel you need to control the discussion. Invite feedback and comments. Identify factors outside the employee's control that may have affected performance. Ask the employee for suggestions on how the job might be improved. Check the action plan for the last appraisal interview to see if the proposed actions have been done. If not, find out why. Providing feedback, paraphrasing what the employee says, and reflecting back their feelings and emotions are all vital behaviours that the manager should adopt during the course of the appraisal interview.

❖ Discuss the strengths and weaknesses of the employee. Praise good performance and accomplishments over the past year. Point out areas where improvement is needed and agree an improvement plan. Provide the resources such as coaching or additional experience if help is needed to improve, and agree a training and development plan. Develop in the employee a positive attitude towards the job and the company.

❖ Jointly set goals. These should be realistic and achievable, stretching and challenging. Concentrate on desired job behaviours rather than personality characteristics. Employees should be allowed go to an appeals process if they disagree with the appraisal. This is a safeguard against the possibility of discrimination.

"Recognising that effective appraisal depends more on sound interpersonal dealings than formal policies or administrative systems and form-filling is critical if appraisal is to become a positive and helpful feature of working life." – George, 1986

After

❖ Write up a report on the performance appraisal interview.

❖ Implement the agreed improvement and training plan.

❖ Keep copies of everything with documentation of a standard to satisfy legal scrutiny. Failure to conduct appraisals in an objective way, such as failing to keep adequate records, may result in legal action being taken by the employee.

❖ Watch for improvement during the year by keeping in touch with the employee and providing feedback as appropriate. Monitor the improvement plan to see that targets are being achieved.

❖ Keep your word, and always maintain confidentiality.

DIAGNOSING PERFORMANCE PROBLEMS

Good job performance is determined by a number of factors such as motivation, aptitude, skill and persistence. The acronym MASTER will help you diagnose performance problems:

❖ **M**otivation. Even if the employee has the knowledge, aptitude, skills and understanding to do the job they may not be motivated to do so. Without motivation nothing gets done. The biggest motivator is probably an inherent interest in the job, although employees may be motivated by a variety of things. As a manager you should find out what motivates employees and take appropriate action to support or create the desired motivators.

❖ **A**ptitude. This is the employee's natural ability to perform the job. Everyone has their own unique strengths and weaknesses determining their capability to do a job. Poor aptitude may mean that the employee may never do the job satisfactorily. There may be a mismatch between the employee and the job requirements – the proverbial square peg in a round hole. Maybe the employee should be in a different job more suited to their abilities?

❖ **S**kill. Skills can be learned up to the limits imposed by aptitudes. The employee may not have the skills, knowledge or experience necessary to do the job effectively. A skill deficit can be improved by coaching, training and appropriate experience. A knowledge deficit can be addressed through mentoring and educational programmes. Experience can be enhanced through job rotation, assignments and special projects. As a manager, it's your duty to address any skill deficit that can be rectified by training.

❖ **T**ask. The employee must understand the nature of the job and the expectations of the manager. Expectations should be clearly communicated. The best way of testing an employee's understanding of the job is to ask insightful questions. Evaluate the level of job understanding by the quality of the answers.

❖ **E**xternal factors. Performance can be affected by factors outside the control of the employee. Poor organisational structures, systems and procedures may hinder performance as well as uncooperative colleagues and managers. Managers should listen to the concerns of employees and identify those factors outside their control impeding progress, and then provide the supports and resources that the employee needs to do the job. In addition, consider whether the employee has the proper authority to make the decisions necessary to be effective. If factors impeding progress are allowed to continue the employee's morale and motivation will be reduced.

❖ **R**esoluteness. We need energy and persistence to get a job done. Employees may be good at starting a project but lack the persistence to finish it. Lack of persistence and procrastination may be caused by boredom, fear of failure or a lack of skills. As a manager it is your job to diagnose the problem and solve it.

CHARACTERISTICS OF GOOD APPRAISAL SYSTEMS

❖ Minimum job performance standards should be clearly specified. This will help the company deliver a better service to customers. Employees should be told how their individual jobs contribute to the overall performance of the company.

❖ There should be a basic assumption that employees want to do a good job and are trustworthy and competent. This operates on the self-fulfilling prophecy principle, i.e. employees will live up to the manager's expectations.

❖ Should be based on principles rather than rules. Principles allow flexibility and choice. Rules create rigidity and bureaucracy.

❖ Line management should drive the system with the support of the HR function. If the system operates the other way round it will not have the commitment of line managers.

❖ It should be designed to create dialogue rather than generate re-cords for planning purposes and allow for continuous feedback dur-ing the year rather than a once-off evaluation.

"Employee reviews should be performed on a frequent and ongoing basis. The actual time period may vary in different organisations and with different aims but a typical frequency would be monthly or quar-terly." — Boice & Kleiner, 1997

❖ Employees should be involved in the design and administration of the appraisal system. It makes sound psychological sense to give them a feeling of ownership over the process. If a system is imposed on them there is a danger that they will just go through the motions and the exercise will not produce results of any real value. Likewise, it should have the support of trade unions and professional associations where these are a feature of the company. Similarly, these should have been consulted during the design stage for their views and inputs.

❖ It should be tailor-made to match the employees with the culture of the organisation. Thus if an organisation is team-based the appraisal should not be based solely on individual performance. It should be easy to operate with the minimum of paperwork. Bought in, generic performance appraisal systems are mostly unsuitable, although some may be customised to meet the particular needs of the company.

❖ Ideally, discussion of training and development issues should be kept separate from assessment, promotion and remuneration.

❖ There should be written instructions on how to conduct an appraisal. Managers should be formally trained in performance appraisal. Different personnel should carry out the appraisal interview and any disciplinary proceedings.

❖ The results of the appraisal should be kept confidential. Employees should have the right of appeal if they consider the appraisal unfair.

PROBLEMS WITH APPRAISAL

Managers' Perspective

❖ Managers may be wary of the appraisal system because under employment law they could be subject to grievance procedures, charges of discrimination or even brought to litigation. The system should therefore be seen to be fair and equitable and the manager will need to keep comprehensive records in the event of things being disputed.

❖ The performance appraisal system may be expensive and time consuming to manage, as the paperwork can be complex and it may turn into an unpopular annual ritual. Busy managers may not treat the exercise with the respect and priority it deserves.

"Effective staff appraisal isn't simply a matter of 'going through the motions', holding ritualistic interviews and mechanically completing forms, before returning to the 'more important' task of getting on with the day-to-day management of the team. On the contrary, appraisal is a tool for managers to use to help them manage effectively." – Moon, 1993

❖ Most managers find it hard to give negative feedback as they find giving bad news to employees difficult, awkward and unpleasant. They are also reluctant to create bad relationships with people they have ongoing contact with.

❖ A once a year appraisal can be ineffective as it may be used to blame and shame rather than improve performance. It would be better if employees were kept informed of their performance during the year. This means that corrective action can be taken on an ongoing basis to put things right. The longer a problem is allowed to continue the more difficult it is to take corrective action. Frequent reviews allow for clarification and revision of objectives and will prevent disappointments and surprises happening on the day of the interview.

❖ Measurement of performance may be judgemental, problematic and inaccurate. Many managers don't have sufficient ongoing opportunities to observe the on-the-job performance of employees and may find it difficult to distinguish the contribution of individual employees from that of the group.

❖ Many companies use rating forms to appraise employees. These rating forms are subjective; two people rating the same employee are likely to give different ratings. In addition, managers may lack skills in rating systems. Some organisations have introduced assessment/development centres to make the process as objective as possible and to identify future senior managers.

Employees' Perspective

❖ Employees can fear appraisal and often feel threatened and uncomfortable during the interview.

❖ The interview may be perceived as very stressful where promotion, pay and a bonus system are linked to the performance appraisal.

❖ Employees may be told they are performing well without any commensurate rewards. This may be seen as patronising and so may discount the appraisal process.

❖ The appraisal may not assess team-oriented behaviours essential for the modern organisation. Depending on the culture of the company, appraisal systems are often designed around individual performance rather than team performance.

❖ The focus on objectives may disregard non-quantifiable factors such as loyalty, commitment, collaboration and the ability to deal with customers.

❖ If there is a poor working relationship between the manager and the employee then trust, mutual respect and a shared sense of commitment will be absent. This will create a lack of credibility and the impartiality of the process will be brought into question. It is difficult for a manager to give a fair appraisal to an employee they don't like.

"Another key to ensuring the effective use of a performance appraisal scheme is keeping and maintaining accurate records of employee's performance. Carefully maintained, they establish patterns in an employee's behaviour that may be difficult to spot by typical incident-by-incident supervision." – Crane, 1991

❖ Employees may feel that managers manipulate the appraisal process for political purposes. Managers may deflate ratings to get rid of a difficult employee, or they may inflate ratings to gain the promotion of a troublesome employee to get them out of their department.

PERFORMANCE–POTENTIAL MODEL

As a senior manager you may have line managers reporting to you. This model will help you to categorise and identify managers with potential for promotion. Management succession is an important aspect of human resource planning. It is an area often neglected in practice, particularly in smaller organisations. The matrix shown in Figure 4 divides managers' potential into four categories: rising stars, core managers, question marks and deadwood managers.

❖ *Rising stars* are managers with the potential to go further. These managers will benefit from career planning, wider experience, mentoring and management training. The company may wish to fast track them by rapid promotion, challenging experience and training and development opportunities. However, there should be no such thing as crown princes, i.e. people who feel they have an automatic right to managerial positions. It must be stressed that getting into senior management positions takes hard work, loyalty and dedication, competing with others and many years of experience. Only the best will advance to these positions.

❖ *Core managers* are those who the organisation depends on to get things done and are seen as its safe and reliable backbone. They are very good at doing their existing jobs but are considered unsuitable for further promotion. They will need training to keep their morale high and expertise up to date. It's important to have incentives in place to keep these managers interested and motivated and they should not be taken for granted. The important role they play in the organisation should be acknowledged explicitly. If you're ambitious and have your eyes set on the top management positions, you don't want to be categorised as a core manager. These managers are going nowhere and often lack flair, creativity and a willingness to take risks and new challenges. They are often set in their ways and are unlikely to be lifelong learners.

❖ *Question marks* are those managers who, for whatever reason, are not making the grade. They may have the ability but lack the motivation, or they may have the motivation but lack the ability. Either way, something must be done about these problem managers. Those with the motivation but lacking ability may be brought up to standard by further on-the-job and off-the-job training. Those with the ability but lacking motivation should be encouraged by an appropriate incentive scheme. Here again, it is not in your interest to be classified as a question mark. You don't want to be written off early and become stagnant in your career. Realise that learning is a lifelong, self-directed process and that you can influence the direction of your career. Anticipate the skills that you may require for future roles and take action to acquire them.

❖ *Deadwood managers* are those who have reached the level of their incompetence and are coasting towards retirement. They are the kind of manager who has literally retired on the job. They are not good for the company and are blocking rising stars from potential promotional positions. Their negative attitudes may be transmitted to younger managers − something the company does not want to happen. You don't ever want to be classified as a deadwood manager. If your career has come to a stop, you should calmly and objectively analyse the reasons why. Consult a trusted colleague to get true objective feedback on your performance. You are too close to the problem to be objective about yourself. A change of direction in your career or a change of company might solve the problem. Early retirement might be a solution if you feel you have marketable skills which could be successfully used by other employers or in a self-employed capacity.

Figure 4: Performance–Potential Model

Source: Armstrong (1993)

TYPES OF BIAS

A biased person has prejudices and preconceived notions about people. They look at everything from their own particular point of view and lack objectivity. When appraising an employee, managers must realise that they too may suffer from bias. Thus it is important that they always get the employee's viewpoint and the viewpoints of independent others. According to Gibbons et al. (1994), there are many biasing factors that may influence a manager (see also Errors of Judgement in relation to Selection Interviewing in Chapter 14). These include the following:

❖ Halo/horn effect. If you like or respect a person you are normally going to think kindly of them. In an appraisal interview a manager might see a person as honest and enthusiastic and then mark them favourably on different traits such as loyalty, courtesy and efficiency even though there is no link between the two. Likewise, a manager may consider one attribute to be of great importance and so they will rate employees as excellent or poor based on that one attribute. The horn effect is the opposite of the halo effect where the manager dislikes a person and marks them down accordingly. Some people find it very difficult to see any good points in a person they dislike. This phenomenon also arises in selection interviewing (see under Errors of Judgement in Chapter 14).

❖ Stereotyping. Stereotyping is a way of simplifying the perception process and making judgements about people. Individuals are judged on the basis of the group they are perceived to belong to. We assume that they share the same traits or characteristics as that group. We may stereotype people as to behaviour, age, gender, race or appearance. This phenomenon also arises in selection interviewing (see also under Errors of Judgement in Chapter 14).

"To know the true reality of yourself, you must be aware not only of your conscious thoughts, but also of your unconscious prejudices, bias and habits." — Source unknown

---

❖ Beauty effect. Attractive people are often preferred over less attractive people and are often assumed to have other appealing characteristics as well such as honesty and intelligence.

❖ Similarity effect. Managers may prefer people who have similar views to them or look and dress like them. Research shows that performance assessment scores were higher when the style and gender of the manager and employee were similar.

❖ Grievance. Managers may react negatively to employees who successfully file grievances against them and view them as troublemakers. This perception may subsequently be used for interpreting all the employee's behaviours.

❖ Subjectivity. If managers and employees are work colleagues it is difficult for them to be impartial. If we work with people frequently we become aware of their good and bad points and will find it difficult to be impartial when the time comes to formally evaluate their performance.

❖ Lack of effort. Managers may choose more severe disciplinary actions when they believe an employee performs poorly because of lack of effort rather than lack of ability.

❖ Central tendency. Managers may be reluctant to criticise and thus rate employees as average, neither very high or very low. This is a particular problem with rating scales, as there is a tendency to move to the centre when marking the scale. For example, if a 1–5 scale is used, 5 being the best, managers will rate a majority of the employees at 3. On the other hand, managers may have a leniency bias. They may have a tendency to rate employees higher than warranted and rationalise why this is appropriate.

❖ Perceptual defence. People are inclined to block out viewpoints that they find threatening or disturbing. They tend to select information supportive of their point of view and choose to ignore contrary information. In other words, they hear what they want to hear and see what they want to see. For example, a manager who is predisposed to making a particular decision may listen to viewpoints that support that decision and ignore ones that question it.

❖ Award ingratiating behaviour. We all like to be admired and appreciated but being surrounded by "yes" people is not a healthy environment in which to operate. It is surprising how managers can be influenced and swayed by sycophants who then receive favourable appraisals and recommendations for promotion.

❖ Recency bias. This is the tendency to remember and assess most recent behaviour because it comes to mind more readily and ignore behaviour that is older because it may have been forgotten. This highlights the need to keep good records of critical incidents during the year. Careful review of the records will help avoid the selective memory effect.

APPRAISAL SKILLS

As a manager you need basic skills to carry out the performance appraisal process effectively:

❖ You need to be very familiar with the performance appraisal procedure and the policies of the company.

❖ You need excellent oral and written communication skills to converse with employees and write up formal reports. You should be able to get across your expectations to staff in a direct, understandable and motivational way.

❖ You must have sound judgement and be able to solve problems and make good decisions.

❖ Develop coaching and counselling skills to help staff reach a desired level of performance. Have a basic knowledge of training and development so that you can suggest ways that the employee may improve performance. You will need conflict resolution skills to handle arguments and disputes effectively.

❖ You need to be able to delegate and empower your staff to take responsibility for their work.

❖ You must have knowledge of employment law so that you understand the potential pitfalls in making appraisals, such as accusations of sexual harassment, discrimination and lack of fairness.

SUMMARY

Performance appraisal is used to evaluate the performance of an employee with the objective of improving job performance. It can also be used to improve job satisfaction, career planning, management succession, manpower planning and as a basis for deciding levels of pay. Each stage of the appraisal interview should be planned. The manager should thoroughly prepare before the meeting. During the meeting they should create a non-threatening climate to encourage dialogue with the employee. After the interview write up a report on the interview and implement the improvement and training and development plan. There are many problems with the annual performance appraisal process. It should be continuous rather than once a year. Employees need to be told how they are doing during the year rather than be surprised at the interview.

The Performance–Potential Model, with its core managers, rising stars, deadwood and question marks, can be used to spot managerial talent. There are many potential sources of bias in appraisal interviews including the tendency to rate employees as average rather than very high or very low. Managers may also hold stereotypes as regards behaviour, age, gender and race. Inferior performance can be due to a skill or aptitude deficit or a lack of resources to do the job effectively. Managers will need a variety of skills for the appraisal interview, including communication, counselling, conflict resolution and problem solving.

CHECK YOUR PEOPLE SKILLS QUOTIENT – 5

	Circle the appropriate response	
1. Most employees go to the interview with fear and trepidation	True	False
2. The annual appraisal interview is the ideal	True	False
3. At the interview you should agree an improvement plan	True	False
4. The manager should do most of the talking at the interview	True	False
5. The manager should not encourage the employee to prepare for the interview	True	False
6. The manager should keep detailed records of the interview	True	False
7. The manager should be familiar with employment law	True	False
8. Managers should retain confidentiality after the interview.	True	False
9. The central tendency means we are inclined to rate people as average	True	False
10. Managers generally prefer people who are different from them	True	False

Total the number of true and false responses and check Appendix 1 at the back of the book for the answers and to determine your score.

FIVE STEPS TO IMPROVE YOUR APPRAISAL SKILLS

1. Encourage employees to prepare for the appraisal interview. Get the employee to review their job description and the performance issues raised at the previous appraisal interview. The employee should do a self-appraisal that can be used as a basis for comparison and discussion during the interview. This gives the manager a helpful insight as to how employees view their own performance.

2. Create a non-threatening climate at the interview and encourage the employee to express their feelings, views and concerns by using open questions. Praise good performance and point out areas where improvements are needed.

3. Use the MASTER model to help diagnose the possible performance problems such as motivation, aptitude, skills and persistence. Provide assistance to help the employee overcome these shortcomings.

4. Keep in touch with the employee during the year and enquire how they are getting on. Provide feedback and support so that the employee can take corrective action before the next appraisal interview. This means that there will no surprises at the appraisal interview.

5. Support the employee to meet their improvement plan by providing coaching and training opportunities. Also find out about the constraints and lack of resources that are holding the employee back from meeting their targets, and eliminate these constraints if possible.

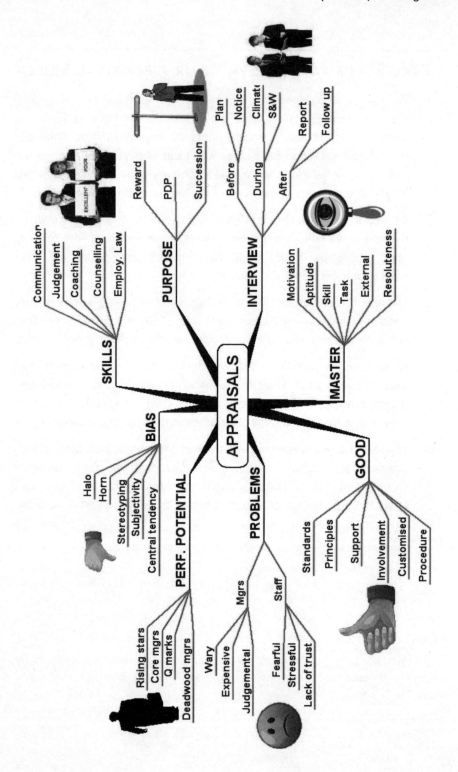

6

Discipline, Grievance and Counselling

- ☑ What are the types of disciplinary problems?
- ☑ What are the disciplinary action steps?
- ☑ How can you conduct a disciplinary interview?
- ☑ What is a grievance?
- ☑ When are counselling interviews needed?

Introduction

If an employee breaches a rule or consistently fails to reach the required level of job performance then a disciplinary situation can arise. Disciplinary problems include absenteeism, failure to obey an order, insubordination, lateness and sub-standard work performance. The disciplinary action steps include informal talk, oral warning, written warning and dismissal. The principles of natural justice include a fair hearing, representation and right to appeal.

When a member of your staff alleges that a manager has acted unfairly against them you have a grievance. Examples include alleged discrimination, sexual harassment, bullying and breaches of the employment contract. Most companies have a grievance procedure for staff complaints. The procedure should be well publicised and widely available. Small businesses are less likely to have formal disciplinary procedures than larger businesses. The grievance process can be considered in two phases. Phase one is gathering information and phase two is resolution. Counselling has been defined as the process of helping employees recognise their feelings about issues, define personal problems accurately, find solutions or learn to live with a situation. The counselling interview can be divided into three parts: before, during and after, with each part requiring detailed planning.

Definition

If an employee breaches a rule or consistently fails to reach the required level of job performance then a disciplinary situation can arise. The manager must exercise sound judgement and be sensitive to employee feelings when taking disciplinary action. The goal of disciplinary action is to improve the conduct of the employee so that similar behaviours will not occur in the future. The disciplinary interview should be run in a fair and equitable manner.

The best discipline is self-discipline. Most mature employees accept that they must follow legitimate orders, do their job to an acceptable standard of performance and that good behaviour is necessary in the workplace. Thus most employees believe in doing a job to the best of their ability, coming to work on time, being honest and refraining from misconduct of any kind. When people come to work they accept that they need to subordinate their personal interests and idiosyncrasies in line with the culture of the company and for the good of the organisation. However, in any organisation there are likely to be a small minority of employees who create problems and will need to be disciplined.

Companies can pre-empt disciplinary problems by implementing a range of employee-friendly policies. These might include employee assistance programmes, holding periodic staff meetings, job flexibility, managers showing understanding about employee's personal problems and generally adopting an informal relaxed attitude in the workplace.

"Right discipline consists, not in external compulsion, but in the habits of mind which lead spontaneously to desirable rather than undesirable activities." – Bertrand Russell

---

TYPES OF DISCIPLINARY PROBLEMS

There are many types of disciplinary problems and a variety of steps can be taken to deal with them. The following are the most frequent types you are likely to come across in the workplace. They can be considered under breaches of rules and inappropriate behaviour.

Rules

❖ Breaking rules, such as for rest breaks and leaving work before finishing time. These should be nipped in the bud early before they develop into a routine and become perceived as a right.

❖ Absenteeism. Chronic or excessive absenteeism is a just cause for dismissal. However, it's important that the reason for the absenteeism be established before any action is taken, as there may be valid and genuine reasons for it.

❖ Lateness arriving to work. This is a minor offence, however lateness over a long period may be considered serious, as managers are likely to view persistent lateness as disrespectful and undermining their authority. It also acts as a bad example to other employees. Here again, there may be valid and genuine reasons for lateness.

❖ Breaking health and safety rules. There is a legal duty on the employer and employee to ensure that health and safety legislation is complied with. Because people's lives may be at stake, it's essential that breaches of health and safety rules be handled with the utmost seriousness. The employer can be held legally responsible for breaches of health and safety laws.

Behaviour

❖ Unacceptable behaviour. This might include discourtesy to customers and serious interpersonal relationship problems with colleagues. Such behaviour is also disruptive to parties not immediately involved.

❖ Sub-standard work performance. Unsatisfactory work performance justifies corrective action. It could be due to carelessness or incompetence. Carelessness may be due to negligence or inattention to established procedures and work methods. Incompetence is the inability to do a job because of lack of aptitude or a deficiency in knowledge or skill. Coaching and training can be used to address a skill deficiency.

❖ Insubordination, such as refusal to obey a legitimate order. This is a cardinal offence since it violates the right of management to direct their employees to carry out the duties of the job and thus undermines their authority.

❖ Alcohol or drug abuse. Drug abuse would include cannabis, heroin and cocaine. This affects the performance of employees and may put their own lives and other lives at risk. Therefore it should never be tolerated. Some organisations run programmes to help employees with alcohol or drug-related problems.

"Disciplinary procedures should not be viewed as a means of imposing sanctions. They should also be designed to emphasise and encourage improvements in individual conduct." — ACAS Code of Practice

---

Disciplinary Action Steps

The following is a list of suggested steps of progressive disciplinary action that many companies have found to be workable:

❖ *The informal talk*. Minor disciplinary issues may be diffused by an informal friendly chat between the manager and the employee. The manager discreetly brings to the attention of the employee that their behaviour is unacceptable in relation to the norms operating within the company. Make sure the employee understands what they are doing wrong and what they need to do to rectify the problem. In most cases this should be sufficient. Take a note of when the issue was discussed, the action agreed and when it should be resolved.

❖ *Oral warning*. If the employee's unacceptable behaviour persists then the manager will warn the employee that their behaviour could lead to serious disciplinary action if it's not discontinued. The vast majority of problems are solved at this stage and go no further.

❖ *Written warning*. This is an official formal warning that becomes part of the employee's record and is the normal procedure in a unionised company. The document will serve as evidence in the case of a subsequent grievance procedure. Invite the employee to a meeting for a formal discussion and remind them that they have the right to be accompanied by a colleague or trade union representative. If you're not satisfied with the employee's explanation you should send a letter to them. This should specify the problem, what needs to be done in the form of improvements you expect to see by a future date, and the steps you will take if there is no improvement.

❖ *Final written warning.* This follows if the previous written warning has had no effect. It should contain details of, and the grounds for, the complaint. It should warn the employee that failure to improve behaviour could lead to dismissal. Managers should always have a colleague with them when issuing a final warning. Employees should be told that they have the right to appeal.

❖ *Disciplinary action such as suspension.* This may be resorted to where the offences have been repeated despite the written and oral warnings. If suspension is not provided for in the contract of employment it may amount to constructive dismissal.

❖ *Dismissal.* This is drastic disciplinary action and should only be resorted to for very serious offences. Never dismiss an employee for a first disciplinary offence, unless it is a case of gross misconduct. If a dismissal is contested in an industrial tribunal it's important that the correct disciplinary procedure has been followed as otherwise it may be considered invalid.

"Informal warnings can range from glancing at a watch if a person is late, or the raising of the eyebrows at some other transgression, to a forceful telling-off that is noted in the manager's diary. By these means a sensible level of control can be maintained which actually reduces the scale of disciplinary problems. If such methods are not used, a vacuum can be created that can cause an organisation to lose control of employee behaviour." – Rees (1997)

DISCIPLINARY INTERVIEW

The disciplinary interview can be divided into three stages: before, during and after.

Before

❖ Consider the purpose of the interview. Decide exactly what you want to achieve by writing down the agenda and interview objectives. Give the employee adequate notice of the meeting. The employee should be informed of the complaint against them and of their right to be accompanied at the meeting by a colleague or union representative.

❖ Check to see if a disciplinary action has been taken against the employee previously. An employee with a good work record and long company service will be viewed more favourably than one with short service, particularly where it's a first offence or one of a minor nature.

❖ Familiarise yourself with the disciplinary procedure and policies for your company. This should be available from the Human Resources Department.

❖ Clarify the authority you possess and the support you have from your own manager for the proposed action. Check this out before the interview to ensure that you are operating within your authority level.

❖ Check out the facts. Try to establish the truth as hearsay, assumptions and opinions are insufficient and dangerous to accept at face value. You must be seen to be impartial.

❖ Think in advance about the likely reactions of the employee so that you're prepared to deal with any counter-arguments.

During

❖ Get down to business quickly. Be serious but polite and courteous by creating a formal business-like climate from the start. Explain the purpose of the meeting.

❖ Describe the offence clearly and without emotion. Present your evidence frankly and tactfully while emphasising the employee's need to improve. The manager's expectations for future improved performance should be made clear.

❖ Get the employee's side of the story. They may explain, justify or deny the offence. Watch for non-verbal communication such as manner, facial expressions and tone of voice as these may betray what the employee is really feeling.

❖ Summarise and adjourn the meeting if necessary to recheck the facts if any doubts arise during the interview. For example, the employee might dispute the factual basis for some of the complaints.

❖ Verify the cause of the problem. Get the view of the employee on how the problem arose and how it might be resolved.

❖ Impose sanctions in line with the company's disciplinary procedure. Explain the reasons for any penalties imposed. You must be seen to be firm but fair. Summarise the proceedings.

❖ Agree an improvement plan on how the desired standard of behaviour will be achieved and monitored. Provide the necessary support such as training.

❖ Agree the review date.

After

❖ Record the proceedings of the interview. A written record of all stages is essential to safeguard against future accusations of unfairness.

❖ Write to the person about what was agreed and about the expectations regarding future attitudes and behaviour.

❖ Organise support such as counselling, coaching or training.

❖ Monitor performance at agreed intervals.

❖ Praise, reward and encourage progress.

PRINCIPLES OF NATURAL JUSTICE

These are basic standards of decency and fairness that you should abide by when dealing with disciplinary or grievance problems.

❖ Fair hearing. This means letting the employee explain their side of the story. They should know what standards of performance are expected and what rules they've broken. They should know what they are accused of and the evidence against them, and be given the opportunity to improve.

❖ Representation. They have a right to be accompanied by a colleague or trade union official to the disciplinary meeting. The meeting must be held at a time and place that are reasonably convenient to the manager and to the employee and their representative.

❖ Right to appeal. If the employee does not agree with the manager's decision they have the right to appeal. The manager has an obligation to explain the appeals procedure to the employee.

❖ Question facts. The employee is entitled to cross-examine their accusers and give evidence on their own behalf.

❖ Defend. An employee has the right to present a defence and explain the background and any mitigating circumstances affecting what happened.

❖ Consistency. Those sitting on the hearing should be impartial. The employee is entitled to due process and to have the rules consistently and fairly applied. Consistency is determined when we compare one employee's treatment to that of others under similar circumstances. Where an employee pursues a grievance and is not treated consistently with that given to others they may in extreme cases claim constructive dismissal.

"The principles of natural justice are an important and integral part of the corrective approach; the employee ought to have a right to fair hearing, the right to representation, the right of appeal, to question the facts as presented and the right to present a defence. – Fenley (1998)

MANAGEMENT HANDLING STYLES

The handling style adopted will vary according to the nature of the issue and the manager's attitude and whether or not the company is unionised. Managers who view discipline as a punishment for employees who are misbehaving will tend to be autocratic. In contrast, managers who see disciplinary situations as problems to be solved will tend to use a participative and open style. Managers may react negatively to employees who file grievances relating to the manager's behaviour. In a unionised company managers may be extra careful in how they handle the situation for fear it could be criticised through union scrutiny. Styles represent a continuum from telling to improve to asking and listening.

Between these two extremes comes the joint problem solving approach, where power and involvement is shared.

❖ Tell to improve or warning. This is an autocratic approach. The manager expects the employee to do what they're told and does not encourage discussion. The employee has no say in the matter and may feel that they haven't been given a chance to tell their side of the story.

❖ Tell and sell. The manager informs the employee of the decision and then tries to persuade them that it's right. The advantage of this approach is the interaction between the manager and employee will be brief and the message about unacceptable standards of behaviour will be clear. However, since the employee is not involved in the decision there's less incentive for them to alter behaviour.

❖ Tell and listen. Here the manager is prepared to listen but has already made up their mind. The input of the employee is unlikely to influence the manager's decision.

❖ Ask and tell. Here the manager is prepared to explore issues and may take the concerns of the employee into account when arriving at a decision.

❖ Joint problem solving. This is where a manager and an employee analyse a problem together and try to find a mutually acceptable solution. This approach is probably more suited to the grievance situation. However, some might argue, since the aim of disciplinary interviews is to change behaviour, a more participative approach is more likely to bring this about.

❖ Ask and listen. Here the employee does most of the talking. The style is very open and the employee has a greater degree of control. However, because of this the manager may be in danger of losing control over the situation.

MANAGER'S CONDUCT WHEN DISCIPLINING

Fenley (1998) advocates the value of metaphor as a means of understanding organisational behaviour, and uses four animal metaphors to describe the distinct types of management conduct in disciplinary situations.

1. *The Lion*, although ruthless, is generally regarded as killing for a specific purpose and good reason. This manager is strong but fair – someone who is meeting good employee relations practice and organisational needs. For example, a rule stating an employee could be dismissed for one instance of "being under the influence of alcohol at work" is clear and justifiable to all. Employees will have little grounds for complaint provided managers conduct a proper and unbiased investigation in line with the disciplinary procedures. Such managers are feared but respected.

2. *The Buffalo*, is the most feared animal amongst natives being regarded as dangerous and unpredictable. Similarly, this manager is strong, but mean and unpredictable. This may be bad employee relation's practice offering no guarantee that the needs of the company will be met. For example, an employee may be dismissed for taking one drink where management previously turned a blind eye to this behaviour perceiving it as a slight infringement of the rule. The policy and rules may not be clear to employees, and there may have been no proper investigation. In these circumstances, the workforce and external bodies will consider the action as illegitimate.

3. *The Elephant*, while appearing slow and ponderous is strong, purposeful and regarded as intelligent. This manager's style is soft, but fair. In the previous circumstances, the manager would give an employee the opportunity to attend an employee assistance programme, as opposed to resorting to extreme forms of action. However, if these methods were unsuccessful the manager may dismiss the employee. The workforce and external bodies would be likely to perceive this as legitimate.

4. *The Zebra* is one moment dormant and docile, but then swift and wild. This manager is deficient and disorganised. They fail to set standards or apply rules, and there is an over-indulgent attitude towards rule breakers. There are blind spots, inconsistencies, overreactions and delayed interventions to situations. An example is a situation where heavy drinking is condoned, without regard to production losses or safety issues, and where rules on alcohol are improperly and inconsistently applied.

Figure 5: Disciplinary Styles Model

Hard	Soft
Punitive (Lion) Dismissable offences Few procedural stages but rules clear, "due process" followed	**Corrective (Elephant)** Few dismissable offences Procedure gives lots of opportunities for "reform" and "due process" imperative
Arbitrary (Buffalo) Management is capricious Fire at will, unpredictable Summary treatment	**Lax (Zebra)** Failure to set standards or apply rules, over-indulgent attitude to rule breakers but inconsistent

Source: Fenley (1995)

GRIEVANCE

A grievance arises when a staff member alleges that a manager has acted unfairly against them. Examples of grievance include alleged discrimination, sexual harassment, defamation, bullying and breaches of the employment contract. Discrimination might relate to work assignments, performance appraisal, pay, promotions or discipline. Sexual harassment claims are usually by women and less frequently by men.

Defamation is the publication of false and derogatory information about an employee. Employers possess and transmit a lot of information about employees, factual and subjective. Truth is an absolute defence in a defamation claim. Nevertheless, employers need to be very careful in the way they handle and disclose information about employees. There is legislation protecting the right to privacy of employees. Bullying is now prevalent in the workplace and anti-bullying policies should be in place. Obviously, the employment contract is a binding document but less obvious are statements of company policy and goals, employee handbooks and promises made to an employee at the recruitment and selection stage.

Most companies have a grievance procedure for dealing with staff complaints. This should be promulgated throughout the organisation. Employees have the right to representation and to appeal decisions they disagree with. A good grievance procedure will handle and resolve employee's complaints in an equitable and timely fashion. If perceived by employees as fair and just, it will be accepted by them even if outcomes are not in their favour. Some employees may be wary of taking or pursuing a grievance because of the fear of reprisal from spiteful managers, despite the official promise that this will not happen.

> "One of the cardinal principles of effective complaints and grievance management is that workers must be aware of and have unencumbered access to well-defined procedures that are easy to understand and use." — Nurse and Devonish, 2007

Initially, the employee should set out their grievance in writing and then approach their immediate supervisor or manager. If it remains unresolved, the matter is passed to higher levels of management or to the employee's union. Remember that prevention is better than cure. Most managers do not like handling grievances, but grievances ignored are likely to fester and become more serious later on. In fact, grievances that are dealt with quickly and as near as possible to the source are the ones most often resolved successfully.

GRIEVANCE PROCEDURE

The grievance procedure can be considered in two phases: gathering information and resolution.

Gathering Information

❖ If you have an opportunity before the grievance interview, check out the facts. Look into the background of the grievance and check what action has been taken in similar cases in the past. Distinguish facts from opinions and assumptions. This may give you the chance to nip the problem in the bud early on. Grievances can become major industrial relations problems if left to fester.

❖ Invite the employee to talk. The employee has the right to be accompanied by a colleague or union representative as witnesses to the proceedings. The manager should handle the issue with great diplomacy and listen with empathy and facilitate the proceedings rather than direct them.

❖ Actively and attentively listen to the grievance by paraphrasing the content and feelings of the case. Probe as necessary, but preferably infrequently, to identify the problems, get additional information and clarify any issues. While listening, study body language such as gestures, facial expressions, manner and tone of voice. Provide the other party with the opportunity to let off steam if needed, but don't allow the situation get out of control.

❖ Factually summarise the details of the grievance and the person's feelings. Suggest a possible solution that is agreeable to the employee.

❖ If an agreed solution cannot be found, adjourn the interview if necessary to recheck the facts and reflect on the issues. Agree a date and time for a resumed interview.

Resolution

❖ Give information about your findings. These may be in agreement with the person making the grievance or you may have come up with alternative versions of what happened. If the differences are minor it may not prevent resolution of the issue.

❖ Jointly explore possible solutions. Search for the best solution to meet both your needs. Agree a resolution of the issue. If it's not possible for a joint resolution, then you may have to impose a solution considered the best in the circumstances.

❖ Follow up to ensure that the action promised has been taken and that the matter has been resolved. Learn from any mistakes made and take steps to make sure that the issue will not arise in the future.

If No Grounds for the Grievance

❖ Discuss with your own manager why the grievance is not valid and get support for your decision. Explain to your manager why the grievance arose in the first place and what steps have been taken to prevent its recurrence in the future.

❖ Explain to the employee tactfully why you are rejecting the claim. Listen to reactions but emphasise again why there are no grounds for the grievance. Be firm but fair.

❖ Explain the appeal process available to the employee. This may be an internal adjudicator such as a more senior manager or an external Rights Commissioner.

COUNSELLING INTERVIEW

Counselling has been defined as the process of helping employees recognise their feelings about issues, define personal problems accurately, find solutions or learn to live with a situation.

> "An employee may need a 'sounding board', that is, someone to listen, as problems are easier to bear when someone listens. As problems are alleviated, an employee's productivity improves. Additionally, an indicator of a good organisational climate is when employees confide in managers by telling them their personal problems." – Wells and Spinks, 1997

Some organisations run formal employee assistance programmes to help staff cope with the anxiety and stress of family, legal and financial problems affecting their on-the-job performance. Others offer an ongoing internal counselling service staffed by company welfare officers. Career counselling in the form of life and career planning are run by the more progressive organisations. Outplacement programmes may be run for employees made redundant because of downsizing. The main purpose is to help them find alternative employment by providing them with CV writing, interviewing and job searching skills.

Counselling may also be used to help an employee identify the reasons for some shortfall in job performance. The objective is to change the employee's behaviour so that their job performance will improve. Counselling may come before disciplining. The manager may notice the employee's performance deteriorating in some way and decide to solve the problem before it develops into a disciplinary matter. The employee may be going through a bad patch in their life and just need a bit of support. The communication style used in counselling should be non-directive and facilitate open discussion.

The counselling interview for a work-related problem is considered under three headings: before, during and after.

Before

❖ Keep an open mind on the person and the problem under consideration by avoiding prejudging or stereotyping.

❖ Accept you may be partly to blame. If so, you will need to challenge and change your own attitudes and behaviour before you attempt to change the employee's attitudes and behaviour.

❖ Decide the purpose of the interview. Your aim is to change the employee's behaviour to improve on-the-job performance.

❖ Consider an appropriate private venue agreeable to both parties where you will not be disturbed by unexpected callers or phone interruptions.

During

❖ Create a friendly, non-threatening and open climate for the interview. Establish rapport by attentive listening and showing a genuine willingness to help. You will need to win the trust of the employee. Adopt the approach of a facilitator so that the employee is encouraged to find their own solutions to their own problems.

❖ Make sure that your statement about the issue is descriptive and factual rather than judgemental and emotive. Show this to the employee with the purpose of getting agreement to it.

❖ Use reflective listening and appropriate body language to feed back the content and feelings of what is said. Paraphrase and summarise the content of the message and use silence as appropriate to encourage dialogue. Show respect for the employee's feelings and point of view.

❖ Get an agreement that performance is below an acceptable standard and a commitment on the part of the employee to improve.

❖ Establish the cause of the problem by the use of insightful questions. Open questions are best to encourage discussion. Closed questions may be used from time to time to refocus the conversation on specific issues. Ask the employee what solutions they think will solve the problem and the advantages and disadvantages of each. Get them to suggest the solution that seems to be the best in the circumstances.

❖ Jointly agree the changes that should be made and when you expect results. It's best that any changes agreed are at the suggestion of the employee in order to win their commitment and support.

❖ Offer support such as training, coaching, mentoring and further counselling, if necessary. Attendance at a stress management programme may be suggested for someone suffering from job-related stress.

❖ Agree an action plan with clear goals and review dates.

"A single conversation with a wise man is better than ten years of study." — Chinese proverb

---

After

❖ Follow up on the agreed dates. Compare actual performance against expected standards and suggest the corrective action, if any, that should be taken.

❖ Praise the improvement, if appropriate, and provide help if targets are not met.

❖ Reward the achievement of desired standards.

SUMMARY

A disciplinary situation arises if an employee breaches a rule or consistently fails to reach the required level of job performance. Disciplinary problems include breaking health and safety rules, unacceptable behaviour and insubordination. The action steps include informal talk, oral warning, written warning and dismissal. The principles of natural justice include the right to question, defence, and to consistency and fairness of treatment.

When an employee alleges that the company or a manager has acted unfairly against them you have a grievance. Examples include alleged discrimination, sexual harassment, bullying and breaches of the employment contract. Most companies have a company grievance procedure for dealing with staff complaints. The process can be considered in two phases. Phase one is gathering information and phase two is resolution.

Counselling is the process of helping employees recognise their feelings about issues, define personal problems accurately and find solutions, or learn to live with a situation. The counselling interview can be considered under three parts: before, where you define the purpose of the interview; during, where you create a non-threatening environment to conduct the meeting and explore the issues; and after, where you follow up to ensure that the agreed solutions have been implemented.

CHECK YOUR PEOPLE SKILLS QUOTIENT – 6

	Circle the appropriate response	
1. The goal of disciplining is to punish the employee	True	False
2. Insubordination is an example of a discipline problem	True	False
3. Disciplinary interviews should be informal	True	False
4. A record should be kept of the disciplinary interview	True	False
5. Grievance and disciplinary situations are similar	True	False
6. The employee initiates a grievance	True	False
7. An employee has no right to appeal	True	False
8. The objective of counselling is to change the employee's behaviour so that job performance improves.	True	False
9. A manager should accept that they might be partly to blame for the poor performance of an employee	True	False
10. Counselling should come before disciplining	True	False

Total the number of true and false responses and check Appendix I at the back of the book for the answers and to determine your score.

FIVE STEPS TO IMPROVE YOUR DISCIPLINE/GRIEVANCE/COUNSELLING SKILLS

1. Use sound judgement combined with sensitivity when taking disciplinary action. Run the disciplinary interview on a fair and equitable basis and in accordance with company rules and policies. Make sure the employee has an opportunity to defend themselves against the accusations. Be seen to be impartial and make sure that you observe the principles of natural justice.

2. Create a business-like atmosphere in the disciplinary interview by being formal but courteous. Explain the purpose of the meeting. Get the employee's side of the story. Impose the discipline in line with disciplinary proceedings but tell the employee of their right to appeal.

3. Use a different approach when dealing with a grievance situation. Handle the grievance with sensitivity and informality. Listen attentively and with empathy to the employee's complaint. Always check out the reason for the grievance to ensure it has a basis in fact.

4. Counsel to change the employee's behaviour with a view to improving job performance. Refer the problem to a psychologist if you feel that the problem is of a delicate nature demanding the help of a professional.

5. Create a friendly atmosphere for the counselling interview. Build rapport and trust by showing a sincere willingness to help the employee. Use reflective listening and silence as appropriate to encourage dialogue.

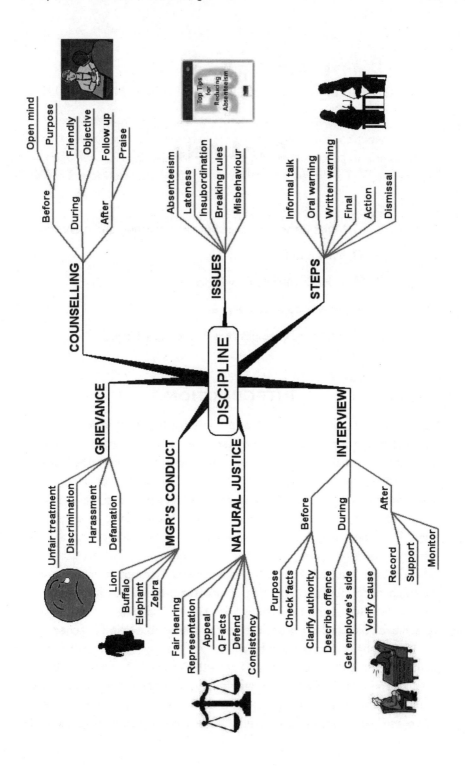

7

COACHING

☑ What is the difference between coaching and mentoring?

☑ Why coach?

☑ What is the coaching process?

☑ How should managers coach?

☑ What are the skills required for coaching?

INTRODUCTION

The first use of the word "coach" in English occurred in the 1500s and meant a particular kind of carriage. Hence the root meaning of the verb "to coach" is to convey a person from where they are to where they want to be. This is still a good definition for coaching. There are differences between coaching and mentoring. Coaching is just-in-time and is skills- and performance-related. It's a one-to-one relationship. The coach may be a line manager or an external consultant. An external coach is usually hired for top executives. Sports coaching is different than business coaching and is based on competition and a win-lose approach. Business coaching is also team-based but has a win-win approach. It has some similarities with sports coaching in that it wants to achieve goals and bring out the best in the people being coached.

Mentoring is usually done by an internal manager other than the line manager and is development- and growth-oriented. A mentor provides specific and practical advice. Training is usually generic, targeting many people at a time, and just-in-case and more short term. Coaching helps us to see blind spots and shortens the learning curve needed to equip us for new positions or perform better in existing ones. Coaching may be for a few weeks or for up to a year or more. One of the disadvantages of coaching is that the learner may become over-dependent on the coach instead of becoming self-sufficient.

The COACH model explained later on can be used to understand the coaching process. Ideally the coach and coachee (learner) should have compatible personality and learning styles. The coach must have good facilitation skills and be available when needed for the person being coached. The coach needs great tact and empathy. The learner should accept that the role of the coach is to ask questions and not necessarily provide answers, and should be willing to accept the pain of constructive negative feedback.

"Once used to bolster troubled staffers, coaching now is part of the standard leadership development training for elite executives and talented up-and-comers at IBM, Motorola, J.P. Morgan, Chase and Hewlett-Packard. These companies are discreetly giving their best prospects what star athletes have long had: a trusted advisor to help reach their goals." — CNN.com

---

DIFFERENCES BETWEEN COACHING, MENTORING AND TRAINING

Coaching

❖ Just-in-time. Coaching is done when the learner needs it. Managers and employees need knowledge and skills to cope with situations as they arise in the workplace.

❖ Focuses on achieving specific objectives usually within a defined time period. It's skills- and performance-related and directed at work issues, and should be tailored to the learner's learning style.

❖ One-to-one relationship. The coach adapts to the needs, aspirations and preferences of the learner. This means that there's a real identification of training needs.

❖ May be done by the line manager or an external coach. Executive coaches are usually hired-in consultants.

❖ Learner goes to the manager for coaching or to an agreed place that's free from interruptions.

❖ Evaluation is relatively easy as results are seen quickly. The skills acquired or desired behaviour adopted can be implemented on-the-job immediately.

❖ Usually lasts over six months or longer and focuses on the future.

Mentoring

❖ Generally done by an internal manager other than the line manager.

❖ Development- and growth-oriented and usually over the long term.

❖ May have the succession needs of the organisation in mind.

❖ Follows an open and evolving agenda, dealing with a range of issues.

Training

❖ Generic. The content is aimed generally and is not tailored to the needs of the individual participants. The content of the training is what the trainer knows or feels the participants need rather than what they actually need.

❖ Usually there's no proper identification of training needs. The training needs are generally assumed rather than individually verified.

❖ The usual training course is between one and three days although it can be much longer. Training professionals usually do the training.

❖ Is just-in-case rather than just-in-time.

❖ Difficult to tailor to different learning styles and the different needs of individual learners.

❖ Evaluation is difficult and there's a low transfer of training to the workplace.

WHY COACH?

Coaching may be done to help people reach their potential, develop management skills or provide a confidant or sounding board to senior managers.

Help People Reach their Potential

❖ Coaching is no longer seen as the preserve of senior management. It's now recognised as a way of helping all staff irrespective of position to achieve their potential.

❖ Helps people see blind spots. This could be in terms of not being aware of shortcomings to not being aware of the tremendous aptitudes or untapped potential people may possess. The higher someone goes up in an organisation, the less feedback they get and the more distorted it is. Many executives never receive honest feedback on how they are perceived by others. Feedback from the coach gives the learner an opportunity to identify these shortcomings and to take corrective action to put them right.

❖ People often don't realise the resources and talents that they possess. The coach should look at the total person and try to unleash previously untapped abilities. For example, people in their lives outside work may be leaders in their local community in charitable or voluntary work. They may have run in marathons and raised money for charity and brought up children with disabilities against insurmountable odds. They may have acquired all kinds of educational and vocational qualifications as well as unique life experiences. People leave these resources and talents behind them when they come to work. One of the goals of the coach should be to help people use their talents by tapping into their hobbies, interests, experiences, qualifications and past achievements and transferring them to the workplace as appropriate.

❖ Helps people deal with problem behaviour such as workaholism, perfectionism and the inability to meet deadlines. Managers with an overbearing manner or an abrasive personality can be taught empathy skills. A lack of sensitivity when dealing with staff can cause problems not only in morale, but also in productivity. Coaching can impart assertiveness skills to managers who are unassertive and avoid confrontation.

❖ Shortens the learning curve for new roles. Coaching will help the learner adapt more quickly to a new position or to a changing environment. The learner doesn't have to re-invent the wheel but can draw on the experience of the coach to help them settle into their new role quickly and minimise the number of mistakes that they're likely to make.

❖ Raises the job performance of staff and increases productivity and quality of output. Improves morale because employees feel valued and connected and thus increases job satisfaction. Consequently labour turnover is reduced.

❖ Develops employees by enhancing their skills and knowledge. Creates a pool of talent from within the company by developing skills and competencies to help people advance as well as changing behaviours that are holding people back. Encourages continuous improvement and lifelong learning. Empowers employees to deliver results and accept responsibility for their actions.

Develop Management Skills

❖ Managers who are unable to delegate and have poor time management skills can be coached to become more personally effective. Managers from a technical background with poor oral and written communication skills may need coaching to communicate more effectively.

❖ Coaching can give line managers who have been promoted to senior management positions leadership, strategic and visionary skills. The coach should pick a behaviour that is easiest to change, and then move to tackle more entrenched behaviours. Small successes will motivate the learner to go from strength to strength.

❖ The move away from hierarchical to team-based organisations means that many managers lack team-building skills. Coaching can help managers become more team-oriented.

"We all know technical and functional wizards whose determination to succeed has pushed them rapidly up the ladder but whose leadership, team-building, change management, collaborative, or interpersonal skills are, to put it mildly, lacking." – MacRae (2002)

❖ Shows managers how to navigate office politics. Provides fresh and invaluable insights into challenges facing the learner in the workplace.

❖ Succession planning. The manager grooms high-performing employees for advancement and promotion by planning their on-the-job training in a systematic and purposeful way.

❖ Brings under-performing executives up to an acceptable standard. Coaching targets precise problems such as communication, time management and interpersonal relationship skills. It can be used to enhance strengths and address weaknesses of managers.

❖ Improves abilities such as problem solving and decision making, strategy and politics, determining priorities, leadership style, rethinking of the future, developing key relationships and personal issues.

Act as Confidant for Senior Managers

❖ The life of senior managers can be lonely and stressful because of the long hours worked. They often have a poor work-life balance and little time to develop personal friendships, but like anybody else they need to talk to someone. Coaches provide a safe environment in which senior managers can explore ideas and discuss decisions with a trusted, highly qualified, independent and impartial facilitator. An external coach will often provide objective feedback and provide different perspectives on problems.

❖ Senior managers prefer to work with external coaches because of the need for confidentiality when dealing with sensitive issues and when a wide range of business experience is needed. External coaches are less afraid and more likely to confront issues and to say difficult things that need to be said. However, there is the danger that an external coach will give wrong advice because of unfamiliarity with the intricacies of the business resulting in disastrous consequences for the manager and the company.

❖ An internal coach is preferred where knowledge of the company's business, culture and politics is critical. An inside coach is also more available and accessible. However, an inside coach from the Human Resources Department might be seen as having a conflict of interest.

"If you treat an individual as he is, he will stay as he is, but if you treat him as if he were what he ought to be and could be, he will become what he ought and could be." – Goethe

Disadvantages of Coaching

❖ Managers may have values that are the antithesis of the coaching philosophy, e.g. "You make your own bed and you lie on it." Managers may believe that employees should be self-sufficient and figure things out for themselves.

❖ Time pressure on managers. Coaching can take a lot of time, the process is a bit esoteric and the results are uncertain. In addition, there may be lack of buy-in and support on the part of the manager if the coaching programme is implemented in the company without adequate consultation.

❖ Lack of integration between coaching, training and development, career planning, succession planning and performance appraisal.

❖ Managers may be poorly qualified to coach because they lack coaching and interpersonal relationship skills. The traditional manager is competitive, likes solving problems, and likes to be in control. These are not desirable qualities for a coach.

❖ A mismatch between the coach and the learner. The relationship is likely to fail if the values and beliefs of the coach and the learner are out of alignment.

❖ The learner develops dependency instead of self-sufficiency. The coach will want to foster self-reliance and expand the learner's capacity to stretch and grow.

❖ Personal agenda of coach. Staff may feel that the line manager as coach may have divided loyalties between their role as manager and role as coach. Consequently, staff may find it difficult to really open up as they feel it might compromise future promotion. In addition, the line manager may just be going through the motions of coaching as it is seen to be currently in fashion in the company.

❖ The coach gives wrong advice because they misdiagnose the problem. They may be treating symptoms as the disease and this may damage the person being coached. The manager also needs to have the judgement to know when the help of a professional clinical psychologist is needed. For example, problem behaviour might be due to personal problems in the learner's life. Adjusting to married life, divorce, illness or struggling with a financial problem can be some of the personal issues in a learner's life. Chronic business behaviours like workaholism, perfectionism and procrastination are often caused by deep underlying psychological problems needing the help of a psychologist rather than a coach.

❖ Coaching can send people on non-business voyages of self-discovery making them unhappy with their present circumstances. The learner might become so self-aware that they decide the job is not for them and decide to leave the company to pursue an alternative career. This may be good for the person but bad for the business because of the cost of replacement and retraining.

❖ The learner must be willing to change. If the person is unwilling to change then the coach's task is impossible. Some people are inflexible and are not willing to undertake new challenges and grow.

"I know you've heard it a thousand times before. But it's true – hard work pays off. If you want to be good, you have to practise, practise, practise. If you don't love something, then don't do it." – Ray Bradbury

---

THE COACH MODEL

The acronym COACH will help you understand the coaching process.

❖ **C**larifying needs. It's often a balance between current performance level, organisational goals and personal development needs. Find out what is important to the learner. What do they want versus business needs? Create a positive focus by believing that people can change. What behavioural patterns are hindering success? How will you know when issues have been resolved? Ask the learner if they're aware about solutions to similar problems.

❖ **O**bjectives. The goals must be meaningful to the learner. The prime objective is that the learner will acquire desired behaviours and eliminate undesirable ones. Set performance measures so that you know the standards to be achieved. Design a method for gauging progress towards the desired outcomes. This will be in the form of a time schedule with interim goals. Objectives should be realistic as unachievable ones will de-motivate learners.

❖ **A**ction plan. Jointly generate and evaluate options before firming up on an action plan. The coach who adopts a perspective of seeing every situation in a fresh light is free to explore novel possibilities. An action plan should be broken down into manageable measurable steps so that the learner is able to constantly assess progress. Small successes are motivational and when combined eventually will make a big difference. It's important that the plan is a collaborative effort between the coach and the learner. The plan will include objectives, actions and outcomes, skills to be improved or learned, behaviours to be acquired, levels of competency to be achieved and a time frame in which all these are to take place. The coach's job is to gain the learner's commitment to action. It's about filling the gap between where the learner is and where they wish to be.

❖ **C**heck and evaluate. What worked? What didn't? What can we do better next time? What is a successful outcome? Learn from successes and failures. Hold the learner accountable for achieving demonstrable outcomes in the workplace. Activities, skills, outcomes and behaviour will be evaluated against the agreed targets.

❖ **H**ands-on approach. Coaching is all about on-the-job learning. It focuses on solutions, practical outcomes and desired behaviours in the workplace. Unlike training, it's specific rather than generic.

"A man can be as great as he wants to be. If you believe in yourself and have the courage, the determination, the dedication, the competitive drive and if you are willing to sacrifice the little things in life and pay the price for the things that are worthwhile, it can be done." – Vince Lombardi

---

COACHING SKILLS

Personal Qualities of Coach

❖ Integrity. The coach must have a high standard of personal and professional ethics. The coach must be a trusted and reliable confidant. Trust enables the learner to say whatever they need to the coach and reflect openly on their mistakes and shortcomings without feeling threatened. Without mutual respect the relationship is unlikely to last. The coach should show regard, consideration and under-standing for the learner's experience and opinions.

❖ Judgement. The coach should know when to refer the learner to other specialists, e.g. psychologists if they feel that there are deeper psychological issues to be addressed and resolved.

❖ The coach should be able to paint the big picture. They should be able to ascertain the long-term potential of the learner and must have the confidence to challenge, inspire and motivate learners to become self-actualised. Their job is to bring out the inherent great-ness in the learners.

❖ Observe performance. They should be able to help the learner identify the values and activities that give them the most passion and fulfilment in life. Work is play and so to be successful at work, the learner must find work that they enjoy.

"It is a paradoxical but profoundly true and important principle of life that the most likely way to reach a goal is to be aiming not at that goal itself but at some more ambitious goal beyond it." — Arnold Toynbee

---

❖ Practise active listening. The coach should reflect back to the learner what has been said. They should paraphrase in their own words so that the learner knows they have been understood and to avoid any misunderstanding.

❖ Rapport. Being able to observe and manage moods and emotions is a core workplace competence. The coach and learner must be on the same wavelength. The coach should be pleasant, courteous and tactful when dealing with the learner and be able to interact, talk, ask questions and listen. They should act as a role model and "walk the talk". They need to retain credibility by keeping their promises and living up to their commitments. Coaching is a journey of self-discovery for both the coach and the learner. Each learns from the other.

❖ Objectivity. The coach should remain detached and operate within boundaries. For example, they should respect the personal bounda-ries of the learner and not interfere in their private life.

Business Skills

❖ Facilitation. Get the learner to reflect on what they have learned. This means to facilitate rather than tell or advise. The coach should guide and support in a non-directive way. They should adopt the belief that the learner is naturally creative and resourceful and wants to improve but may occasionally need advice, opinions or suggestions. However, both parties must understand that the learner is free to accept or reject what is offered and must always take the ultimate responsibility for actions taken.

"The core skills of coaching can be divided into mental and interpersonal skills. The mental skills include observation and analysis, and the ability to structure the coaching process for the learner in question. Key interpersonal skills include questioning; listening; giving and receiving feedback; communicating and motivating." — Phillips (1995)

❖ Business acumen and experience. Learners expect their coach to have a good track record with considerable business experience. Coaches should have the necessary political skills to pass on to the learner and the knowledge of how complex organisational systems work. They should understand group dynamics and organisational behaviour. They need a broad understanding of leadership if they want to pass on the knowledge and skills of leadership to learners.

❖ Communication. We listen at three levels which can be called the 3-H's: at the head level we listen for thoughts, at the heart level for emotions and feelings, and at the hands level for actions. What is the commitment of the learner to perform and actually do things to change?

❖ The coach needs the ability to ask challenging but non-threatening questions which prompt and motivate the learner to discover the answers for themselves. "Where have you been?" This helps you think of your journey to the present – you are what you are because of your past. "Where are you now?" This takes stock of your present position – a strengths and weaknesses analysis would be helpful here. "Where do you want to be?" This should consider your learning goals – visualise the situation you want to achieve. "How can you get there?" You can get there via an action programme. "How will you know when you've arrived?" This presupposes a mechanism for determining how much learning has taken place.

❖ Provide feedback. The coach should always make feedback constructive. Some experts believe that sandwiching negative comments between two positive ones softens the blow. Offer feedback in a safe setting. Feedback should be two-way so that the coach should also ask for feedback from the learner. Reframe situations to enable the learner to see them differently.

"The purpose of coaching and mentoring is to help and support people, in an increasingly pressurised and competitive world, to take responsibility for managing their own learning in order to maximise their potential, develop their skills, improve their performance and proactively become the people they want to be." — Eric Parsloe, Oxford School of Coaching

---

❖ Problem solving and decision making skills. The coach should be able to offer new perspectives and insights to problems. Their role is to be curious, to ask questions, to challenge ideas and assumptions, to uncover problems and explore ways of solving them. The learner is ultimately responsible for solving their problems.

❖ Understanding learning. The coach needs a good knowledge of training and development techniques and approaches. They should understand how adults learn and be able to apply this knowledge to help them learn more effectively.

❖ Make learners more self-aware. Assessment tools will help the manager identify behaviours in the learner that need to be eliminated or improved. The Johari Window, the Myers-Briggs Type Indicator (MBTI) psychometric tests, emotional intelligence tests, and 360-degree feedback can be used for this purpose. These will improve the learner's perception of how they're perceived and impact on others. For example, the MBTI will indicate whether people are extroverted or introverted, whether they take an empirical or an intuitive approach to information or whether they're more inclined to rigidity or spontaneity, logic or emotion. Knowing what your personality type is can be useful to both the coach and the learner. The application and interpretation of this test requires professional expertise.

"I never cease to be amazed at the power of the coaching process to draw out the skills or talent that was previously hidden within an individual, and which invariably finds a way to solve a problem previously thought unsolvable." — John Russell, MD, Harley-Davidson Europe Ltd

---

RELATIONSHIP BETWEEN COACH AND LEARNER

Coach

❖ Exercise emotional IQ. The coach needs to develop their emotional IQ to help them understand and acknowledge the feelings and emotions of the learner in a tactful way. The coach should understand the learner's perspective.

❖ Be supportive. The coach should encourage the self-belief of the learner that they're capable of achieving goals. They should awaken the enthusiasm of the learner to achieve results and engage in life-long learning. They should act as a role model by leading by example, and be there for the learner when needed.

❖ Respect. The coach should create an environment in which the learner receives unconditional positive regard irrespective of their personal feelings towards them. This means acceptance is never conditional; it is never withheld or withdrawn. It's just there. This creates an environment of mutual trust and respect where the learner's concerns are listened to in a non-judgemental way.

❖ Confidentiality. The coach is a trusted confidant and should exercise great discretion when dealing with the learner. It just takes one careless remark to undermine trust. The learner should feel safe to reflect openly on mistakes and weaknesses and to be honest with themselves and others. Confidential matters should never be discussed in front of others. Therefore, it's important that the time and place to raise confidential matters is chosen with great care and consideration.

❖ Professionalism. The coach should be the epitome of professionalism. They should be organised with good time management and office skills and have high ethical standards and values. The coach should have integrity, honesty and a genuine concern for the welfare of the learner and tell the truth and keep their promises.

❖ Communication. The coach should be able to inspire, motivate and get the learner's commitment to achieve the goals of the coaching plan. They should be able to draw out the creativity of the learner to think of different ways to achieve goals.

Learner

❖ Should be open and honest. The learner should tell the coach if they have a specific reason for wanting or not wanting to do something. They should accept that the role of coach is to ask insightful questions, generate ideas and not necessarily provide answers.

❖ The learner needs to be assertive to ask questions, explore issues and make it clear what they want. They should create networks inside and outside the company to help further their career.

❖ The learner should be self-aware and know their strengths and weaknesses and thus know when to look for coaching in different situations.

❖ The learner should accept responsibility for their learning and training and development plans. Thus the learner should maintain a learning log where they record their experiences and then review and reflect on them.

❖ The learner should be willing to experiment through independent action. They should practise desired behaviours between sessions and prepare in advance for coaching sessions. They should be prepared to accept challenges, options and new behaviours on the journey towards reaching his goals.

❖ The learner should maintain a positive interpersonal relationship with the coach to enhance the productivity of the arrangement. They should accept that the coach has their best interests at heart and wants the learner to improve and reach their potential.

❖ The learner should expect to receive sound guidance and ongoing feedback, both positive and negative, to improve their skills and behaviour. The learner should be aware of their successes as well as their mistakes and be prepared to accept the pain of constructive critical feedback.

"Personal growth, unaided, can be slow and discouraging. With the help of a coach, people can tap into broader resources, faster. Moreover, they have the help of someone who brings experiences and perspectives that they might not access on their own." — Richard Haasnoot, Coach

---

❖ The learner should meet with the coach at least once a month for several sessions and after that as needed. They should take the initiative to see the coach as necessary as the coach may be unaware that they need help. The learner should have access to the coach between sessions by email and telephone. They should meet in the coach's office or other agreed place free from distractions.

❖ Before finally committing themselves to the coaching agreement they should make sure that their coach has the required business and technical skills to help them improve and reach their goals. They should pick a coach that they feel comfortable with. If there is a lack of chemistry between the coach and the learner then they should look for somebody else.

❖ They should receive a formal written agreement and plan for the coaching sessions and clarify with the coach the degree of confidentiality to be observed.

SUMMARY

There are similarities and differences between coaching, mentoring and training. All of these approaches can be used to improve the productivity of managers and staff. Coaching is just-in-time and is skills- and performance-related. It's done in the workplace. The coach may be a line manager or an external consultant. Mentoring is usually done by an internal manager other than the line manager and is development- and growth-oriented. It's also normally done in the workplace. Training is usually generic and just-in-case and more short term. It's usually done off the job in a training centre. Coaching helps to develop employees and improves job performance, productivity and morale. It may have shortcomings such as a mismatch between the coach and the learner or the coach may lack good coaching skills.

The COACH model may be used to understand the coaching process. It stands for **c**larifying needs; **o**bjectives for behaviour change; **a**ction plan; **c**heck and evaluate; **h**ands-on approach

There should be a good match between the coach and the person being coached, and ideally they should have compatible personality and learning styles. The coach should have good facilitation skills and be available as needed. They need great tact and empathy and to be able to customise their approach to the needs of the learner. The learner should accept that the role of the coach is to ask questions, clarify issues and not necessarily to provide answers. The learner should be prepared to accept the pain of constructive negative feedback.

CHECK YOUR PEOPLE SKILLS QUOTIENT – 7

	Circle the appropriate response	
1. Coaching and mentoring are the same	True	False
2. A line manager should do the mentoring	True	False
3. Training is generic and just in case	True	False
4. Coaching is skills related and just-in-time	True	False
5. Coaching integrates learning into the workplace	True	False
6. A good coach acts as a facilitator	True	False
7. A good coach clarifies issues rather than answers questions	True	False
8. A manager does not need formal training to coach.	True	False
9. If trust is undermined then the coaching relationship is ruined	True	False
10. The learner should accept responsibility for own learning	True	False

Total the number of true and false responses and check Appendix 1 at the back of the book for the answers and to determine your score.

FIVE STEPS TO IMPROVE YOUR COACHING SKILLS

1. The manager as coach should develop facilitation skills. This means the coach should suggest rather than tell, act as a sounding board, get the learner to work out their own solutions, be non-directive by guiding and supporting the learner, and clarify issues and suggest alternatives for consideration rather than giving definitive answers.

2. The coach and learner should jointly agree a coaching action plan. The coach then needs to get commitment to this plan and set down the expected outcomes and the time schedule for their achievement. They should organise meetings to discuss progress towards the attainment of interim goals.

3. The coach should practise communication skills such as active and reflective listening, asking questions, clarifying issues, acting the devil's advocate, reframing situations and giving and receiving feedback.

4. The coach should create rapport with the learner by establishing sound interpersonal relationships and building mutual respect and trust. The coaching relationship is confidential and this must be strictly observed. Trust takes a considerable time to establish but can be destroyed quickly even with as little as one careless comment.

5. The coach should remind the learner of their responsibilities. These include being open and honest; asking questions and looking for feedback; taking the initiative if necessary to see the coach; developing the maturity necessary to accept the pain of negative constructive feedback; maintaining a learning log; and accepting responsibility for their own learning.

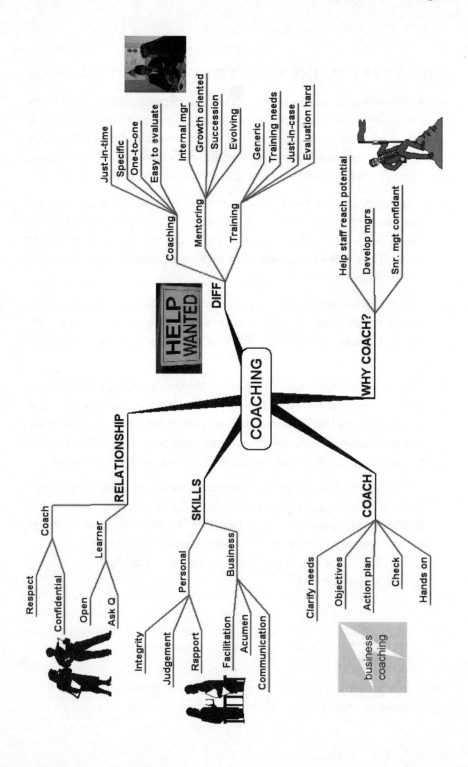

8

LEADERSHIP SKILLS

☑ What are the traits of good leaders?

☑ What are the styles of leadership?

☑ What is the difference between a manager and a leader?

☑ What are the sources of power and influence?

☑ What are the best leadership practices?

INTRODUCTION

Leaders create a vision and inspire others to achieve goals. The traits of leadership include integrity, toughness, confidence, humility, enthusiasm, intelligence and warmth. The functions of leadership include planning, leading, organising and controlling. The styles of leadership are directive, visionary, affiliative, participative, pacesetting and coaching. The types of leaders are functional, appointed, charismatic, traditional and situational.

Everyday leadership is about demonstrating confidence and optimism and meeting challenges head on. There are differences between managers and leaders. Managers do things right while leaders do the right things. Managers promote stability while leaders promote innovation and change. The sources of power and influence include physical, resource, personal, position, and expert power. Leadership's dark side includes narcissism and fear of letting things go. The best practices of leadership include communicating an inspirational vision and encouraging continuous improvement and lifelong learning.

Definition

Leaders paint a vision and inspire others to pursue goals. Leadership presupposes followership.

"To lead people, walk beside them.... As for the best leaders, the people do not notice their existence. The next best, the people honour and praise. The next, the people fear; and the next, the people hate.... When the best leader's work is done the people say, 'We did it ourselves'." — Lao-tsu

---

LEADERSHIP TRAITS

The debate as to whether nature or nurture is dominant in creating leaders still goes on. It's generally agreed that some traits are genetic, such as physical size, energy and personality, while others are acquired during our development and as we mature. Most experts agree that many of the attributes of a good leader can be learned or acquired; hence the rise of management schools and leadership courses.

Leaders come in different shapes and sizes and clearly many great leaders lack some of the traits listed. Some studies indicate that physical traits such as height and appearance are an advantage because they give presence, but there are exceptions to this as well. For example, many US presidents were tall, such as Abraham Lincoln and Bill Clinton, but other leaders such as Hitler and Napoleon were small. All agree that a certain level of intelligence and a high level of energy are needed although leaders don't necessarily have to be exceptionally bright. Many suggest that good interpersonal relationships are crucial although we all have had the experience of dealing with senior managers who lack social skills and manners. In truth, the most unlikely people often make good leaders and there seems to be no magic formula that guarantees leadership skills.

Desirable Traits

However, the following are some traits that would be advantageous to have in some combination or other as a leader:

❖ Integrity. Fairness, honesty and ethics are the hallmark of a good leader. Followers expect their leaders to treat them fairly and consistently in relation to others. They expect them to be honest and to keep their promises and to display high ethical standards when dealing with suppliers, customers and employees. Leaders should always be seen to do the right thing.

❖ Toughness. Leaders are not afraid of conflict or giving constructive criticism. They are prepared to make tough decision if the situation warrants it. For example, leaders may have to downsize a company to reduce costs if the financial situation is poor, which is often met with fierce union opposition. In these circumstances it takes toughness, determination and resilience to make the right decision to secure the future of the company.

❖ Confidence. Self-efficacy is the most important ingredient of confidence. Leaders with self-efficacy have a total belief in their own abilities to bring about a desired outcome. They have ambitious goals, implement action plans to achieve them and visualise successful outcomes. They tend to have optimism tinged with realism.

❖ Humility. The ideal leader has the humility to admit when they have made a mistake and have no hesitation in listening to the ideas of others and adopting them if they think they are useful. They realise they don't know everything and have the sense to make use of others' abilities and expertise as needed.

❖ Enthusiasm. Great leaders feel passionate about their work and their goals. Leaders with passion are animated, energised, enthused and committed. They love their jobs because they are inherently interested in what they do and so are totally self-motivated. This enthusiasm is contagious.

❖ Intelligence. Common sense is possibly more important than high intelligence. We all know people who are very bright but who lack the common touch and a sense of reality. Leaders with lots of common sense but average intelligence can be very successful in running large companies. Nous is often the trait that separates the great from the mediocre. Very intelligent people often make business problems more complicated than they actually are. Good leaders are capable of going straight to the critical issues.

❖ Warmth. A good leader has good interpersonal relationship skills and takes a genuine interest in the welfare of their followers. They are friendly, considerate, supportive and respectful. This trait will win the loyalty and commitment of employees.

❖ Drive and ambition. It stands to reason that people who get to leadership roles have great drive and ambition. They display exceptional energy, commitment, willpower and determination on their way to the top. Leaders normally are prepared to work long hours to achieve their goals and so need a great deal of energy and stamina to succeed.

"No institution can possibly survive if it needs geniuses or superman to manage it. It must be organised in such a way as to be able to get along under a leadership composed of average human beings." – Peter Drucker

---

FUNCTIONS OF LEADERSHIP

Functions are things leaders do. They can be recalled by the acronym COMBINED:

❖ **C**ontrolling. Controlling is about making sure that what is planned gets done efficiently. Control is achieved through discipline, targets and budgets. Actual results are compared with targets, variances are highlighted and corrective action taken to put the plan back on track. This cyclical process will help a business achieve goals and stay on target.

❖ **O**rganising. The leader achieves personal effectiveness through the adoption of time management skills. They know time is precious and can prioritise tasks so that the critical issues are dealt with first. The leader organises the business through proper structures, systems, procedures, resources, manpower and administration to achieve goals.

❖ **M**otivating. Leaders motivate and inspire their followers with a compelling vision and then win the commitment of employees to achieve it. Henry Ford is reputed to have said, "Without vision, the people perish", and Napoleon Bonaparte once said, "Imagination rules the world".

❖ **B**riefing. The leader must consistently use clear communication when dealing with others, by articulating ideas, espousing good values and giving and receiving feedback. Part of good communication skills is the ability to listen. Active and attentive listening affirms the other person by showing that you're interested in their views.

❖ **I**mplementing plans. Without plans and follow-through nothing gets done. The leader must be seen as a person who gets things done through action and delegation.

❖ **N**eeding to lead by example or "walk the talk". Leaders must live up to their own expectations and the expectation of their followers. They must do what they say and follow through on their commitments.

❖ **E**nthusiasm. See under traits.

❖ **D**efining the task. The task should be clearly defined so that everybody knows exactly what's required and what the leader's expectations are.

STYLES OF LEADERSHIP

There are four basic styles of leadership.

❖ *Dictatorial.* This style advocates force by threats, penalties and punishment and so operates on the basis of fear. It's rarely seen in modern business but still prevalent in some political systems in countries throughout the world. The psychological contract is one of coercion.

❖ *Autocratic.* In this style the leader makes all the decisions. Obedience and deference to leaders is the norm. Participation by employees in decision making is not encouraged. This style is still practised by owner-managers who build up their own companies and have a hands-on approach. However, when companies grow beyond a certain size this style becomes impracticable. The style is still in evidence in the army, police and hospital services. In hospitals, nurses find it difficult to question consultants even when they are wrong because they are put up on a pedestal and treated like gods.

❖ *Democratic.* This is a participative style of leadership. Decision-making is decentralised and shared and the involvement and empowerment of employees is encouraged. The rise of the knowledge worker and better-educated employees has facilitated this process.

❖ *Laissez Faire.* The leader exercising this style takes a back seat and gives no direction. They allow employees to set their own goals and make their own decisions. This style may be suitable in a research environment with highly qualified professional employees who need little supervision. They know what must be done and should be given the freedom to do it within budgetary constraints.

The Ashridge Styles

The following styles are based on the work of the Research Unit at Ashridge Management College in the UK. Using everyday language they describe the leadership styles as "tells", "sells", "consults" and "joins". They are in fact similar to the dictatorial, autocratic, democratic and laissez faire styles mentioned above.

❖ The autocratic or "tells" style is characterised by one-way communication between the leader and employees. The leader makes all the decisions and issues instructions expecting them to be obeyed without question, discussion or participation.

❖ The persuasive or "sells" style is where the leader makes the decision and then tries to persuade employees of its merits. At least the leader acknowledges the employees and makes some attempt to win them over and deal with resistance.

❖ The "consults" style is where the leader consults employees but still retains the right to make the final decision. They may or may not take account of employees' views and may have made up their mind beforehand. This approach may therefore be only a façade by pretending to listen to their advice and suggestions.

❖ The democratic or "joins" style is a consensus approach to decision-making. This style is best where employees have the knowledge and expertise to make a meaningful contribution to the decision.

The findings of the Ashridge studies included the following:

❖ Employees prefer the "consults" style of leadership. Despite this they claimed that leaders mostly exercise the "tells" and "sells" styles.

❖ The attitude of employees towards their work varied in relation to the style of leadership. The most favourable employee attitudes were those who perceived their manager to have a "consults" leadership style.

❖ Employees with the least favourable attitudes perceived the style of their manager to be inconsistent and unpredictable. It seems employees are unsettled by a manager who frequently changes between "tells", "sells", "consults" and "joins" styles of leadership.

Figure 6: Tells, Sells, Consults and Joins Leadership Model

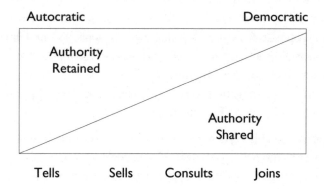

"I don't necessarily have to like my players and associates but as the leader, I must love them. Love is loyalty, love is teamwork, love respects the dignity of the individual. This is the strength of any organisation." – Vince Lombardi

The Six Styles of Leadership

Spreier et al. (2006) describe the following six styles of leadership:

❖ *Directive.* A directive style is strong and coercive behaviour. It is command and control style of leadership where the leader tells staff what to do, when to do it and what will happen if they don't. The directive approach is useful in a crisis or when the leader must manage a poor performer, but overuse stifles initiative and innovation. High achievers working under stress favour this style.

❖ *Visionary.* This style is authoritative but focuses on a clearly communicated vision. The leader gains employees' support by clearly expressing their challenges and responsibilities in the vision. This makes goals clear, increases employee commitment and energises a team. Usually leaders driven by the need for power favour this style.

❖ *Affiliative.* This style emphasises harmony and relationships and puts the emotional needs of employees first. It's appropriate in certain high stress situations, for example when employees are going through a personal crisis. It's most effective when used in conjunction with the visionary, participative or coaching styles but is seldom effective alone.

❖ *Participative.* This style is collaborative and democratic where leaders involve staff in decision making. It's great for building trust and consensus in situations where the leader has limited knowledge or lacks formal power and authority. The style is suitable for teams or project-based organisations. It's favoured in stressful conditions by leaders with a need for affiliation.

❖ *Pacesetting.* This style involves leading by example. Leaders using this style set the pace with high standards and make sure those standards are met, even if they have to do the work themselves. This style can get results in the short term, but it's demoralising and exhausting for employees in the long term. It's a style for high achieving leaders working under low stress conditions.

❖ *Coaching.* A coaching style focuses on long-term development through coaching and mentoring of staff. It's a powerful but underused approach that should be used by all leaders. Leaders who like to involve themselves in a one-to-one situation with staff prefer this style. It's used in low stress conditions.

"If your actions inspire others to dream more, learn more, do more and become more, you are a leader." — John Quincy Adams

---

There is no one best style of leadership. Each has its own strengths and limitations. The most effective leaders are adept at all six leadership styles and use each in the proper context.

Blake and Mouton's Managerial Grid

This theory was put forward by Blake and Mouton (1962) as a two-dimensional model of leadership (see Figure 7). It has a common sense approach and is intuitively appealing. Leadership is about getting the job done effectively through people. The grid has two axes: concern for people and concern for production.

❖ *Impoverished manager.* This is the 1.1 position on the grid. This manager is low on concern for production and low on concern for people. This style is ineffective and the manager avoids taking responsibility for actions. They have little contact with employees and show no commitment to problem solving, making decisions or achieving targets.

❖ *Country club manager.* This is the 1.9 position on the grid. This manager is very high on concern for people but low on concern for production. The manager's key goal is harmonious relationships with employees at all cost. Conflict and disagreement are avoided, mistakes are ignored and even constructive criticism is not given because it might disrupt interpersonal relationships.

❖ *Task manager.* This is the 9.1 position on the grid. This manager is high on concern for production but low on concern for people. They are very competent technically but take little account of employees' feelings or views. They expect schedules to be met on time and delays are viewed as employee mistakes. It's an autocratic style of management. Traditionally, this was the leadership style that was favoured in the car manufacturing industry with its scientific management approach.

❖ *Middle of the road manager.* This is the 5.5 position on the grid. This manager balances the need to achieve acceptable production levels while maintaining satisfactory relationships with employees. This manager has good common sense and is seen as firm but fair.

❖ *Team manager.* This is the 9.9 position on the grid. This is a high performance manager who is good at relationships and good at achieving production targets. This is the ideal manager for the modern organisation. They aim at the highest possible standards while maintaining excellent interpersonal relationships. This is a participative style of management where employees are involved in decision-making and goals are seen as challenges. Conflict is seen as inevitable and positive and is dealt with in a transparent fashion. There is mutual respect and trust between the manager and the employees.

This grid can also be used for the performance appraisal of managers. A manager can be scored on the grid in relation to task and people and will be able to see how their performance as a leader can be improved in relation to the ideal style of team manager. Leaders can then take the appropriate action to improve their style.

Figure 7: The Blake and Mouton Grid

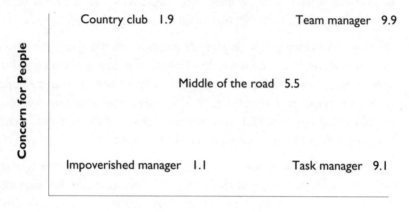

Concern for Production

TYPES OF LEADERS

The acronym FACTS will enable you to bring these to mind:

❖ **F**unctional. This is a contingency theory of leadership. The leader needs to adapt their style in relation to context, task, group and individual needs. For example, if the leader's followers are mature and professionally qualified, it is unlikely that they would need much supervision. In such a situation the leader can step back and let the employees get on with the job with the minimum of direction.

❖ **A**ppointed. This is the bureaucratic leader who derives power from their position in the hierarchy. Obviously the more senior the position held the more power the leader has. The powers of the position are clearly defined. However, the appointed leader may not be able to implement them because of lack of credibility, weak personality or lack of training.

❖ **C**harismatic. The leader's influence is derived from their unique personality. These leaders set high expectations, motivate followers and express confidence in their ability to achieve goals. Some people have a problem with this type of leadership style as followers are inclined to blindly follow the charismatic leader. For example, Hitler was able to persuade his followers to commit heinous war crimes and some religious leaders have been able to persuade their followers to commit mass suicide.

❖ **T**ransformational. This is the leader who recognises the need for change, creates a vision to guide that change, and then implements the change effectively. This type of leadership requires unique skills and is needed during times of great change such as company expansion or contraction. In times of rapid expansion the company may merge, acquire new companies or set up their own subsidiaries. In times of contraction the opposite might occur with the need for disinvestment, downsizing and other cost cutting measures.

❖ **S**ituational. The situational leader arises during exceptional circumstances. The unique abilities of the leader match the requirements of the situation. In an emergency a leader may emerge who has the capabilities of dealing with a particular problem. As soon as the emergency is dealt with the leader resorts to their previous role as a follower.

"I should say that tact was worth more than wealth as a road to leadership.... I mean that subtle apprehension which teaches a person how to do and say the right thing at the right time. It coexists with very ordinary qualities, and yet many great geniuses are without it. Of all human qualities I consider it the most convenient — not always the highest; yet I would rather have it than many more shining qualities."
— M.E.W. Sherwood

DIFFERENCES BETWEEN MANAGERS AND LEADERS

Managers

❖ Do things right rather than doing the right things. Efficiency is the primary goal of management. However, there is no point in being efficient at doing the wrong things.

❖ Manage things such as manpower, materials, money and machines within the constraints of budgets.

❖ Promote stability by making sure that existing operations are run smoothly.

❖ Implement the policy handed down by the board of directors.

❖ Command, control and direct activities by exercising authority. Control by comparing actual results with targets and taking corrective action to put things back on track again.

❖ Problem solving and decision-making. Solve problems of a tactical or logistical nature and make decisions with short-term implications.

❖ Tend to be more analytical, structured and controlled.

"Management is efficiency in climbing the ladder of success; leadership determines whether the ladder is leaning against the right wall." — Stephen R. Covey

---

Leaders

❖ Create and communicate a vision and set a direction for others to follow. Energise, inspire, motivate and empower others to achieve the vision. Leadership is the art of engaging the hearts and minds of employees and creatively releasing their energies to accomplish the vision of the organisation.

❖ Lead their people forward. Leadership is based on goodwill. It means total commitment to helping followers achieve the goals of the organisation. Build trusting relationships and expect loyalty in return.

❖ Do the right things. The primary goal is effectiveness. Are ethical when achieving business results. Co-ordinate the activities of others. Let managers and employees do the work while they concentrate on the strategic thinking.

❖ Formulate and enunciate policy and make decisions with long-term implications. Focus on strategic results and make sense of the world around them and advocate change for the better.

❖ Influence others. The key to successful leadership is influence and not the exercise of authority. The good leader relies more on partnership and collaboration than on power or position to get things done.

❖ Tend to be more creative, experimental and flexible and are happy to acknowledge their mistakes and move on.

"Leadership is not magnetic personality, that can just as well be a glib tongue. It is not 'making friends and influencing people', that is flattery. Leadership is lifting a person's vision to higher sights, the raising of a person's performance to a higher standard, the building of a personality beyond its normal limitations." — Peter F. Drucker

---

Theory X and Y

This theory about how managers perceive employees was enunciated in Douglas McGregor's book *The Human Side of Enterprise*. It has two extremes called Theory X and Theory Y. In practice managers can be a bit of both and even adopt different attitudes to employees in different contexts.

❖ *Theory X*. This assumes that people are lazy, dislike work and will avoid it if they can. This management philosophy thus has an emphasis on controls and external rewards. If managers adopt this attitude they will not trust employees to do their work. Consequently, they will adopt a very autocratic style of leadership and will direct and control employees. Managers will be reluctant to delegate.

❖ *Theory Y*. This assumes the opposite. People are naturally energetic and they like work and will use their initiative to achieve their objectives. Therefore, employees can be trusted to perform efficiently and effectively. In such circumstances managers will not hesitate to delegate work.

SOURCES OF POWER AND INFLUENCE

In his book *Understanding Organisations*, Charles Handy identified six types of power from different sources. These can be recalled by the acronym PROPER:

❖ **P**hysical or coercive power. This is the power to punish or withhold reward and is used to coerce others to do something. It is based on fear and rare in most modern organisations, though it still comes to light in the form of bullying, harassment and intimidation. Traditionally, it was the type of power resorted to in the armed forces and prison service.

❖ **R**esource or reward power. This is the responsibility for, and control over, resources. Senior managers may have the right to grant pay increases, award bonuses or recommend employees for promotion. Unions have resource power to take their members out on strike.

❖ **O**wn or personal power. This is charismatic power or the power of personality. A popular leader may have influence over their followers because of the power of their personality. Such leaders exude a personal magnetism that draws people towards them and have an air of confidence and a strong self-belief that others find irresistible. The leader senses the needs of people and promises success in meeting them.

❖ **P**osition power. This is legitimate power being associated with the position in the management hierarchy. The higher up the greater the potential for position power. This might include access to information or contact with board members or the chief executive. Some managers may have the power to determine conditions of employment or make other major decisions.

❖ **E**xpert power. This is the power a manager has because of their expertise or know-how. Specialist managers in organisations such as information technologists, engineers, accountants and lawyers may have this power provided they are recognised as experts in their field. It depends on education, training and experience and is an important source of power in a company.

❖ **R**efusal or negative power. This is the power not to do something and disrupt operations. A manager may deliberately provide misinformation or delay information in order to undermine another manager or sabotage a decision. Negative power is destructive and potentially very damaging to a company's efficiency. Even ordinary employees have considerable negative power.

THE DARK SIDE OF LEADERSHIP

Just like in any profession there are good leaders and bad leaders. These are some of the negative characteristics of leaders or the negative things that they do.

Negative Characteristics

❖ Emotional inadequacy. These are bureaucratic leaders who rigidly follow rules and regulations. They are typical organisation men, disciplined, cold and dispassionate with an inability to empathise with others. This means they find it difficult to foster good interpersonal relationships. They like working in a structured environment and tend to lack creativity. They drive out excellent people because of their mediocrity, lack of vision and conventional approach.

❖ Narcissism. Narcissistic leaders are egocentric and easily provoked to anger. They have little self-awareness of their weaknesses and faults. Criticism is not tolerated and if given provokes the leader's wrath. They have little empathy for others. They have feelings of grandiosity often demonstrated by explicit or implicit arrogance, dominance and devaluation of others. According to Coutu (2004), the problem with narcissistic leaders is that they activate their followers' latent narcissism. The followers idealise and praise the leader who then becomes addicted to the follower's idealisation and loses touch with reality. Tragically, some leaders get to the point where they fire individuals who don't praise them sufficiently.

❖ Fooled by flattery. Some leaders surround themselves with sycophants who fool them with flattery and isolate them from uncomfortable realities. Leaders like those who like them and are more easily influenced by people that they like and feel comfortable with. Leaders should instead surround themselves with people who will tell them the way things really are and keep their feet solidly rooted on the ground. A leader should never underestimate the value of dissent. Well run 360-degree feedback programs and executive coaching can help a leader stay in touch with reality.

❖ Fear of letting go. Some leaders try to hang on to power as long as possible even though their power base has been eroded and they are advancing in years and not up to the job. They tend to be workaholics and see no future for themselves beyond the present job. They constantly fear the possibility of younger and more able people taking over their jobs and thus are basically very insecure.

Toxic Things They Do

❖ Withholding information. These leaders see information as power and are reluctant to share it with others, especially those they see as rivals. Some leaders may even provide misinformation to further their own aims.

❖ Machiavellian tactics. These are named after a sixteenth century, Italian author, Machiavelli, who admired unethical selfish leaders who exercised power by force. He suggested that fear was an acceptable way of enforcing power on others and is reputed to have said, "it is much safer to be feared than loved". This management philosophy advocates that the end justifies the means. Leaders with this philosophy are motivated by the need for power and use it to control others. They tend to be rational and unemotional and will not hesitate to use lies and deceit to achieve their goals. They put little emphasis on loyalty and friendship and enjoy manipulating others for their own purposes. This philosophy, though frowned upon, is still alive and well in modern business. The need for checks and balances in companies grew out of the need to counter such behaviour in organisations.

❖ Unethical practice. Some leaders are ruthless and relentless in the pursuit of business results, often cutting corners, cheating and breaking the law. Out of control ambition and greed have seen senior executives before the courts for fraud and accounting irregularities. Examples include Enron and WorldCom where false accounting was used to defraud shareholders and resulted in the collapse of the company and the jailing of senior executives.

❖ Creating a false impression. Leaders who create a false image and pretend they are something they're not. Because people can see through this façade they lose the respect and trust of others. Followers expect their leaders to be honest and transparent in their views and opinions.

❖ Life–work balance. Many leaders are workaholics with few interests and friends outside the job, being obsessed about their work and talk about nothing else. Once they become successful they find it very hard to slow down. All they know is how to do their job. In the meantime, their personal and family relationships are in tatters because of neglect over the years. However, retirement looms for everyone and when that happens they are likely to become very depressed because they have no interests or friendships to fall back on outside of work.

BEST LEADERSHIP PRACTICES

Personal Attributes

❖ They take calculated risks. There is risk attached to any decision and this risk must be balanced by the potential returns. However nothing gets done if you're not prepared to make decisions and take some risk.

❖ Good leaders communicate a vision that others can believe in and adopt as their own. They identify and communicate three to five priorities that are needed to achieve that vision and mobilise staff to make it happen by getting them to commit to goals.

"Leadership is the ability to establish standards and manage a creative climate where people are self-motivated toward the mastery of long-term constructive goals, in a participatory environment of mutual respect, compatible with personal values." – Mike Vance

---

❖ They possess the necessary commitment and drive to be successful, and decide what needs to get done and then develop action plans to do them. They have the ability to act and reflect so that they can learn from mistakes and not repeat them in the future. They take responsibility for making decisions and encourage their followers to do likewise.

❖ They display humility and realise that they don't know everything. They are able to tap into the knowledge and expertise of others and build a network of confidants to help them accomplish goals.

❖ They motivate others by involvement and caring, and are prepared to roll up their sleeves and chip in when an emergency arises.

❖ They run productive meetings. This requires deciding the format of the meeting and sticking to the agenda.

❖ They prioritise their time in relation to key tasks. They ensure that staff prioritises their time in a similar fashion. They do important things first and one thing at a time.

❖ They win respect by demonstrating expertise and competence. Followers admire leaders who know what they're talking about and have the ability, reputation and track record to prove it.

❖ They listen actively and acknowledge the ideas of others. They practise two-way feedback and encourage dialogue with other managers and staff. They ask insightful questions and seek out answers rather than give them.

"The leader is one who mobilises others towards a goal shared by leaders and followers. Leaders, followers and goals make up the three equally necessary supports for leadership." – Gary Wills

---

Learning

❖ They seek out a good mentor. Most successful leaders have access to the ear of a good mentor who will guide and advise them on their careers.

❖ They turn mistakes into learning situations, and avoid the blame game or looking for fall guys. They see problems as opportunities to be exploited and concentrate on possibilities rather than obstacles.

❖ They acquire deep knowledge of their company and the industry they operate in. They know that they must constantly keep up to date if they want to remain on top and keep their company competitive.

❖ Leadership cannot be taught; it can only be learned through experience. Leaders may acquire knowledge and ideas from books but experience is the real teacher as practical work experience is the most important source of learning. Knowledge is useless until it's translated into deeds.

❖ They adopt a role model by studying great leaders and taking on some of their behaviours and methods. They in turn act as a role model for staff. They exude an air of confidence, enthusiasm and optimism in everything they do.

❖ They encourage staff to undertake training and development and provide the means of doing so. They provide staff with opportunities for growth in the form of secondments, assignments and job rotation. They promulgate the philosophy of lifelong learning and practise and believe in the concept themselves.

❖ They encourage continuous improvement in all areas of the organisation. They know that costs must be managed vigorously if a company is to remain profitable.

Being Employee-centred

❖ They are employee-centred and operate a participative leadership style. They take a genuine interest in their employees' backgrounds, families and interests. At the same time they maintain a discreet psychological distance so that authority is respected and accepted without over-familiarity.

❖ They create a climate of trust by treating employees fairly and justly. They operate to high ethical standards, have a strong sense of integrity and are honest, authentic and transparent. They encourage mutual respect because employees admire and follow those they respect and trust.

"Curiosity is more important than knowledge." — Albert Einstein

---

❖ They create a happy work environment as they realise that happy workers are productive workers.

❖ They focus on the needs of internal and external customers. They are more concerned about outcomes than activities.

❖ They create self-belief and self-efficacy in staff by giving them tasks they can do successfully. They provide necessary encouragement, support and resources to their staff without being intrusive.

❖ They have a team orientation and believe that teams achieve the best results. The leader selects team members for their different contributions and brings out their talents through training and development. A team is successful when the members augment and complement one another. The leader acts as a coach facilitating the team to achieve its goals.

"The leaders who work most effectively, it seems to me, never say 'I'. And that's not because they have trained themselves not to say 'I'. They don't think 'I'. They think 'we', they think 'team'. They understand their job to be to make the team function. They accept responsibility and don't sidestep it, but 'we' gets the credit.... This is what creates trust, what enables you to get the task done." — Peter F. Drucker

---

❖ The leader picks good support staff to do what needs to be done. They demand high levels of performance without exercising close supervision, as they believe most employees are capable of doing a good job if left alone. They delegate but don't abdicate by deserting employees when they need their advice, guidance or support.

❖ They trust but verify and thus always establish the facts. They are conscious of sycophants who fool you with flattery and isolate you from uncomfortable realities. To counteract this they surround themselves with people who will give honest feedback and sound advice.

"I think that the best training a top manager can be engaged in is management by example. I want to make sure there is no discrepancy between what we say and what we do. If you preach accountability and then promote somebody with bad results, it doesn't work. I personally believe the best training is management by example. Don't believe what I say. Believe what I do." — Carlos Ghosn, CEO of Renault-Nissan

SUMMARY

Leaders create and communicate an inspirational vision to gain the commitment of staff to achieve goals. Ideal leadership traits include integrity, intelligence, toughness, confidence, humility, enthusiasm and warmth. Leaders build a climate of mutual trust and respect. The functions of leadership include planning, leading, organising and controlling. Leadership styles are autocratic, democratic and laissez faire. In practical terms they are tells, sells, consults and joints. The types of leader are functional, appointed, charismatic, traditional and situational.

There are differences between managers and leaders. Managers implement policy while leaders create and enunciate policy. Managers direct activities while leaders lead people. The sources of power and influence include physical, resource, personal, position and expert. Leadership's dark side includes withholding information and emotional immaturity. The best practices of leadership include creating a no blame culture by encouraging employees to learn from their mistakes and accept responsibility.

CHECK YOUR PEOPLE SKILLS QUOTIENT – 8

	Circle the appropriate response	
1. Leaders inspire followers to achieve goals	True	False
2. An autocratic style is the ideal style for leaders	True	False
3. A situational style of leadership takes the context into account	True	False
4. Managers do the right things	True	False
5. Leaders do things right	True	False
6. Many companies are over-managed and under-led	True	False
7. Managers focus on long-term results	True	False
8. Leaders should seek out a good mentor	True	False
9. Leaders should turn mistakes into learning opportunities	True	False
10. Leaders should trust but verify	True	False

Total the number of true and false responses and check Appendix I at the back of the book for the answers and to determine your score.

FIVE STEPS TO IMPROVE
YOUR LEADERSHIP SKILLS

1. Create an inspirational vision and mobilise and motivate staff to make it happen. Set a direction for others to follow through goals, targets and action plans.

2. Build a climate of mutual respect and trust. Employees follow and are loyal to those they trust. Rely on partnership and collaboration rather than power or position to get things done.

3. Encourage continuous improvement and lifelong learning. Act as a role model in this regard. Advocate change only when needed for improvement and cost reduction.

4. Beware of sycophants. Reward truthful feedback from trusted employees. Surround yourself with people who will give you honest feedback and advice such as an external coach.

5. Acquire a deep knowledge of the company and industry in which you operate. Keep up to date with best practices.

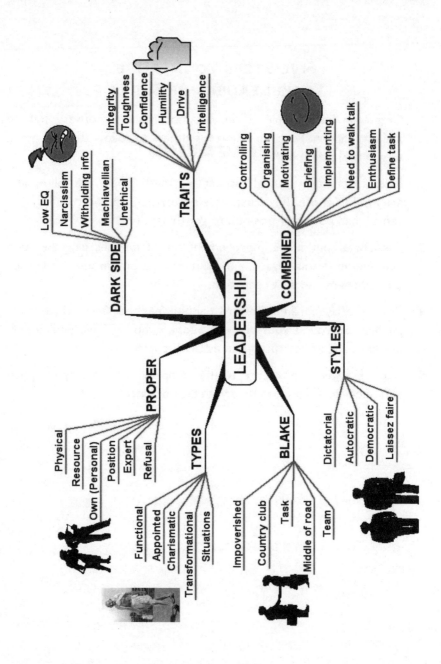

LEADERSHIP

DARK SIDE
- Low EQ
- Narcissism
- Witholding info
- Machiavellian
- Unethical

TRAITS
- Integrity
- Toughness
- Confidence
- Humility
- Drive
- Intelligence

COMBINED
- Controlling
- Organising
- Motivating
- Briefing
- Implementing
- Need to walk talk
- Enthusiasm
- Define task

PROPER
- Physical
- Resource
- Own (Personal)
- Position
- Expert
- Refusal

TYPES
- Functional
- Appointed
- Charismatic
- Transformational
- Situations

BLAKE
- Impoverished
- Country club
- Task
- Middle of road
- Team

STYLES
- Dictatorial
- Autocratic
- Democratic
- Laissez faire

9

DELEGATION

☑ How can you delegate effectively?

☑ What are the benefits of delegation?

☑ Why do managers fail to delegate?

☑ What is the systematic approach to delegation?

☑ What is the trust–control dilemma?

INTRODUCTION

Delegation is getting work done through other people. The benefits of delegation include having more time to manage and being able to call on the expertise you need. Managers might be reluctant to delegate because of lack of self-confidence or fear of losing control. Employees may be reluctant to accept delegation because they fear criticism for mistakes or they are already overworked. There are certain things a manager should not delegate including confidential work, difficult jobs and ones requiring the status or special expertise of the manager.

There are some principles of delegation. You can delegate authority but you can't delegate responsibility. If you make an employee accountable to you for work delegated you should give them sufficient authority to carry it out. The trust–control dilemma suggests that the more you trust your staff, the more you will delegate to them and the less control you will exercise. On the other hand, the less trust you have in your staff, the less you will delegate to them and the more control you will exercise.

"Give up control even if it means the employees have to make some mistakes." – Frank Flores

---

Definition

Delegation is getting work done through other people by entrusting them with authority and responsibility to do the work delegated to an acceptable standard. It is a two-way process and a social skill. A manager must be aware of people's psychological needs, attitudes, aptitudes and skills to delegate effectively. The work you delegate should be SMARTER tasks. Unclear or vague tasks are impossible to complete and control. It's best if your requirements are clearly communicated. SMARTER stands for:

❖ **S**pecific. Be specific about what you want done and how you want it done. This requires clear communication on your part. Specify the extent of the employee's discretion and the sources of relevant information and knowledge needed to do the job.

❖ **M**easurable. Design controls and checkpoints for interim stages so that you know the job delegated is going according to plan. This will give you the opportunity to put things right before a catastrophe occurs when it may be too late to rectify the situation.

❖ **A**chievable. Make sure the job delegated can be done satisfactorily with the allocated resources and within the time specified.

❖ **R**ealistic. Make sure the job is within the capabilities of the staff to whom it is delegated. You may need to provide further coaching or training to bring them up to the standard required to do the job.

❖ **E**thical. Make sure you are not breaking the law or being unethical. Remember Enron and what happened there! If senior managers are unethical the staff will follow their example.

❖ **R**ecorded. The terms of reference should be brief and preferably in writing so that there is no uncertainty about the expectations.

BENEFITS OF DELEGATION

The benefits of delegation can be considered from two perspectives: management and staff.

Management

❖ It will give you more time to handle the real responsibilities of management such as thinking about the future and coaching staff. Successful delegation will help to overcome Gresham's Law of Planning, which states that routine work tends to drive out non-routine work. Routine work involves decisions that are repetitive while non-routine works involves ones that are novel and unstructured. Some managers bury themselves in the routine instead of attending to their main responsibilities.

❖ It will develop you for promotion and career opportunities. Because you will have more time you can concentrate on developing the skills needed to get to the next level of management.

❖ It creates less stress for the manager by reducing the workload.

❖ It helps to achieve a work–life balance. Work smarter, not harder. You can work less, achieve more and be more productive if you delegate effectively.

❖ It's essential where an organisation is geographically dispersed. Such organisations by their nature are decentralised with delegated structures and decisions made as close to the operations as possible.

❖ Delegation is sound economics. It's a question of opportunity cost. There is no sense in having high level people doing lower level tasks. Decisions should be made at lower levels and as near the customer or site of operations as possible. Decision-making will be quicker, better and more informed. Delegation increases efficiency.

❖ The 80/20 rule, which states that 20 per cent of tasks really make a difference to your business, means that it makes sense to delegate the other 80 per cent so you can concentrate on the issues that really count.

Staff

❖ It uses the under-utilised expertise of staff. Some of your staff may be better qualified, experienced and more capable of doing the work delegated than you are.

❖ Training and development of staff. It's a way of testing staff's suitability for promotion and undertaking more responsible work. It provides staff with a varied experience making them multi-skilled. It develops the specialist knowledge and skills of staff.

❖ It gives an even spread of work to employees. Overworked managers can offload some of their more routine work to others.

❖ It improves the morale of staff through better job satisfaction, participation and commitment.

"If you want to grow one year of prosperity, you can grow grain. If you want to grow 10 years of prosperity, you can grow trees. If you want to grow 100 years of prosperity, grow people." — Chinese Proverb

---

REASONS FOR LACK OF DELEGATION

Manager

❖ The manager may lack self-confidence and feel insecure and exposed when delegating to staff. They may feel that if staff do the work very well they will get the credit and the manager's own competence will be questioned. In point of fact, if the staff member does a good job it will reflect favourably on the manager.

❖ Perfectionism. The manager may feel that nobody else can do the work as well. The manager may be risk averse and not want to take the chance that the work delegated may not be done properly.

❖ The manager has no confidence in the capability of the staff to do the work delegated – a Theory X view of staff. They believe that staff are naturally lazy, lack initiative, avoid responsibility if they can, can't be trusted and therefore must be coerced and threatened to do a good job. Such a manager will only be interested in limited delegation. The manager doesn't realise that the more you trust staff the more their confidence grows and the more capable they become.

❖ The manager wants to stay in control. They fear the surrendering of authority to others and want to stay in touch with everything that is going on. There may also be a lack of controls to act as early warning systems to alert the manager when things go wrong.

❖ The manager has received no training in the art of delegation and doesn't understand the philosophy involved or its importance to the development of staff. They may also lack the communication skills to give clear instructions and persuade staff of the benefits of taking on delegation.

❖ The manager feels that it would take too much time to instruct or coach staff to do the work and that it would be quicker doing the work himself. The first time around this may be true but it's a false notion of efficiency. In the long term, staff will become capable and confident and the manager will reap the benefits of delegation.

> "The best executive is the one who has sense enough to pick good men to do what he wants done, and self-restraint enough to keep from meddling with them while they do it." — Theodore Roosevelt

❖ The company has a non-supportive blame culture. Mistakes are viewed negatively rather than seen as opportunities to learn. Staff in the past have been criticised and reprimanded in front of colleagues for making mistakes undermining their self-esteem.

❖ Managers are reluctant to delegate tasks that they are particularly good at doing and that led to their promotion in the first place!

Staff

❖ They are reluctant to accept delegated work because there are no monetary or non-monetary incentives to do so. They find it easier to ask the manager to help them.

❖ They fear criticism for mistakes and the responsibility involved.

❖ They are already suffering from work overload and lack the information, time and resources to do the delegated work.

❖ The may view delegation simply as extra work. In addition, they may not have been sold on the benefits to their training and development of taking on delegated work.

ART OF DELEGATION

When Not to Delegate

❖ Don't dump tasks on your staff just because you don't like the work.

❖ Don't delegate the preparation of confidential reports.

❖ Don't delegate controversial jobs. The staff will perceive you are avoiding potential sources of conflict and setting them up for failure.

❖ Don't delegated HR jobs like motivation, training, team-building, performance appraisal, counselling, discipline and rewards.

❖ Don't delegate jobs requiring the status of the manager such as hiring and firing, attending meetings, policy issues, control and dealing with key customers. However, the attendance at routine meetings can be delegated to staff.

❖ Don't delegate personal jobs like picking up the dry cleaning or shopping. This is unethical and degrading for staff and will only provoke their resentment and undermine your authority.

❖ Don't accept upward delegation such as partially finished jobs. If you do you may end up doing a lot of the work you previously delegated.

❖ Avoid being a "drive-by delegator" – someone who assigns tasks to a staff member when they meet them by chance in the office corridor. Instead, assign the task formally in your office. Take the time to thoroughly explain the task and give the employee the opportunity to ask questions and receive the resources needed to do the job.

"Delegating means letting others become the experts and hence the best." — Timothy Firnstahl

---

Do Practise the Following

❖ Start by delegating one task at a time. As your confidence in staff grows and they prove themselves capable of doing the work you can delegate more tasks. By delegating gradually in line with their experience you will build up the confidence of your staff. From the employee perspective, there is nothing worse than to be given work that you feel you haven't the competence to do. This may become a self-fulfilling-prophesy creating a cycle of failure.

❖ Do motivate staff by recognising success and avoiding blame. If people do a good job don't hesitate to praise them. This will build up their esteem and self-confidence.

❖ If necessary, break very difficult jobs into parts. Delegate parts to different people, although it is generally better to delegate complete jobs if possible. Complete jobs provide greater satisfaction and the outcome is more likely to be better thought out and integrated.

❖ The first time you delegate work have the patience to accept that it will usually take longer for staff to complete it and get it right. After all, they are just novices and still learning the job while you have been doing it for years!

❖ Review the delegated work at appropriate checkpoints, without breathing down people's necks, to solve problems before they develop into a crisis.

"The great leaders are like the best conductors — they reach beyond the notes to reach the magic in the players." — Blaine Lee

---

PRINCIPLES OF DELEGATION

❖ You can delegate authority but you can't delegate responsibility. Therefore it's important that the manager picks the right person at the right time with the right experience and competence for the work delegated.

❖ Authority should match responsibility. Many employees complain that they lack the authority to do the job effectively.

❖ There's a difference between authority, responsibility and accountability. Authority is the power to give orders, make decisions, spend resources and take action. Authority is supported by the management hierarchy and organisation structure. The manager is ultimately responsible for the work of the section, however. When the manager delegates work to an employee they can make the employee accountable for the satisfactory performance of the work delegated.

"You can delegate authority, but you can never delegate responsibility for delegating a task to someone else. If you picked the right man, fine, but if you picked the wrong man, the responsibility is yours, not his." — Richard E Krafve

❖ Delegation is not abdication. The manager should support staff in every way by providing the necessary resources such as equipment and knowledge to do the job. The manager should monitor performance without interference or continually checking. They should operate by the Management by Exception principle, which means only checking those items that are not going according to plan and that require attention.

❖ Macro-manage rather than micro-manage. Breathing down employees' necks is not the way to manage when you delegate. Just tell the employee that you know that they are capable of doing the job but if they run into trouble that they can call on you for support. Delegation requires trust, confidence and courage.

"If there is one axiom that I have tried to live up to in trying to become successful in business, it is the fact that I have tried to surround myself with associates that know more about business than I do. This policy has always been very successful and is still working for me." — Monte L. Bean

❖ The manager should not encourage reverse or upward delegation. This occurs when the staff member tries to offload the work delegated back to the manager. Obviously, this defeats the purpose of delegation.

❖ The manager should inform other departments about the nature and extent of the delegation. This will facilitate the staff member when they seek the co-operation of other departments.

THE SYSTEMATIC APPROACH TO DELEGATION

❖ What to delegate? Tasks that can be better performed by staff because they have superior skills, experience and knowledge to do them. If you keep an activity log for a few weeks it will help you identify the routine jobs that you could delegate. Make a list and determine how long it takes to do them. Work that a manager finds routine may offer development, variety and challenge to someone who has never done it before.

❖ To whom should you delegate? Match the needs of the task with the competencies of the employee. Employees must have the time and be willing and able to do the work. Inexperienced staff will need coaching and training to bring them up to the standard required to do the delegated tasks. Initially, these people will require close supervision but it will be worthwhile in the long term.

❖ How do you delegate? Give staff the right degree of authority to do the work delegated. Prepare staff for the work by briefing or coaching and explain the purpose of the job and your expectations regarding standards of performance. The exact method of how they do the job should be left to the employee's discretion. Make sure you provide the necessary resources for the employee to do the job.

"Never tell people how to do things. Tell them what to do and they will surprise you with their ingenuity." – General George Smith Patton, Jr.

❖ The schedule for delegated tasks? Employees are motivated by deadlines. Install controls to review and evaluate the work done. If there are various tasks involved indicate the priorities, and agree a time schedule with dates for the completion of interim stages.

❖ The purpose of delegation? Explain to the staff member why the job or responsibility is being delegated and why they were chosen to do the delegated task. Indicate the importance of the job and how it fits into the overall scheme of things.

Handy's Trust–Control Formula

Handy (1985) advanced the $T + C = Y$ formula, called the trust–control dilemma, where T equals trust, C equals control and Y is a constant unchanging value. The more managers trust their staff, the more they will delegate and the less control they will exercise. In other words, the more experienced and reliable the employee is, the more freedom you can give. The less managers trust their staff, the less they will delegate and the more control they will exercise. This is the dilemma that faces management.

"The first rule of management is delegation. Don't try and do everything yourself because you can't." — Anthea Turner

---

Delegation Styles

Each of these styles gives progressively more control and freedom to staff to do the delegated task. Level one gives little or no freedom while level six gives complete freedom to do the job.

1. Level one. This gives the employee the freedom to examine the problem and collect the facts. The manager reserves the right to decide what to do based on the information received. The manager has total control. The employee has little freedom and exercises few thinking skills.

2. Level two. In addition to examining the problem and getting the facts, the employee is allowed to generate alternatives and make recommendations as to what course of action they think is best. The manager retains control, but the employee does exercise considerable thinking skills in generating alternatives and making recommendations.

3. Level three. This gives the employee permission to examine the problem, collect the facts, generate alternatives, make recommendations and advise what they intend to do. However, they must wait for the manager's approval before they proceed. The ultimate control is still with the manager, however the employee exercises considerable thinking and decision-making skills.

4. Level four. This gives the employee a free hand to do all of the previous three and to proceed until told otherwise. The manager still

retains some of the control, but a lot of authority has been passed to the employee.

5. Level five. This gives the employee a free hand to do all of the previous four but the manager expects to be kept informed about what is done. Most of the control has passed from the manager to the employee. The manager has great trust in the employee to do the work delegated.

6. Level six. No further contact with the manager is needed. At this level the manager has complete confidence in the staff to do the work delegated and lets them get on with the job.

"You need courage to risk delegating. Managers typically avoid taking chances, but delegation is a calculated risk, and you must expect that over time the gains will surpass the losses. You must recognise the risk and adjust emotionally and intellectually in order to delegate effectively. Delegation is risky because you're never absolutely sure of the outcome of a task you delegate." — Dr. Frank F. Huppe

---

SUMMARY

Delegation is getting work done through other people. Since it is impossible to do everything yourself it pays to engage the skills and expertise of others. Managers can thus free themselves up to attend to the tasks of management such as planning, leading, organising, controlling and staffing. The benefits of delegating include less stress and the opportunity to train and develop staff for promotion or more responsible work. Managers might be reluctant to delegate because they fear their staff will do a better job and they will be shown up as less competent. Employees may be reluctant because they are already overworked and they fear the criticism and responsibility if they make mistakes. A manager should not delegate human resource duties such as appraisal, discipline and hiring and firing.

There are some principles of delegation, such as you can delegate authority but you can't delegate responsibility. The manager is ultimately responsible for the work of their section. Delegate but don't abdicate. If you delegate work to your staff give them sufficient authority to carry it out. Follow a systematic approach when delegating by asking the questions, What? Whom? How? and When? The trust–control dilemma suggests that the more you trust staff, the more you will delegate and the less you will control. The less you trust staff, the less you will delegate and the more you will control. This is the dilemma of management. The delegation styles give progressively more control and freedom to staff to do the delegated task.

CHECK YOUR PEOPLE SKILLS QUOTIENT – 9

	Circle the appropriate response	
1. You can delegate responsibility but you can't delegate authority	True	False
2. You should ensure that authority matches responsibility	True	False
3. You should micro-manage rather than macro-manage	True	False
4. The manager is ultimately responsible for the work of his section	True	False
5. You should delegate rather than abdicate	True	False
6. You should delegate human resource duties	True	False
7. To delegate requires confidence, trust and courage	True	False
8. You should delegate controversial jobs	True	False
9. The manager should delegate work requiring his status	True	False
10. Authority is the power to make decisions and take action	True	False

Total the number of true and false responses and check Appendix 1 at the back of the book for the answers and to determine your score.

FIVE STEPS TO IMPROVE
YOUR DELEGATION SKILLS

1. Build up the expertise of staff through coaching and training so that you are confident that they will be able to do the delegated work satisfactorily. The staff you delegate to should be willing and able to do the work. It is your responsibility to ensure that they possess the necessary competencies. Accept that staff will make mistakes and initially take longer to do the work delegated because they are novices.

2. When you delegate work make sure you give the employee sufficient authority and resources to carry it out. Make them accountable to you for the correct performance of the tasks delegated. Give them general guidance but let staff decide for themselves the methods they will use to do the work delegated. There are different ways of doing any task and encourage staff to be creative.

3. Monitor staff performance without undue interference or continually checking. Give your staff scope to use their initiative while at the same time telling them you're available if needed for guidance and support.

4. Delegate but do not abdicate. Keep in touch with what's going on by installing appropriate checks and reviews. Give staff the necessary supports such as equipment and information to do the work satisfactorily. At the end of the day, if anything goes wrong you're responsible. It pays to ensure that everything runs smoothly and that there are no surprises.

5. Don't just delegate routine jobs or ones you don't like. Pick those jobs that will challenge and stretch employees so that you are catering for their growth and development. Nevertheless, even jobs that you find routine may challenge and interest the novice. Over time, and as you gain more confidence in your staff, gradually increase the complexity of the tasks you delegate.

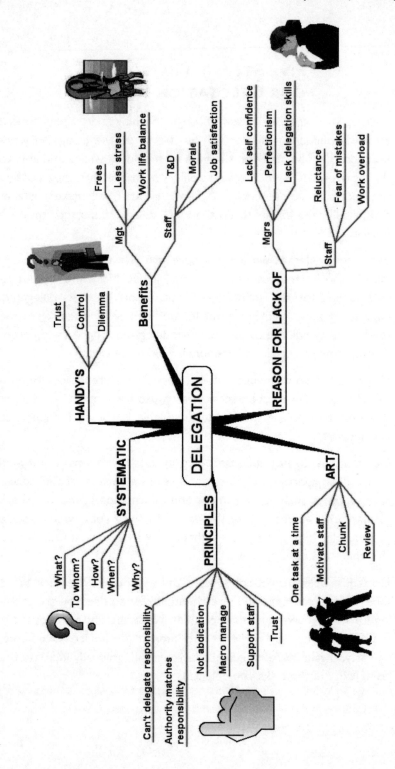

DELEGATION

HANDY'S
- Trust
- Control
- Dilemma

Benefits
- Mgt
  - Frees
  - Less stress
  - Work life balance
- Staff
  - T&D
  - Morale
  - Job satisfaction

REASON FOR LACK OF
- Mgrs
  - Lack self confidence
  - Perfectionism
  - Lack delegation skills
- Staff
  - Reluctance
  - Fear of mistakes
  - Work overload

SYSTEMATIC
- What?
- To whom?
- How?
- When?
- Why?

PRINCIPLES
- Can't delegate responsibility
- Authority matches responsibility
- Not abdication
- Macro manage
- Support staff
- Trust

ART
- One task at a time
- Motivate staff
- Chunk
- Review

10

MOTIVATION

☑ How can you motivate staff?

☑ How can you motivate yourself?

☑ What are the main demotivators?

☑ What is the power of expectation?

☑ What are the theories of motivation?

INTRODUCTION

Motivation is complex because different things motivate different people. The triggers of motivation change over time. There are two sources of motivation: internal and external. Internal motivation comes from within and tends to be long term and very strong. External motivation comes from outside and tends to be short term and varies in strength with the source. There are numerous ways of motivating staff. A shared vision, clearly communicated, will energise staff to achieve goals. A good way of motivating yourself is to become a lifelong learner and seek out ways of continually improving performance. Office politics and poor systems are some of the things staff find de-motivating. The power of expectation is a great motivator, as employees like to live up to their manager's expectations. There's a strong body of knowledge and theory supporting the concept of motivation in organisations that a manager should be familiar with. The more well-known of these are Maslow's hierarchy of needs, Vroom's expectancy theory, McClelland's need for achievement theory, Herzberg's two-factor theory and the importance of goal-setting for motivation.

> "Remember, what you get by reaching your destination isn't nearly as important as what you become by reaching your goals — what you will become is the winner you were born to be!" — Zig Ziglar

Types

Different things motivate different people and motivation changes over time. Intrinsic motivated is self-generated and comes from internal needs, drives and desires and tends to be long term. A person will be highly motivated if they have a passion for the work and for personal growth and development. A person may be driven by curiosity and interest to learn something new. Employees are more creative when motivated primarily by the interest, enjoyment, satisfaction and challenge of the work itself. When intrinsic motivation is lowered, creativity dips. On the other hand, extrinsic motivation comes from outside and tends to be short term. It may be rewards such as salary, fringe benefits, incentives, praise or promotion. Over time employees get used to these and the effect gradually wears off.

HOW TO MOTIVATE STAFF

❖ Find out what motivates your staff. Undertake regular employee satisfaction audits to determine their views. Generally, some of the things that motivate staff include autonomy, recognition, opportunities for achievement, career advancement, participation and having interesting and worthwhile work. To motivate staff you need to meet their hopes, aspirations and expectations and make them feel important. At the minimum, you need to provide them with a decent living.

❖ Seek staff suggestions. A formal suggestion scheme should be implemented to encourage and reward staff who suggest ways to improve work methods and operations. The more involved staff feel the more motivated they will be. They love to feel that their views are valued and important to management and that they are making a worthwhile contribution to the company's success.

❖ Respect that staff need a work–life balance and realise that they have a life outside work. As a manager you've a duty to help staff achieve a healthy work–life balance.

"People who are unable to motivate themselves must be content with mediocrity, no matter how impressive their other talents." — Andrew Carnegie

- ❖ Create a sense of involvement of staff. Explain to them the importance to the organisation of the work they do. Employees' motivation will be high if they perceive their work as significant. Keep in touch with your staff by managing by wandering about (MBWA) and being available on a daily basis to discuss their concerns. Allow staff to plan, control and continually improve their work. Delegate whole tasks so that they can readily see the impact of their work.

- ❖ Communicate clearly a shared vision and goals. Goals should be specific, realistic and challenging. Most employees want an interesting and challenging job rather than an easy and boring one. Knowledge of results should be accurate and timely. Participation in the formulation of goals leads to commitment and high performance.

- ❖ Do continuous performance appraisals rather than once a year appraisals. This will help staff rectify problems as they are highlighted and also continually identify training needs. They will know where they stand with their manager rather than the uncertainty of waiting 12 months to find out.

- ❖ Recognise achievement with praise as appropriate. Only praise work that's exceptional or outstanding. Praise must be earned to be worthwhile as this makes staff feel they're doing important work. Praising everyday performance diminishes its worth and may only arouse cynicism in staff. Give credit as soon as possible, after the event deserving praise, for immediate impact. When showing appreciation you should specifically describe the desired behaviour, state why the desired behaviour was helpful and express sincere thanks.

"Thoughts lead on to purposes; purposes go forth in action; actions form habits; habits decide character; and character fixes our destiny." — Tyron Edwards

❖ Avoid the blame culture. Criticise behaviour and not people and treat employees as special to build their self-esteem. Celebrate success to motivate people to go on to achieve further success.

❖ Create an attractive environment and make work more interesting by job enrichment, job enlargement, job rotation and job redesign. Build on the strengths of staff by delegating assignments to help them grow and develop. Introduce flexible working hours if requested by staff.

❖ Have equitable pay and working conditions. This makes staff feel they are working for an ethical and reputable organisation. There's a link between the level of pay and a sense of self-worth.

❖ Adopt a Theory Y approach to staff by showing that you trust them and expect them to show initiative and be productive. Treat employees with respect. Show employees that you like them, are interested in their welfare and value their views, loyalty and commitment. Do this and you are sure to have a motivated staff.

"No horse gets anywhere until he is harnessed. No stream or gas drives anything until it is confined. No Niagara is ever turned into light and power until it is tunnelled. No life ever grows great until it is focused, dedicated, disciplined." – Harry Emerson Fosdick

---

MOTIVATE YOURSELF

❖ Be motivated yourself. If you are genuinely enthusiastic and committed this is likely to rub off on the staff. If you are not prepared to do something, why should the employees? The excitement and passion you create will be contagious. Enjoying what you do is probably the greatest energiser and motivator of all.

❖ Be genuine, honest and sincere. Walk the talk and keep your promises. There is nothing more de-motivational to staff than dealing with "phoney" managers – those pretending to be something they are not. Provide support and try to help staff with personal problems.

❖ Set SMART goals. These should challenge, stretch abilities and drive you forward to achieve desired outcomes.

> "You get the best out of others when you give the best of yourself."
> — Harry Firestone

❖ Cultivate a desire to achieve. Ambition fires drive and provides the motivation to succeed. Celebrate your own successes no matter how small as this provides you with the motivation to keep on going.

❖ Use positive self-talk or affirmations. Develop a strong self-belief in your abilities. Have a positive attitude by visualising successful outcomes. Mentally rehearse the way you want some future situation to work out so that you're subconsciously propelled forward to reach your dream.

❖ Avoid unfavourable comparisons with others, as these can be demotivational. Try to improve on your previous best performance.

❖ Look after yourself mentally and physically – a healthy mind in a healthy body.

❖ Adopt a role model to guide you towards better performance and act as a role model to staff by leading by example. Become a lifelong learner and encourage others to do likewise. Review your performance and reflect on and learn from your mistakes and shortcomings.

❖ Discover what motivates you. Motivators might be values such as success, praise, recognition, respect or just the feeling you get when you've done a worthwhile job. More physical things such as a house, a car, a cause or an education might be motivators as well. The scientific school of management believed that money was a prime motivator and that people were driven by incentives. Behavioural scientists consider responsibility, relationships, power and achievement to be more important.

❖ Welcome difficulty and challenge. Solving complex problems is interesting and challenging and the process is motivating in itself. The journey is often more motivational than the arrival.

DEMOTIVATORS

The signs of de-motivation include high staff turnover, absenteeism and poor industrial relations. They can be caused by a variety of factors.

Organisational Issues

❖ Command and control culture. A bureaucratic-type organisation is unlikely to reward risk taking and innovation. In fact, it often rewards conformity, mediocrity, lack of decisiveness and a conservative approach to work issues. If employees feel they are over-managed and have no control over their work situation they will tend to be de-motivated.

❖ Confusing instructions, poor communication and unclear expectations mean that employees do not know precisely what is expected of them. Employees can spend a lot of time on the wrong tasks, achieving the wrong results and consequently becoming frustrated.

❖ Unproductive meetings with ambiguous outcomes. Everybody should be clear on what's supposed to be done when a meeting concludes. A results-oriented meeting with an action plan will keep people focused and motivated.

"Don't wait until everything is just right. It will never be perfect. There will always be challenges, obstacles and less than perfect conditions. So what. Get started now. With each step you take, you will grow stronger and stronger, more and more skilled, more and more self-confident and more and more successful." – Mark Victor Hansen

---

❖ Poor human resource policies. For example, where there is no clear relationship between effort and reward employees will have no incentive to be more productive. Where there is an incremental scale awarded on the basis of service rather than effort, or where there is a lack of equity in pay and reward systems, employees will feel disgruntled. Where there is a culture of bullying, intimidation and harassment in the company employees will feel a sense of injustice. Where employees generally are not treated with dignity and respect they will feel demoralised and resentful.

❖ Not walking the talk. Management saying one thing and doing another. For example, a company may encourage feedback from employees and then do nothing about it. I once worked for a company that undertook a costly staff survey in response to frequent industrial relations problems and then did nothing about the findings. Hypocrisy is rampant in business. A company may introduce a cost cutting programme, ask employees to defer wage increases or accept wage cuts and at the same time award its chief executive a huge salary increase.

❖ The company operating a policy of not keeping staff fully informed about what's going on. Lack of information is a major source for employee stress. When an information vacuum occurs misleading rumours fly around the organisation to fill it, often causing anxiety and unease. Some companies are good at keeping their employees informed, even about the financial performance of the company. Unfortunately, others prefer to keep them in the dark.

❖ Work overload causes people to feel stressed all the time and may lead to burnout. Work underload is where people are bored because they have too little to do. Also, staff may not be getting the opportunity to use their discretion, unique expertise, qualifications and abilities in their job.

❖ Office politics. This includes competition for power, influence, resources, favour and promotions. Office politics can be the unwritten subtle determinant for success in an organisation. Some people seem to be better at playing the game than others. The latter find it difficult to read situations and ascertain what the politically correct behaviour in an organisation is. Consequently, they often feel anxious in case they upset powerful people and hinder their chances of promotion. Ideally, if office politics were eliminated from an organisation people would feel they have an equal chance for success.

"In 1998, Mitsubishi paid $34 million in a sexual misconduct settlement. The company's North American division paid awards of $10,000 to $300,000 to 486 female workers to settle allegations that women on an assembly line were harassed and managers did nothing to stop it." – Curtice (2005)

Staff Issues

❖ Boredom. The work is tedious and there is no desire or effort on the part of management to make it more interesting.

❖ The staff is not consulted about plans, goals, targets and strategies. The staff is not forewarned about changes such as downsizing or expansion. Sometimes the first employees know about problems in the company is when they arrive to work on a Monday morning to find the company gate shut and a receiver appointed.

❖ There is negative thinking and lack of self-belief among staff. Employees are treated like automatons rather than thinking human beings.

❖ Constant change. Some change can be highly motivational provided it is needed, results-oriented, well-planned and communicated and clearly in the interests of the company and its employees. People are unsettled by constant change, however. Change ideally should be incremental, the reason for the change should be clearly communicated by management to employees and their concerns openly and honestly addressed. Managers should focus on the positive aspects of the change and the improvements it will bring.

❖ There are dysfunctional relationships among employees and departments. There is a lack of co-operation between departments with ongoing battles for power and territory. Good interpersonal relationships in the workplace have a positive influence on morale and productivity.

❖ There are inadequate resources for staff such as equipment, materials and space. There is little support in the form of coaching and information from managers.

❖ Low quality standards. Short-term cost reduction considerations are often the reason for quality compromises. Employees should be involved in goal setting and process improvement. Tapping into their creativity will often mean that quality standards need not be sacrificed for cost considerations.

❖ The staff is given negative feedback for poor performance but never praised when performance is exceptional. Employees who hear nothing but destructive criticism inevitably feel demoralised, inadequate, worthless and resentful.

❖ The staff feels they are underpaid for the type of work they do and the level of responsibility they have. They may be aware that similar positions are earning more in competitive companies.

❖ Managers and supervisors steal the ideas of their staff without giving acknowledgement or credit. This is standard practice in many organisations as managers consider their staff to be adjuncts of themselves and therefore exist to bolster their positions and make them look good. Staff deserve recognition for their ideas.

"Security is mostly a superstition. It does not exist in nature, nor do the children of men as a whole experience it. Avoiding danger is no safer in the long run than outright exposure. Life is either a daring adventure, or nothing." — Helen Keller

---

Blocked Desires

Blocked desires cause frustration and lead to a lack of motivation. Employees will feel frustrated if they haven't the right equipment and support systems to perform to a level that they desire. Likewise, they will feel frustrated if their ideas are not acknowledged or implemented. The acronym RAFT will help you remember the typical responses to frustration.

❖ **R**egression. This is where employees revert to childish behaviour such as tantrums if they feel they lack the facilities to help them do a good job or their wishes are continually ignored.

❖ **A**ggression. This may take the form of physical attack or verbal abuse on those in authority who they blame for the lack of facilities. In extreme cases employees may go on strike for trivial issues or even commit acts of sabotage.

❖ **F**ixation. This is where employees persist in unproductive behaviour of no value such as delaying work for no particular reason. This is in response to their feelings of frustration.

❖ **T**otal withdrawal. This is where employees show apathy, indifference and resignation in response to an unfavourable situation, such as lack of resources needed to do the job, instead of doing something positive about it.

POWER OF EXPECTATION

❖ If the manager communicates high expectations then the staff will tend to live up to them. This is known as the Pygmalion effect, or the self-fulfilling prophesy. Expectations should be realistic and achievable. With new recruits the initial management expectations set mould subsequent behaviour. Managers should possess the self-belief to train and develop staff to achieve results.

❖ Staff has greater respect and belief in competent managers with proven track records and who live up to their promises. The tone of the manager should be congruent with the words spoken. Words used to describe situations should be appropriate, simple and direct and in line with behaviour

❖ The manager should use non-verbal cues when communicating their expectations. The body language should be in harmony with the message. Lean slightly forward with your body keeping your posture open and direct. Maintain eye contact. Use hand gestures, head and facial expressions to support the positive nature of your message.

CONCEPTS OF MOTIVATION

Motivation is extremely complex. Different concepts provide different frameworks and perspectives. It's useful for practising managers to have some acquaintance with these theories. Most training programmes on management will cover all or some of them. The following are the most important:

❖ Maslow's hierarchy of needs

❖ Vroom's expectancy theory

❖ McClelland's theory of Motivation

❖ Herzberg's two-factor theory

❖ Goal-setting.

Maslow's Hierarchy of Needs

In his motivation theory, Maslow argued that people had five innate needs.

1. *Physiological needs.* These are also called basic or physical needs. They are the need for food, water and shelter. In an organisational sense they would include a reasonable wage and good conditions of employment. Once these are satisfied the next set of needs kick in.

2. *Safety needs.* These are also called security needs and include freedom from threat and coercion. In an organisational sense they would include pension, health insurance, a safe working environment and secure employment. Once a person becomes secure they then become interested in making friends and becoming accepted by those around them.

3. *Love needs.* These are also called social and relationship needs. This is the need for friendship and collaboration in the workplace. People like to feel a sense of belonging. This can be achieved by creating a family-type atmosphere in the workplace. Once socially accepted, people like to be loved and respected by others.

4. *Esteem needs.* People like to have the respect and recognition of their work colleagues. At work, promotion may win status and respect in the perception of others. Once people have won the respect of others they then strive to become self-actualised.

5. *Self-actualisation needs.* This is when you reach your full potential or what you're capable of becoming. This is often something you strive for all your life. Lifelong learning and continuous improvements are part of this philosophy.

Figure 8: Maslow's Hierarchy of Needs

Maslow maintained that as soon as one need is met another one takes its place. A need that's satisfied no longer motivates an individual. The need for self-actualisation can never be totally satisfied and is an ongoing search. Many people spend their lives trying to meet their lower level needs and never get the opportunity to satisfy their higher level ones for self-esteem and self-actualisation.

Maslow's theory can not be empirically proven but it has intuitive appeal and has stood the test of time. Obviously, the primary survival needs of food and shelter take precedence over all other needs. It is only when these have been met that a person considers status or recognition to be issues worth striving for.

Maslow's theory is of limited practical use but is a good generic concept of motivation. It cannot be applied at an individual level because different people are motivated by unique needs. Some people may have little desire for promotion, and the responsibility it brings with it. One person may seek to satisfy a need for esteem by getting promoted or becoming the best at doing their particular job. Another person might get active in a trade union and win the esteem of their work colleagues by challenging authority. Some of these issues are dealt with by other theories, such as Vroom's expectancy theory.

Vroom's Expectancy Theory

This theory states that the strength of an individual's motivation depends on the extent to which they believe that their efforts will bring about a desired outcome. If employees believe that their efforts will lead to the rewards that they desire then they will be motivated to improve their performance. Mathematically it can be expressed as:

$E \times V = F$

Where E = Expectancy or the strength of their expectation that their behaviour will bring about the desired outcome.

V = Valence or the value they place on the outcome.

F = Force of motivation

This theory, unlike Maslow's, is not a generic theory. It takes into account each person's unique motivation. For example, an individual's promotion valence may be nil, i.e. they place no value on promotion.

This might be because they do not want extra responsibility. Therefore the strength of their motivation would be zero.

McClelland's Theory of Motivation

McClelland maintained that three things motivated managers:

1. The need for achievement
2. The need for power
3. The need for affiliation.

He felt, however, that managers were more motivated by achievement and power than affiliation. Power has been described as the greatest aphrodisiac. Managers like to be challenged and to exercise personal responsibility. The major concern with high achievers is that they are task-oriented rather than relationship-oriented. This is a major disadvantage in team-based organisations.

Herzberg's Two-factor Theory

Frederick Herzberg, in his book *Work and the Nature of Man*, introduced the two-factor theory of motivation. This identified the elements causing job satisfaction and job dissatisfaction. He called these hygiene, or maintenance, factors and motivator factors. The hygiene factors minimise dissatisfaction but do not give satisfaction. For example, we know that good sanitation minimises threats to health but does not provide good health. Satisfaction with hygiene factors varies over time and is short term. The hygiene factors are:

❖ Company policy and administration

❖ Salary

❖ Supervision

❖ Interpersonal relationships

❖ Working conditions and

❖ Job security.

The motivators are:

❖ Status

❖ Advancement or promotion

❖ Recognition

❖ Responsibility

❖ Challenging work

❖ Achievement, and

❖ Opportunities for growth.

A lack of motivators will concentrate employee's minds on the hygiene factors such as pay and working conditions. However, this is less likely to happen if the work is challenging, interesting and offers scope for advancement. Herzberg recommended that managers concentrate on the motivators to improve motivation. Therefore, it is better to make the job more challenging than improving working conditions. He specified three methods of making work more motivational. These are:

1. *Job enrichment.* This is the process of giving an employee more responsible and demanding tasks to do. Typically, this might be delegating more interesting and problem solving-type work to an employee. This approach can increase motivation and improve job satisfaction. Job enrichment provides more opportunities for achievement, recognition, esteem and responsibility, and can add meaning to a task by providing a challenge to learn something new.

2. *Job enlargement.* This gives the employee a greater variety of tasks to do. Typically, it might be increasing the number of operations an employee is engaged on and so moving away from a narrow specialisation of tasks. Herzberg mentioned that this is more limited in value, since a worker is unlikely to be highly motivated by a variety of tasks if the tasks are still repetitive and tedious to do.

3. *Job rotation.* This rotates employees between different tasks within a section or different jobs between departments. The primary role of job rotation is to improve employee's problem-solving and decision-making skills while at the same time broadening their experience and giving them an overall perspective of the company and the interface between departments. It's particularly useful for the training of junior managers.

Goal-setting

It's well known that setting goals can motivate people. A manager may influence the behaviour of employees productively by setting clear achievable goals. Goals that are challenging and require mental effort are more motivational than goals that require little effort. However, the goals must not be so difficult that they are unattainable. Employees often feel elated when they achieve a worthwhile goal, accomplish a task or solve a problem. Even making progress towards a goal can create the same sensations. In contrast, employees who are blocked from achieving their goals will become frustrated, unhappy and de-motivated by their work.

Reinforcement fosters motivation. In other words, an employee who is rewarded for achieving a difficult goal is more likely to strive towards the next one. Goals must also be specific and capable of measurement if they're to be motivational. Employees are more likely to accept and be committed to goals if they participated in setting them. They expect managers to provide the necessary resources and supports to enable them to achieve their goals.

"People are always blaming their circumstances for what they are. I don't believe in circumstances. The people who get on in this world are the people who get up and look for the circumstances they want, and, if they can't find them, make them." – George Bernard Shaw

SUMMARY

Motivation is complex as evidenced by the different concepts offered by management theorists. Different things motivate people and what motivates one person will not necessarily motivate another. The triggers of motivation change over time. There are two sources of motivation: internal and external. Internal motivation comes from within such as needs, drives and desires, and tends to be long-term and strong. External motivation comes from outside such as salary, fringe benefits and promotion, and tends to be short term and vary in strength with the source.

There are numerous ways of motivating staff. A shared vision, clearly communicated will energise staff to achieve goals. People will feel more motivated if they're consulted and involved in decision-making. A good way of motivating yourself is to become a lifelong learner and seek out ways of continually improving performance. Office politics, bureaucracy and poor systems are some of the things staff find de-motivating. The power of expectation is a great motivator, as staff like to live up to the manager's expectations. A variety of motivational theories of practical use to managers were discussed.

CHECK YOUR PEOPLE SKILLS QUOTIENT – 10

	Circle the appropriate response	
1. Internal motivation tends to be long-term and strong	True	False
2. A clear vision, clearly communicated motivates staff	True	False
3. Adopting Theory X is a good way of motivating staff	True	False
4. Use positive self-talk to motivate yourself	True	False
5. Praise should be delivered long after the event	True	False
6. SMART goals will motivate staff	True	False
7. Overwork will stress and de-motivate staff	True	False
8. Staff with little to do will be more motivated	True	False
9. Staff tend to believe managers with proven experience	True	False
10. The Pygmalion effect is also called the self-fulfilling-prophesy	True	False

Total the number of true and false responses and check Appendix I at the back of the book for the answers and to determine your score.

FIVE STEPS TO IMPROVE YOUR MOTIVATION SKILLS

1. Use internal motivators such as an inherent interest in the job or opportunities for personal growth and development to motivate staff. Managers should ensure that the job is designed to make it as interesting as possible. Job enrichment, job enlargement and job rotation may be used make work interesting.

2. Make sure there is a clear relationship between effort and reward. Reward staff commensurate with their efforts and in line with the going rate within the industry.

3. Get employees involved in problem solving and decision-making. Recognise their achievement by praise and thanks. Employees like to feel that their ideas and work is valued.

4. Motivate yourself by lifelong learning and a desire to continually improve performance. Act as a role model in this regard so that your staff will be motivated to do likewise.

5. Set high expectations for staff and they will live up to it, as they like to be stretched by goals that are challenging but realistic.

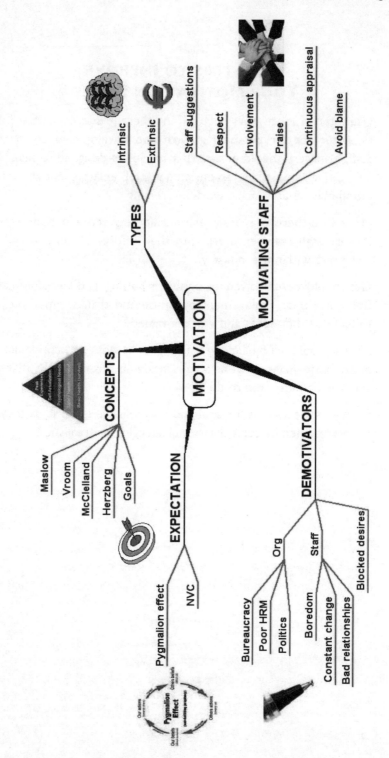

MOTIVATION

TYPES
- Intrinsic
- Extrinsic

MOTIVATING STAFF
- Staff suggestions
- Respect
- Involvement
- Praise
- Continuous appraisal
- Avoid blame

CONCEPTS
- Maslow
- Vroom
- McClelland
- Herzberg
- Goals

EXPECTATION
- Pygmalion effect
- NVC

DEMOTIVATORS
- Org
  - Bureaucracy
  - Poor HRM
  - Politics
- Staff
  - Boredom
  - Constant change
  - Bad relationships
- Blocked desires

11

TEAM MANAGEMENT

☑ What are the stages of team development?

☑ What are the roles needed in a team?

☑ How can the line manager act as facilitator?

☑ What are the traits of effective teams?

☑ What are the principles of team building?

INTRODUCTION

A team is two or more people with complementary skills who are committed to a common purpose. The development of teams goes through five stages: forming, storming, norming, performing and adjourning. The roles of teams are shaper, people person, evaluator, chairman, innovator, finisher, resource allocator, co-worker and specialist. The functions involved in keeping a team going can be grouped under task and maintenance. Group think can prevent a team from functioning effectively.

Facilitation means to make things easy. In the modern business context the manager is now moving from a directive style to a facilitative style. This approach is needed to manage teams and to encourage the sharing of information. The manager as a facilitator should observe behaviour and be fair, friendly and unassuming. They should be people of emotional stability with great empathy to the wishes and concerns of others.

The traits of effective teams include collaboration, enthusiasm and rapport. To run an effective team leaders need to inspire commitment and be available when needed by the other team members. Team members need good interpersonal relationship skills and problem-solving techniques. To build an effective team you will need to foster morale, and develop trust, confidence and respect. Team goals and behaviour should be congruent with the culture of the company.

Definition

A team is two or more people, and ideally not more than eight, with complementary skills who are committed to a common purpose. Clear performance goals and monitoring help a team keep track of progress and hold itself accountable. The goal might be improved customer service, increased sales, higher productivity or cost reduction. The team members are individually and collectively accountable for the work of the team. A TEAM can be defined as "Together Everyone Achieves More." This acknowledges the synergistic effect of teams. Teams are developed through training and experience. Skills needed for effective performance are a combination of the technical, organisational and interpersonal.

There are different types of teams. The best known are quality circles, project, self-management, departmental, policy-making and change teams. Quality circles are set up to improve quality and reduce costs. Project teams are drawn from different departments, set up to complete a project and are disbanded when it's accomplished. Self-management teams are responsible for the work of their team and are empowered with the authority, resources, information and accountability to do the job. Departmental teams operate within a department to solve a particular problem. Policy-making teams are brought together from all departments to develop company policies and philosophy. Change teams are set up to manage the change process in a company. Change may happen through expansion by merger or acquisition or contraction by disinvestment.

"There is no 'I' in TEAMWORK." — Source unknown

DEVELOPMENT STAGES

The development of teams happen over five stages. Tuckman (1965) identified these as forming, storming, norming, performing and adjourning.

1. *Forming*. This is the stage of coming together and building the team. There is concern about structure, direction, support, timetables,

resources and goals. People want to know the terms of reference for the team, their roles within it and how it is going to function. They are trying to get used to each other by finding out about backgrounds, interests and competencies. They want to know who the leader is going to be and what are the expectations for team members. They are trying to get to grips with the task they have been given to do and how they are going to do it. They will want to know where team meetings will be held. At the forming stage there is suspicion, uncertainty and anxiety and a certain amount of testing the waters to ascertain each other's tolerance limits and personalities. Investing time in this stage helps teams move forward.

2. *Storming*. This stage is often characterised by confusion and aggression and is sometimes called the infighting stage. Debate, dissent, disagreement, personality clashes, and competition for power and influence fuel the conflict. There is open and hidden hostility and resentment between members of the team. The storming stage can be an unsettling and traumatic period for members with a need for conflict resolution to calm things down. Teams that avoid managing conflict constructively may drive it underground and build up resentments and problems for the future. This stage is quite normal and most teams will work their way through it before proceeding to the next stage.

3. *Norming*. At this stage standards or norms of behaviour are being established and it is often called the getting organised stage. Norms are rules to be drawn up to resolve contentious issues, make decisions and complete tasks. Plans are formulated and agreed, work standards put down. People are settling in and roles for each member are being identified, having regard to unique abilities and skills and the needs of the team. Trust is established between the members of the team with co-operation, collaboration, cohesiveness and commitment between team members. The norming stage is a stage of productivity with norms made explicit so that they can be reviewed and renewed as needed. Failure to do so may result in negative norms being established frustrating the goals of the team.

4. *Performing*. Interpersonal relationship problems have been resolved with roles, rules and behaviour norms agreed and structures in place. There is synergy between members as their unique compe-

tencies are blended. Rapport has been built up and members now get down to achieving the goals. People are highly motivated to get things done. The leader empowers the team and then lets them get on with the job. Consequently, there is a high level of morale, satisfaction and productivity in the team.

5. *Adjourning*. The task has been successfully completed and the team celebrates their accomplishments. The team should reflect on what it has learned from the project. At the same time, there is a sense of grieving for lost friendships or letting go as the members contemplate going back to their old jobs or to the next team.

A team may move back briefly to the forming stage when a new member has been accepted. However, the process of breaking in a new member should be faster and they will quickly move on to the performing stage.

"Teamwork is the ability to work together towards a common vision. The ability to direct individual accomplishments toward organisational objectives. It is the fuel that allows common people to attain uncommon results." — Andrew Carnegie

---

TEAM ROLES

In a successful team, members adopt specific roles. The acronym SPECIFICS based on the work of Belbin (1981) will help you recall these roles:

❖ **S**haper. The shaper is action-oriented, thrives on challenge and shapes decisions in an optimum way. They provide dynamism and drive for the team members and encourage them to overcome obstacles. They see problems as challenges, however in the pursuit of getting things done they may be insensitive to the feelings and perceptions of others.

❖ **P**eople person. The people person has excellent social skills and maintains relationships within the team. They promote unity by diplomacy; attentive listening, facilitating and resolving conflicts through excellent negotiating skills. They recognise the interests, attitudes, concerns and achievements of others but may be indecisive in critical situations, unwilling to take sides.

❖ **E**valuator. The evaluator is a critical thinker. They analyse ideas, evaluate options and solve arguments. They spot potential problems and test the feasibility of solutions. They tease out issues by acting as the devil's advocate and so help the team avoid ill-judged projects. However, they may lack the drive and ability to inspire others.

❖ **C**hairman. The chairman keeps the team on course, exercising discipline and control as necessary. They exercise a democratic leadership style but may need to be assertive at times to show who's in charge. They clarify goals and control and co-ordinate the activities of the team to achieve those goals. They justify decisions so that everybody knows exactly what's going on. They delegate wisely by matching activities with the unique abilities of team members but may be perceived as manipulative if thought to be offloading personal work.

"Strength lies in difference, not in similarities." — Vincent Lombardi

---

❖ **I**nnovator. These are the unorthodox, creative or ideas people with unique insights into problems. The team needs a thoughtful original thinker who can help it brainstorm alternative ways of looking at problems and generating solutions. Innovators are often too preoccupied to communicate effectively being a little bit like the caricature of the absentminded professor obsessed with ideas.

❖ **F**inisher. The finisher is the person who motivates and inspires the team to implement things and get things done. They create a sense of urgency, are good at time management and prod the team forward to complete tasks on time. They are concerned with schedules, deadlines and the consequences if things go wrong. They are inclined to worry unduly about minor details and are reluctant to delegate tasks that they don't trust anybody else to perform.

❖ **I**nvestigator of resources. These people are good at research and network with people outside the team to see what resources are available to do the job. The team will need information, expertise, equipment and material resources to get the job done. The investigator of resources keeps in touch with the wider world and is often inspired by ideas picked up from outside. They may be over-optimistic and may lose interest once initial enthusiasm has passed.

❖ **C**o-worker. These people are very good at administration and converts plans into actions. They organise, follow up and keep ongoing records of work-in-progress and completed tasks. They advocate clear objectives and procedures so that the team knows exactly what to do. They may become perfectionist in their pursuit of keeping the paperwork in order.

❖ **S**pecialist. The specialist is the technical expert with the unique expertise, skills and knowledge to guide the team forward. They have a great depth of knowledge and enjoy sharing it with others. If they do not know the answer to something they will gladly find out. The team may need specialists who can contribute engineering, accounting, information technology or marketing skills. The specialist is inclined to concentrate on technicalities and tends to have a narrow viewpoint.

FUNCTIONS

Team functions can be considered under two headings: task and maintenance.

Task

This is the behaviour of team members affecting the way the work gets done. Part of the task function is deciding how decisions are arrived at: by consensus or by majority rule. Will leadership be rotated? Will a systematic approach to solving problems be used? The team leader (facilitator) might suggest suitable problem solving models be used such as decision trees, the cause and effect diagram, the fishbone technique or brainstorming. The acronym SLICE will help you recall the task functions of a team:

❖ **S**ummarising. This is the task of co-ordinating ideas, summarising and arriving at conclusions for team acceptance.

❖ **L**ooking for or giving information. This is the task of seeking and providing ideas, facts and suggestions. Dialogue and debate should be encouraged between members.

❖ **I**nitiating. This is proposing activities and goals and defining problems and suggesting solutions.

❖ **C**onsensus-testing. This is checking on how much agreement has been reached before decisions are made.

❖ **E**laborating. This is providing options and illustrative examples and clearing up issues so members understand what is going on.

> "Work and self-worth are the two factors in pride that interact with each other and that tend to increase the strong sense of pride found in superior work teams. When people do something of obvious worth, they feel a strong sense of personal worth." — Dennis Kinlaw

Maintenance

The facilitator should draw up terms of reference to act as ground rules for the functioning of the team and ensure that members follow them. An important aspect is conflict resolution and maintaining good interpersonal relationships. The acronym SCHEME will help you recall the maintenance or building functions of a team:

❖ **S**etting standards. Standards are needed as targets for members to achieve. The leader should encourage the team to stay focused on the task and develop norms of behaviour to build team cohesiveness and morale.

❖ **C**ompromising. Sometimes members must compromise on their own position to maintain the cohesion of the team.

❖ **H**armonising. Collaboration is needed to achieve the goals of the team. Differences must be reconciled and tensions reduced by resolving interpersonal relationship problems that are inevitable in any group of people. The leader acting as a facilitator should reflect on the process of handling conflict and direct it in a positive and constructive way.

❖ **E**ncouraging. Members encourage collaboration by being warm and friendly and by accepting and recognising each other's contributions.

❖ **M**aintaining dialogue. Communication skills are needed to encourage and maintain dialogue between members.

❖ **E**xpressing feelings. Interpersonal relationships are built and maintained by sharing and exploring feelings, emotions and concerns. If these are not expressed openly and honestly then the harmony of the team may be undermined.

LINE MANAGER AS FACILITATOR

Facilitation comes from the Latin word *facilis* which means to make easy. Facilitation is the provision of opportunities, resources, encouragement and support to achieve objectives, identify and solve problems and make decisions. It helps people to work together effectively, improve the process for doing so, and empowers people to take control and responsibility for their own efforts.

> "The first responsibility of a leader is to define reality. The last is to say thank you. In between, the leader is a servant." — Max DuPree

A facilitator will help a team work together smoothly and is trained to ensure that relationships, beliefs and values are taken into account, helping it perform more effectively. A facilitator may be required to lead, mediate, coach, act as a peacemaker, observe, take notes or simply be there if team members need expertise and guidance. Personality conflicts between members can hinder performance. Unless such conflicts are addressed and brought to the surface they will fester and impact negatively on the performance of the team. A good facilitator will be aware of these issues bringing them out into the open to resolve them. The approach adopted depends on the context and the type of people dealt with.

TRAITS FOR FACILITATION

The line manager becomes a facilitator by practising the following behaviours, which can be recalled by the acronym FAITHFULNESS:

❖ **F**riendliness. They should adopt an open, pleasant and approachable manner.

❖ **A**gility of mind. They should have the flexibility of mind to generate alternative ways of doing things. They should be able to assess a situation, identify problems, make decisions and guide the process along by keeping the discussion moving.

❖ **I**ntegrity. They must be someone with a high standard of ethics. Anything they hear during the course of facilitation should be treated with the strictest confidence. The boundaries of confidentiality should be agreed, recognised and respected with the team.

❖ **T**act. They should have the sensitivity to be aware of people's expressed and unexpressed feelings and not to upset them in any way. They should have the acumen to be able to steer conflict in a positive constructive way without antagonising anybody.

❖ **H**umour. They should know when to use humour to manage and relieve tensions and defuse situations.

❖ **F**air. They should be fair and impartial, and treat people as equals.

❖ **U**nassuming. They should have no airs and graces and have the humanity and flexibility to deal with people at their own level.

❖ **L**earning ability. They should be interested in lifelong learning so that they can continually develop. Likewise, they should assist others to reach their potential. They should create a non-threatening environment where people feel safe to learn and can trust each other and provide the resources and opportunities for others to learn. This means a complete acceptance that mistakes are learning opportunities and will inevitably lead to success.

❖ **N**atural. They should be natural and humane. They should be able to congratulate people and praise them in a genuine, natural way.

❖ **E**motional stability. They should have self-understanding and be able to empathise with others. This creates a willingness to make and accept feedback. They need good interpersonal relationships and should be sensitive to the company culture, knowing the political pitfalls to avoid and guiding the team away from them.

❖ **S**ensitivity. They should be sensitive to the company culture, know the political pitfalls to avoid and guide the team away from them.

❖ **S**incerity. They should be sincerely interested in the welfare of the group and be prepared to work with them to achieve their goals.

"The wise facilitator's ability does not rest on techniques or gimmicks or set exercises. Become aware of process — and when you see this clearly, you can shed light on the process of others." — From the Tao

---

FACILITATION PROCESS

Facilitation is an activity or process and can also include non-action such as silence. The outcome of facilitation should be to help the team arrive at its own conclusions, solve its own problems, make its own decisions and take responsibility for its own actions. The process can be recalled by the acronym COASTER:

❖ **C**hallenge. Challenge people directly to think for themselves by asking incisive questions or through constructive feedback.

❖ **O**bserve the behaviour of people by being aware of what's happening in the group and the needs of individuals. The facilitator must have good judgement and be able to assess human situations and make sound decisions. Where they see a member of the team not pulling their weight or doing their fair share of work they should intervene to ensure an equal contribution from all members. Likewise if some members are not observing the ground rules they can intervene to bring this to their attention.

❖ **A**sk penetrating questions. The facilitator should know how to open up discussion and clarify issues where people are confused. They should not control situations and force their own wishes or needs on the team but instead explore situations by asking open questions. The information they get will help them understand the situation. They should use questions to challenge and clarify expectations and show alternative ways of achieving things. They should encourage individual contributions and acknowledge them in an appreciative way.

❖ **S**peak powerfully but infrequently. The facilitator should persuade, encourage, support, inspire, confront and motivate. They should act as a catalyst to bring forth the untapped creative energy and knowledge of the team.

"Few facilitators realise how much how little will do." – Source unknown

---

❖ **T**otal focus. The facilitator should keep the topic on track and stick to the agenda. They should make sure that a co-operative stance is adopted by encouraging team members to focus on the same objectives.

❖ **E**ars to ground. The facilitator should listen for what is said and for what is not said. Unexpressed feelings can be gauged through body language. They should be aware of the feelings and emotions that lie behind what is said by listening for intent, commitment and purpose. They should give feedback at appropriate stages by summarising what has been said.

❖ **R**espect. The facilitator should value people by recognising and respecting differences so that they are acknowledged personally and not afraid to speak out. They should treat people as equals and show consideration for their feelings by being fair, unbiased and considerate to all viewpoints. They should win trust by creating a non-threatening environment and addressing people's concerns and fears. They should follow the TOUCH acronym to win the respect of the team: **T**rust, **O**penness, **U**nderstanding, **C**onsideration and **H**onesty.

"Run an honest, open group. The fewer rules the better. Every law creates an outlaw. Good facilitation means doing less and being more." — From the Tao

---

INTERVENTION

Interventions may be needed to help a team improve the way it identifies and solves problems, works together and makes decisions. Facilitators help teams keep focused on their tasks, achieve their goals and increase the productivity of members. They help it bond together by creating team spirit.

Techniques

The techniques of facilitation can be a judicial mixture of supportive, persuasive and directive approaches:

❖ *Supportive.* Sometimes doing nothing is the best approach and just sit back and let the team get on with the task. The facilitator should use silence as appropriate to encourage dialogue between members. Use clarifying questions when needed to make issues clear.

❖ *Persuasive.* The facilitator may use questions to move the team along such as where to go next, suggest choices, paths to follow and actions to take. They should encourage the exchange of information and the sharing of ideas between members.

❖ *Directive*. This approach is adopted infrequently. Sometimes the facilitator needs to provide some guidance or direction to the team on what should be done next, especially where they have the special expertise to do so.

"When I give up trying to impress the group, I become very impressive. Let go in order to achieve. The wise facilitator speaks rarely and briefly, teaching more through being than doing." — From the Tao

---

Handling Conflict

Conflict should be managed positively. The facilitator should be competent in managing conflict and when no conflict exists they should be able to create constructive conflict to elicit debate and enhance team performance. Conflict can help the members look at a situation from different perspectives. This will help the team become more creative and make more effective decisions. The objective should be to encourage the development of win-win solutions. A conflict resolution model is shown in Chapter 4.

THE GROUP THINK PROBLEM

This is where a team becomes arrogant, feels invulnerable and looks on outsiders with suspicion and disdain. The team becomes insulated from outside opinion and fails to exercise critical thinking when solving problems or making decisions. The following are some of the characteristics of group think:

❖ Sense of invulnerability. The team becomes excessively optimistic about their strengths. As a result they pursue excessively risky activities and progressively lose touch with reality and common sense.

❖ Rationalising. They discount negative feedback and justify the soundness of their position without the benefit of objective analysis and expertise from independent sources.

❖ Moral blindness. They are self-righteous and ignore the ethical dimension of issues that may prove to be inimical to their goals. There is nobody willing to shout "stop" and say that what they are doing is wrong and unethical.

❖ Stereotype outsiders. They are over-confident and stereotype outsiders as stupid and inferior to them.

❖ Group pressure. Group norms are exercised to keep people in line by imposing sanctions or ostracising those who disagree. Consequently, members are afraid to express different viewpoints so that unpopular ideas are suppressed and an artificial sense of harmony created.

❖ Self-censorship. The group closes rank to outside influences and ideas so that personal doubts are not brought into the open and thus suppressed. Members want to maintain consensus at all costs and so put pressure on dissidents not to "rock the boat".

In addition to group think, other disadvantages of teams include:

❖ Members might feel their individual creativity is stifled and lost within the team. They may resent that their unique contribution is not sufficiently recognised.

❖ There is a great cost in time and effort of building a team. They are not created overnight but take a long time to evolve and bond together.

❖ Decisions may be compromised on the basis of keeping members happy rather than reaching the best possible decision. There is the danger that members may be influenced by group pressure to conform and maintain harmony at all costs.

SKILLS

The following are the skills needed by leaders and members to work effectively in a team:

Leaders

❖ They are visible and available when needed by other members. They practise the process of management by walking about.

❖ They know that team building is critical to success and that it's a continuous process.

❖ They have a participative style of leadership and thus create a team spirit.

❖ They know the values, beliefs, attitudes and interests of the members.

❖ They are trained facilitators. They praise exceptional performance and provide support and feedback to the team. They encourage members to discuss problems and encourage creativity by responding constructively to ideas.

❖ They define roles and relationships so that members know exactly what to do and will work together effectively to achieve goals.

"Trust men and they will be true to you; treat them greatly, and they will show themselves great." — Ralph Waldo Emerson

---

❖ They create a shared vision that energises and commits the team to the achievement of goals. They set high expectations and recognise the successes and achievements of the team through praise and reward. They make every member accountable for their contribution to the team.

❖ Their sense of integrity and high ethical values wins the respect of members. They behave in an exemplary manner and realise that they are a role model to other members. They exhibit self-belief that creates and sustains the self-belief of members.

❖ They promote team norms so members respect and support each other and are realistic in their expectations for each other. They foster trust, confidence and commitment among members.

Members

❖ They need to be trained in problem-solving and decision-making techniques. They need to be familiar with analytical techniques such as decision trees, break-even analysis, the fish bone technique, cause and effect diagrams, critical path analysis, cost benefit analysis, Pareto analysis, and flow-charting. They also need to be familiar with creativity techniques such as brainstorming, value analysis, force-field analysis, swot analysis and mind mapping.

❖ Time management. They need to cultivate time management skills so that they are aware of adopting the best methods and prioritise tasks and be conscious of time wasting activities.

❖ Results-oriented. Members should be goal-directed and all actions should be determined by the need to achieve objectives.

❖ They need interpersonal-relationships skills to be assertive, co-operate with others, resolve conflicts and encourage shy members to contribute. They need to create a team atmosphere that is in-formal, relaxed, comfortable and non-judgemental. Communication skills are needed to listen, encourage dialogue and to give and ac-cept constructive feedback.

❖ Emotional IQ. This is needed to be sensitive and helpful to the needs of other members while being in control of their emotions to avoid friction.

❖ Flexibility. They need to be flexible to consider other viewpoints, generate alternatives and consider possibilities. They need adaptive behaviours to be able to work effectively with other members.

❖ Leadership skills. They should be able to take turns at chairing meetings and be capable of alternating roles as initiator and fol-lower. They should be able to exercise task and maintenance func-tions as appropriate.

"Team player: One who unites others towards a shared destiny through sharing information and ideas, empowering others and devel-oping trust." – Dennis Kinlaw

---

TEAM BUILDING

Organisational Context

❖ Teams should be supported by the strategic plan and by the top management and the unions. Managers should provide clear goals and parameters in which the team can operate. They should also provide it with the necessary resources to get the job done.

❖ Teams should be congruent with the company culture. This means a culture of collaboration rather than competition.

❖ The composition of the team should ensure that members have complementary skills.

❖ Members should be trained in leadership, team building skills, continuous improvement, lifelong learning and problem solving.

"A group becomes a team when each member is sure enough of himself and his contribution to praise the skills of others." — Norman Shidle

---

❖ A performance appraisal scheme should be designed acceptable to members.

❖ Good communication channels so that the team can converse with other teams and senior management within the company.

❖ Managers should have realistic expectations regarding how long it will take the team to form and be effective and the training necessary for team building.

Motivating Your Team

The factors involved for a leader to motivate a team can be recalled by the acronym AGAINST:

❖ **A**ccountability. Make the members accountable and then let them get on with the job. Overcome obstacles to performance by providing the necessary resources and supports. Provide opportunities for participation and consensus decision-making and recognise the contribution of all members by rewarding exceptional performance.

❖ **G**oal. Clarify your own goal as a manager and agree the goals for the members so that everybody knows what has to be achieved.

❖ **A**cquaint yourself with the strengths and weaknesses and personalities of the members. Create an atmosphere that is informal, relaxed, non-threatening and non-judgemental.

❖ Incentivise members through praise, reward and recognition. Foster morale, trust, confidence and respect among the members.

❖ Need to be tough but fair when necessary. Members trust and are loyal to leaders who are firm but fair in their dealing with members and who respect confidentiality.

❖ Sincere emphatic listening to members. Attentive listening is the most important communication skill. Foster a team spirit by providing constructive feedback by focusing on the behaviour rather than the person and by creating a sense of collective partnership.

❖ Training and development. Encourage the training and development of members through coaching, on-the-job training and attending course programmes.

SUMMARY

A team is two or more people with complementary skills who are committed to a common purpose. Team development goes through five stages: forming, storming, norming, performing and adjourning. The roles of teams are shaper, people person, evaluator, chairman, innovator, finisher, resource allocator, co-worker and specialist. The functions involved in keeping a team going can be grouped under task and maintenance. Task functions include summarising, initiating, consensus testing and elaborating. Maintenance functions include setting standards, compromising, harmonising, encouraging and maintaining dialogue.

Facilitation means to make things easy. The manager needs to move from a directive to a facilitative style of management to manage teams effectively and encourage the sharing of information among members. The facilitative manager should observe human behaviour, listen and ask probing questions to clarify issues as necessary. He should be fair, friendly and unassuming and practise empathy to listen to the concerns of others.

Group think can prevent a team from functioning effectively. Group think occurs when teams become arrogant and feel invulnerable to outside threats. The traits of effective teams include collaboration, enthusiasm and rapport. To run an effective team leaders need to inspire commitment and be supportive, visible and available when needed by members. Members need good interpersonal relationship skills and have training in problem-solving and creativity techniques. An effective team

needs to foster morale and develop trust, confidence and respect between members. Teams should be congruent with the culture of the
company being collaborative rather than competitive.

CHECK YOUR PEOPLE SKILLS QUOTIENT – 11

	Circle the appropriate response	
1. A team consists of two or more people	True	False
2. Self-managed teams are totally responsible for their work	True	False
3. Sequentially team development stages are forming, norming, storming, performing and adjourning	True	False
4. The shaper is the creative person	True	False
5. The finisher implements and completes tasks	True	False
6. The functions of a team can be grouped as task and maintenance	True	False
7. Maintenance functions include setting standards	True	False
8. Task functions include maintaining dialogue between team members	True	False
9. Group think is characterised as excessive optimism	True	False
10. A facilitator directs operations	True	False

*Total the number of true and false responses and check Appendix 1 at the
back of the book for the answers and to determine your score.*

Five Steps to Improve Your Team Building Skills

1. Be aware of the stages that teams go through so that you can anticipate problems and plan for dealing with them when they arise. Realise that it takes a long time for a group to evolve into a team.

2. Complementary roles are essential for the successful running of teams. Learn the SPECIFICS acronym so that you become aware of the roles required in effective teams. Pick members with these roles in mind. Some of the roles may be combined in the one person.

3. As a manager you should move from a directive to a facilitative style by taking a back seat. This means you should empower members by encouraging them to accept responsibility, share information, generate ideas and see mistakes as learning opportunities.

4. Memorise the acronym COASTER to intuitively practise the process of facilitation. Challenge people to think by asking questions, clarifying issues and giving constructive feedback. Speak powerfully but infrequently but keep the discussion on track and stick to the agenda. A good facilitator will be able to bring conflict to the surface to defuse it and deal with it effectively. Remember constructive conflict can enhance team performance.

5. Make sure that members have problem solving, social and time management skills. They should have a philosophy of lifelong learning and continuous improvement.

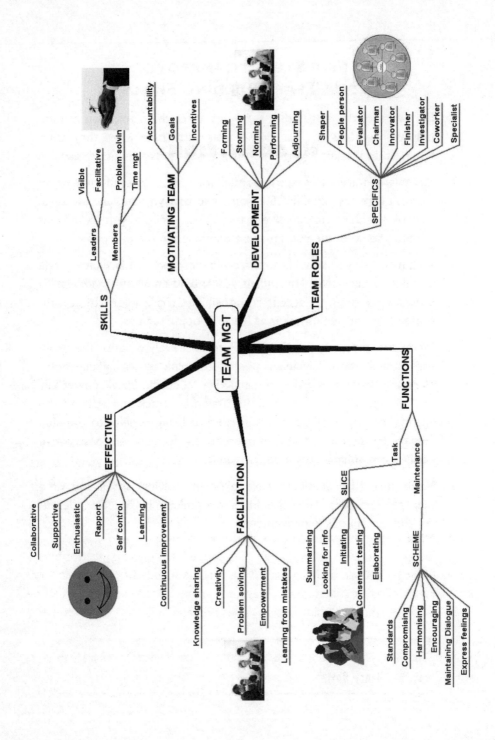

12

NEGOTIATION

- ☑ What are the basic skills of negotiation?

- ☑ What are the negotiation strategies?

- ☑ How can you persuade someone to your viewpoint?

- ☑ What are the common mistakes of negotiation?

- ☑ How can you make a compelling case?

INTRODUCTION

The basic skills of negotiation can be recalled by the acronym POCKET explained below. There are numerous negotiating strategies that are effective in different situations. These are referred to as salami, limited authority, withdrawal, pretence, deadlines, good guy–bad guy, standard contract and fait accompli. Persuasion skills will help convince others to do what you want. A co-operative style is recommended where the aim is to have a win-win solution.

Support your case by relying on precedent, quoting an impartial eminent source or claiming that it has been conceded to others in the past in similar circumstances. There are many mistakes you can make when negotiating including poor preparation and failure to compromise.

"The most important trip you may take in life is meeting people half way." – Henry Boyle

BASIC SKILLS

Negotiating is a process of bargaining by gradually moving from opposing positions closer together. Unless both parties move there is no negotiation. Successful negotiation generally results in a contract. As a manager you will negotiate with other managers, customers, suppliers, employees and trade unions. For example, with suppliers you will negotiate payment terms, quantity, quality, timing, after-sales service and delivery. Even in a private capacity you negotiate with your friends, children and partner. Examples include getting the best deal on a trade-in against a new car, negotiating a pay rise, negotiating with an auctioneer to buy a house, or seeking estimates from builders for an extension to your home. Use the acronym POCKET to recall the basic skills needed to be an effective negotiator:

❖ **P**lan. The purpose is to make a deal, ideally one that is a win-win solution. You must achieve your critical goals and the minimum baseline that you won't go below. Also consider the other party's target and resistance point (i.e. a point that they will not go below). Preparation is the key to success and will lead to better outcomes. Before the meeting practise reverse role-play so that you can get into the other person's shoes and experience where they are coming from. Have a clear view of the outcomes you desire. Now weigh up the strategies you will adopt to achieve your objectives. Consider where the meeting will be held and the seating arrangements. A neutral venue is probably the best as the home advantage is avoided. A round table promotes a non-confrontational atmosphere for negotiating, while a rectangular table encourages an adversarial approach with people sitting on opposite sides. If the negotiations are going to be done by a team, pick the best people for the purpose. People with previous experience as successful negotiators would be an obvious choice. The more attractive you are perceived by the other party the greater your persuasiveness. Attractiveness here includes sense of humour, friendliness, appearance, dress, attentiveness, sensitivity and competence.

❖ **O**pening position. Before you begin make sure the other party has the necessary authority to conclude the negotiations as otherwise you can waste a lot of time. Know your own needs and what you want to achieve. Categorise your goals into "must haves" and "desirables". The "must haves" are items that you consider critical to the negotiation. Failure to agree on these would mean the negotiations would fail. It might be useful to classify the "desirables" into strong and weak. The weak are the ones you would concede first. Be aware of your own and others' perceptions. Avoid partisan or biased viewpoints and see others as your equal. Identify differences between your point of view and the other party's point of view. Try to bridge the gap by identifying common ground. Create a positive climate and promote feelings of goodwill. Establish the facts but read between the lines by studying body language and innuendo. Never go into a negotiation without knowing what your BATNA (**b**est **a**lternative **t**o **n**egotiated **a**greement) is. You are then in a position to compare the deal made with the BATNA. Also know the other party's BATNA.

"You and I have a conflict of needs. I respect your needs, but I must respect my own, too. I will not use my power over you so I win and you lose, but I cannot give in and let you win at the expense of my losing. So, let's agree to search together for a solution that would satisfy your needs and satisfy mine, so no one loses." — Thomas Gordon

---

❖ **C**ommunicate. Use your powers of persuasion and be assertive as appropriate. Speak using clear, constructive and logical language. Listen attentively. Use the technique of reflective listening such as "you feel that ..." This will help avoid confrontation while at the same time giving you an opportunity to find out what the other party thinks. Use silence as necessary to encourage the other person to speak or continue speaking as silence creates a vacuum encouraging the other person to fill it. Flag or signpost what you are about to say next. Ask and you shall receive. It is surprising what people will tell you when they are encouraged to do so and you take an interest in them. Self-disclosure on your part is likely to be reciprocated. Respect confidential information. Avoid emotive language and insults by always maintaining your composure.

❖ **K**now your opponent. Information is your greatest weapon and so forewarned is forearmed. Find out as much as you can about the other party and what they want from the negotiations. Confirm what their goals are and try to address their problems and concerns. Identify trade-offs, make concessions and seek a compromise. Bargaining is all about trading concessions. You offer something to get something in return. A win-win deal will be perceived as fair.

"Never forget the power of silence, that massively disconcerting pause which goes on and on and may at last induce an opponent to babble and backtrack nervously." — Lance Morrow

---

❖ **E**xplore options by asking "what if" questions to find out what the other party would settle for. The more options considered, the more likely that a win-win solution will result. Win-win solutions are arrived at through asking questions, considering alternatives and problem solving. They require openness, imagination, trust and goodwill. Most deals are driven by a 50 per cent emotional need, and a 50 per cent economic need. So be sensitive to the emotional needs of the other party. To address the economic needs only promise what you can deliver.

❖ **T**erminate or conclude the deal. Proposals have been made and concessions given by both sides. The deal is concluded when the option satisfying both parties is selected. Celebrate agreement with a smile and a handshake, with the deal confirmed in writing to avoid misunderstandings. Copies of the agreements should be circulated to all interested parties. Relationships are maintained when both parties stand by their agreement and this is more likely if the agreement is in writing. Carry out a post-mortem to see which tactics worked and which didn't. Reflect and learn from your experience.

The model of conflict management discussed in Chapter 4 can also be used in negotiation (see page 82).

NEGOTIATION STRATEGIES

A good negotiator will be familiar with numerous strategies that can be used appropriately:

❖ Salami. This strategy is to divide and conquer. Getting one slice at a time and being patient may mean that eventually you get almost the whole salami. Chunk objectives down into sub-objectives. It is easier and more manageable to agree things by stages than all at once. As each stage is concluded it can be written up and put aside. This will give you a feeling of accomplishment and motivate you forward to achieve more sub-goals. Start with the items where there is little disagreement.

❖ Limited authority. This is a ploy where you pretend that you have to refer back to a higher authority for approval. The strategy may backfire in that the other party may call your bluff and insist that they go to the higher authority. Pre-empt the other party from employing this strategy by enquiring what level of authority they have at the start of the negotiations. If you find they have insufficient authority then you should stop the negotiation.

❖ Withdrawal. This is the sham of taking umbrage at what is being said or what is being offered and then storming out of the negotiations. You may believe that the offer on the table is not reasonable and the withdrawal gives the other party time to reconsider. It may be used as a tactic hoping to get a better offer on return. The success of the ploy depends on one's acting ability and determination to persist.

> "Trades would not take place unless it were advantageous to the parties concerned. Of course, it is better to strike as good a bargain as one's bargaining position permits. The worst outcome is when by overriding greed, no bargain is struck, and a trade that could have been advantageous to both parties, does not come off at all." — Benjamin Franklin

❖ "Flying a kite" to gauge a situation. This might be a ploy to gauge a reaction to a proposal by testing the waters. If the proposal is not agreeable then it can be dropped. It's based on the principle of "you don't know how deep the puddle is until you step in it". Unions usually come in with a high wage demand partly to test the waters and see what reaction they'll get from the employer. Politicians often leak some "confidential information" about a proposed new controversial policy to see what the public reaction is likely to be. If the reaction is favourable they will then pursue the policy. If the reaction is negative they will quietly drop it.

❖ Deadlines. A specific deadline will concentrate minds and energies. However, deadlines themselves are nearly always negotiable. If the other party has set the deadline you can always test it to see if it can be changed. Consider the Belfast Agreement talks where brinkmanship was the name of the game with the deadlines continually being pushed back.

❖ Good guy–bad guy or the hard line versus the soft line. This is often the scene in cop films where two cops are interrogating a suspect. One detective acts the nice guy, while the other acts the tough guy to break down the suspect's resistance. Sometimes the good guy may ask the bad guy to calm down. In negotiations one person may take the soft line and be friendly, approachable and reasonable while the other takes a hard line being difficult and uncompromising. When the hard-liner leaves the room the other person offers a deal that in the circumstances looks comparatively attractive. This may backfire as the person taking the hard line is ignored completely and all the negotiation is done with the person taking the soft line.

❖ Standard contract. A standard contract suggests it can't be changed. Saying this is the norm for the industry implies that everybody accepts it without question and that you should do so also. An employer may make a pay offer claiming it's what has been accepted generally in the industry, while in fact it may be possible to negotiate more favourable conditions. Details of the standard contract can usually be changed and negotiated to accommodate your needs.

❖ Fait accompli. The deed is done and is irreversible. It's like taking your car to the garage to get an estimate for repairs but when you go back to collect your car you find that the job has been done. This may backfire in that you are entitled to insist that they were not authorised to repair the car until after you had seen the estimate and agreed it. However, most people don't bother going to the trouble and just accept it as a fait accompli. Builders have been known to demolish buildings with a preservation order and contrary to planning laws. This is a risky strategy and can go very wrong if the local authority insist on the building being reinstated!

PERSUASION

There are many approaches you can adopt to persuade others to your viewpoint. The following are some of the persuasion techniques commonly used:

❖ Style. There are two basic styles – competitive and co-operative. The competitive style is confrontational, adversarial and aggressive. It assumes the pie for sharing is finite and aims for a win-lose outcome. The co-operative takes an integrative problem-solving approach and aims for an agreed solution. This style assumes the pie for sharing is expanding and aims for a win-win outcome. Back up your arguments with case studies as well as hard evidence and deliver your message in a confident and authoritative way. Seek to be collaborative and build up rapport. For example, when productivity deals are agreed with trade unions both the company and the workers benefit. Productivity increases the wealth of the company for sharing so that everybody gains.

❖ Talking/listening. To persuade someone you need to spend about half the time talking and half listening. In fact, you should give the other party the opportunity to talk more than you. People like the sound of their own voice and are more likely to be persuaded if they are given plenty of opportunity to speak. The aim of a good negotiator is to build a good relationship with the other party.

"Remember not only to say the right thing at the right time in the right place, but far more difficult still, to leave unsaid the wrong thing at the wrong moment." – Benjamin Franklin

---

❖ Get the other person's point of view. Pay attention to what the other party is saying, and try to see the world through their eyes. Stress the benefits of your proposals to meeting their needs by emphasising what's in it for them.

❖ Probing questions. Use probing questions to assess the strengths and weaknesses of the other person's argument. Focus in on their weaknesses to dilute the strength of their arguments. Do this in an unobtrusive and sensitive way, as you do not want to antagonise them. Don't assume that you know what the other party is looking for, as reading minds is counter-productive. Ask them what they want from the negotiation, as knowledge is power to be used with advantage.

❖ Adjournments. These can be used for rest and recreation or to discuss proposals or develop and consider solutions. They can also be used to break a deadlock or to consider new information presented by the other party. Breaks give people time to cool down and reflect on both sides of the argument in a dispassionate fashion. Also, a bit of humour will help the negotiations along.

❖ Win compromise by making concessions. It's better to sell the wool than the sheep. Bargaining is all about give and take and making trade-offs. When people receive they like to reciprocate in return. The ability to bargain is a managerial skill necessary for personal and organisational success. Great negotiators always have a sweetener in reserve to clinch a deal. Putting all "the cards on the table" at an early stage in the negotiations is not a good idea. Trading mutually advantageous concessions is the hallmark of professional negotiation. If appropriate, emphasise the scarcity value of some of the concessions given, as items perceived to be hard to get tend to have more value and appeal.

❖ Summarise in writing what has been agreed in the negotiations. This is a public declaration of commitment that people will feel obliged to honour. It will also consolidate your position to date and prevent the parties from going back over old ground.

"Your ability to negotiate, communicate, influence, and persuade others to do things is absolutely indispensable to everything you accomplish in life. The most effective men and women in every area are those who can quite competently organise the co-operation and assistance of other people toward the accomplishment of important goals and objectives." – Brian Tracey

---

❖ Reaching agreement. Timing is very important and so you will need to gauge that the mood is favourable before you decide to conclude. The posture, gestures and facial expression of the other party should provide clues as to when the right moment for agreement has arrived. When you have agreed, test the understanding of the other party to make sure you are of the same mind. Establish monitoring and review procedures to ensure that the agreement is implemented satisfactorily.

Supporting Your Case

The following are some tips to make your case more compelling.

❖ State explicitly what you want. Don't assume that the other party is a mind reader.

❖ Use precedents, examples or case studies from comparable situations to back up your case.

❖ Support your case with impartial facts researched from an eminent reliable source. Make a clear and explicit conclusion to your argument.

❖ Make the case that it is the industry norm. For example, a trade union may refer to comparable percentage increases obtained by other workers in the same industry that year.

❖ Support your case by demonstrating that it has been conceded to others in a similar situation in the past.

❖ Acknowledge what the other side sees as important.

NEGOTIATION MISTAKES

The following are some of the mistakes that are frequently made when negotiating:

Attitude

❖ Adopting a win-lose attitude. You view negotiation only as getting the best deal for yourself and as a contest to beat the other side. Consequently, you miss opportunities for a mutually beneficial trade-off.

❖ Being too committed to your viewpoint and unable to objectively consider the other's point of view. You are stuck in an entrenched position, without being able to see the possibilities for breakthrough with no give and take or win-win values. As a result, you may win the battle and lose the war. The other party is dissatisfied and will be waiting in ambush to retaliate in the future.

❖ Seeing your own side as more talented and capable than the other. For example, if you see the other side as stubborn, the self-fulfilling prophecy may operate so that the other side lives up to your expectations and behaves in an inflexible and uncooperative fashion.

"The team needs to establish ground rules for the negotiation. Details such as who will lead the negotiation, when the lead will change hands, who will document the negotiation, what processes will be used to develop alternatives.... The team's game plan must be clearly understood by all members." – Zack (1995)

Poor People Skills

❖ Using abusive behaviour. Being confrontational and continually interrupting the other party is not the way to win friends and influence people. Even your body language may show coldness and inadvertent signals of lack of trust, disrespect and hostility. Building good relationships and mutual respect should be your aim.

❖ Not listening to the other person's point of view and finding out exactly what they want. Engaging in a monologue rather than a dialogue.

❖ Failing to build up a trusting relationship. Trust is at the heart of negotiation. If we are suspicious or wary of people we may find it extremely difficult to engage and make agreements with them.

❖ Ignoring the signs of conflict and failing to defuse situations. Don't personalise issues by concentrating on the person's physical appearance or personality rather than their behaviour. Be soft on the person but hard on their behaviour.

❖ Patronising the other person. This is often evident when the other party is a woman or when a specialist is dealing with a non-specialist and is contemptuous of their lack of knowledge.

❖ Using irritators. Irritators are words or phrases used by one side that irritate, annoy or offend the other. Examples include phrases such as "that is an unreasonable demand" or "you are being unhelp-ful". Often people use these without any thought and don't realise the negative effect they have on others.

Planning

❖ Poor preparation. Don't jump into a situation without having all the necessary facts and considering the options available – agree in haste, repent at leisure. Failure to plan is planning to fail and so you should plan the negotiation process.

❖ Lack of clear objectives. You need to know your goals and bottom line, otherwise you may agree to something you don't want. You also need to know the goals of the other party and what their base line is.

❖ You don't anticipate what deadlocks might emerge and therefore have no contingency plans in place to deal with them.

❖ You have poor problem-solving skills and thus don't approach is-sues in a systematic way. You are swept along by a tide of emotion rather than by logic and reason.

❖ Impatience. Negotiations can be a tedious process. Patience, persis-tence, attention to detail and thoroughness in your approach will see you successfully through in the end.

"Always anticipate that the other side will use surprise as a tactic. You will come across as cool and collected no matter what happens." – Jack Pachuta

---

SUMMARY

The basic skills of negotiation can be recalled by the acronym POCKET. There are numerous negotiating strategies that you can use in different situations. These are salami, limited authority, withdrawal, pretence, deadlines, good guy-bad guy, standard contract and fait accompli. Per-suasion skills will help you get others to do what you want. Some of these include creating good relationships, making concessions and sum-marising what has been agreed to date. A co-operative style is recom-mended.

Support your case by relying on precedent, quoting an impartial eminent source or claiming that it has been conceded to others in the past in similar circumstances. There are many mistakes to avoid when negotiating including poor preparation and failure to compromise.

CHECK YOUR PEOPLE SKILLS QUOTIENT – 12

	Circle the appropriate response	
1. The best negotiation philosophy is win-lose	True	False
2. Salami is achieving negotiation goals by stages	True	False
3. A standard contract is the norm for the industry	True	False
4. Deadlines are not negotiable	True	False
5. The competitive style is best for negotiating	True	False
6. You should adjourn to try and break a deadlock	True	False
7. It's okay to become angry when negotiating	True	False
8. Trade-offs are a normal part of bargaining	True	False
9. You can support your case by calling on precedent	True	False
10. Compromising totally satisfies both sides	True	False

Total the number of true and false responses and check Appendix 1 at the back of the book for the answers and to determine your score.

FIVE STEPS TO IMPROVE YOUR NEGOTIATION SKILLS

1. Learn the basic skills of negotiating by memorising and practising the skills and behaviours in the POCKET acronym. This will help you become a more effective negotiator.

2. Chunk the negotiating objectives into sub-objectives and as agreement is reached record them in writing. This will win commitment and save time by preventing you from backtracking.

3. When using a team approach to negotiation have one person take the lead, the second presents the case and the third will observe and take notes.

4. Become familiar with the range of common mistakes people make when negotiating and make sure you do not commit them.

5. When making a case support it with precedent, case studies, reputable sources, accepted industry practice or the fact that it has been conceded in similar circumstances. Explicit signs of planning and preparation impress negotiating parties.

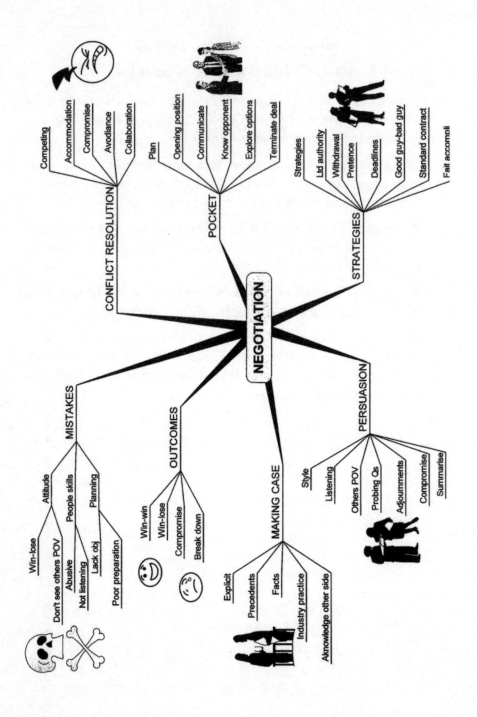

13

MEETINGS

☑ How can you organise an effective meeting?

☑ What are the pitfalls to avoid?

☑ What are the duties of a chairman?

☑ What are the types of meetings?

☑ What are the three elements of a meeting?

INTRODUCTION

A meeting is the coming together of two or more people to transact business. They are useful when a manager wants to make something widely known. The three elements of a meeting are task, maintenance and process. Before the meeting you should plan and prepare an agenda. During the meeting you should start promptly, keep it on track and finish on time. After the meeting you should write up the minutes and circulate the action plans. Some of the pitfalls of meetings include group conformity and allowing talkative people to dominate proceedings. The chairman should ensure that the rules of the meeting are adhered to and give participants an equal chance of contributing.

An effective meeting will have clear objectives and stick to the agenda. The main advantage of a meeting is it facilitates face to face communication. The main drawbacks are that there are opportunity costs involved and it's time-consuming. The key role of participants at a meeting is to come prepared, obey the rules and make a contribution.

TYPES OF MEETINGS

❖ Policy planning. To develop policy and initiate planning with management.

❖ Information giving. If the meeting is just for providing information, however, then this might be done more effectively by communicating in writing.

❖ Information seeking. This is where a manager asks a group of people for their views and opinions. The chairman should give everyone present an equal opportunity to speak. The chairman will summarise the views of those present.

❖ Problem solving and decision making. Put forward proposals for consideration and discussion. The meeting may be requested to make suggestions regarding appropriate decisions.

❖ Brain storming. The purpose of this meeting is to generate as many ideas as possible to solve a particular problem. The best alternatives are considered and the most effective solution determined.

❖ Team briefing. The team leader usually does the team briefing. This could take the form of information giving and receiving and general discussion. Information relayed from higher management and material of specific relevance to the team may be discussed. Team members may raise issues or discuss proposals

---

"Great things are done when men and mountains meet. This is not done by jostling in the street." — William Blake

---

PURPOSES OF MEETINGS

❖ When managers want to announce something to a large group of people. A meeting is an efficient way of disseminating information.

❖ When managers lack expertise and need to get advice and information from a diverse source of people from different departments. When there's a need to pool ideas, knowledge and expertise.

❖ When a proposed decision affects participants, when implementation is important, and the manager wants to gauge their reaction in advance of making the decision; when the decision is complex and needs the expert input of others; when managers want to empower participants through consultation or getting them involved in the decision making process.

❖ To socialise and get to know as many staff as possible. Meetings may be a bonding exercise.

THREE ELEMENTS OF MEETINGS

Task

Doing the task element right means the administration part of the meeting is done effectively and efficiently. This should take up about 85 per cent of the time allowed.

❖ The purpose of the meeting should be clearly stated.

❖ Setting an agenda with time allocations for each item.

❖ Gathering and summarising information during the meeting.

❖ Analysing data and drawing conclusions.

❖ Making decisions based on facts rather than hearsay or opinion.

❖ Sharing views and opinions so that all feel involved and motivated.

❖ Following up to ensure that agreed actions have been satisfactorily carried out.

"The length of a meeting rises with the square of the number of people present." — Eileen Shanahan

---

Maintenance

The benefits of effective maintenance are improved relationships and a better environment in which to hold the meeting. This should take up about 10 per cent of the time allowed. Ineffective maintenance may hinder the task. Most maintenance takes place at the start and end of meetings.

❖ Relationships. Focus on ideas not personalities. Acknowledge your own feelings and the feelings of others.

❖ Individual comfort or how people feel. The room should be suitable for its purpose, well-ventilated and lit, and comfortable chairs with tables should be provided. Everybody should be able to see everybody else. There should be adequate breaks for refreshments, bonding, and to allow people attend to their personal needs.

Process

The benefits of an effective process are greater participation and shorter meetings. This should take up about 5 per cent of the time allowed.

❖ Reflect on how the meeting is going and take corrective action as needed to get it back on track.

❖ Use facilitation skills to encourage discussion and debate.

❖ Get feedback describing rather than judging what is happening.

❖ Control proceedings and make decisions.

❖ Draw shy people in so that everybody gets a chance to contribute.

ORGANISING EFFECTIVE MEETINGS

Before the Meeting

❖ Consider alternatives to a meeting such as video conferencing, phone calls, e-mail or one-to-one discussions. If these are viable options they would be less costly than holding a meeting. Only hold meetings that are absolutely necessary.

❖ Purpose of meeting. The purpose of the meeting should be agreed with the participants. Consider the desired outcomes and again whether these outcomes be achieved by other means. What do you want to achieve? What do you need to discuss? What decisions will need to be taken? Who needs to be there? How long should the meeting be?

❖ Plan the meeting. Visualise in advance what you feel the meeting should be like and the outcome you expect. Research the potential participants so that you know your audience and anticipate their attitudes and the positions they will take. Consider the people that are likely to make a meaningful contribution.

❖ Adequate notice. Proper notice must be given to every person entitled to attend the meeting. Decide the date and time and pick a
place that is convenient for the participants to attend. Only invite
those who are essential for the business of the meeting. These
might be people affected by the problem or those who can contribute to the discussion, experts on the subject or people who are
good at problem solving or generating ideas. Sometimes it might be
a good idea to invite an objective outsider for an impartial view on
matters arising during the meeting.

❖ Prepare an agenda. The agenda should be complete, specific and designed towards achieving the desired outcomes. The purpose of the
meeting should be written clearly at the top of the agenda. Create a
timeframe for each item on the agenda and keep it focused on a few
key issues rather than have numerous items. An agenda allows the
chairman to limit discussion to relevant subjects and control the way
time is spent. The agenda should be circulated along with supporting
documentation to potential participants before the meeting.

❖ Only include relevant items on the agenda. The fewer the better.
Prioritise items in relation to their importance. Decide who will
lead the discussion. Provide background information as appropriate
for items on the agenda.

❖ Book the room and prepare the necessary paperwork. Consider
the layout appropriate for the meeting. You may need a personal
computer and a flipchart or other equipment such as an overhead
projector if you consider visuals necessary. Make sure there are no
obstacles in the view line of participants.

❖ Organise coffee breaks. If you anticipate the meeting is going to be
long, schedule breaks of 15 minutes every two hours. The time span
of attention is about 20 minutes and certainly not more than an
hour.

"The real process of making decisions, of gathering support, of developing opinions, happens before the meeting or after." — Terrence Deal

During the Meeting

❖ Start on time. Show by example that you practise time management. A quorum must be present at the meeting to validate decisions made. This is the minimum number of people that need to be present at a meeting to lawfully transact business. Where an organisation has no rule a majority of those invited must be present. If a quorum is not present, the meeting should be adjourned.

❖ The function of a chairman is to tell participants the purpose of the meeting and set out the ground rules. Voting is usually by show of hands, or where secrecy is needed by ballot. The chairman should demonstrate objectivity, personal control and efficiency at all times.

❖ Encourage open debate by inviting contributions from the floor. The chairman should ask questions to clarify issues and generally keep the debate on focus.

❖ The chairman should reach decisions and periodically summarise what has been agreed. People will try to test limits, upstage others, divert attention, entertain with wisecracks, manipulate and waste time by getting off the point. It is the chairman's job to stay on target and be firm but fair with people who try to dominate proceedings.

❖ Take minutes. These should include the names of those who attended, key points of the meeting, decisions made and action required. It should include the name of the person who makes a motion, the person who seconded it and whether it is carried or defeated. Minutes record what's decided rather than what's said and are not a verbatim record of the proceedings. The mind map technique is very useful for taking preliminary minutes in key point form for completion after the meeting.

❖ When the business on the agenda has been done the chair declares the meeting closed.

"A meeting is a group of people who keep minutes and waste hours."
— Source unknown

After the Meeting

❖ The chairman will write up and fine-tune the minutes. These will be presented at the next meeting for approval by the chair.

❖ The chairman will reflect and review the effectiveness of the meeting and learn from the experience. This will ensure that the same mistakes are not repeated.

❖ They will circulate action minutes showing who is responsible for taking action, what action needs to be taken and when it should be done by.

❖ They will follow up to ensure that everything gets done according to plan and on time.

AVOID MEETING PITFALLS

One of the biggest time wasters in the workplace is the endless stream of meetings, many of them unnecessary. A significant part of a manager's working day is now spent at meetings. There are staff meetings, budget meetings, work-in-progress meetings, appraisal meetings, disciplinary meetings and many others. Make sure your meetings are necessary and productive by avoiding the following pitfalls.

"A meeting is a gathering of people who singly can do nothing, but together can decide that nothing can be done." – Source unknown

---

❖ Group conformity. Meetings may become insular and fail to take the broader view.

❖ Chairman dominates the meeting with own personal agenda. The chair manipulates the meeting, and deals in personalities rather than issues.

❖ Failure to control the meeting. Discussion becomes unfocused and people constantly wander off the topic. The roles of participants at the meeting are not clear.

❖ Interruptions. People are called out from the meeting to attend to urgent tasks or to take telephone calls.

❖ Talkative people are allowed to dominate the meeting. The simplest way to deal with this problem is to limit the speaking time for each person and stick rigidly to it.

❖ Decisions are made based on hearsay and assumptions rather than facts. A systematic problem solving approach, establishing the facts and considering alternatives, leading to solutions is not engaged in.

❖ The goals for the meeting are vague, there is little monitoring of progress and no emphasis on achieving outcomes or results.

❖ The appropriate people are not present or there are too many people present. People who should have been invited but left out of a meeting will feel annoyed. They will have little commitment to any decisions made, and may be offended to the point of working against the decision.

❖ The room is not suitable. It is too large or too small, poorly ventilated and arranged like a classroom. Some people's line of view is blocked.

❖ The agenda is too long and items are not prioritised or limited to a time slot.

❖ Where the boss is the chairman, participants tell the boss what the boss wants to hear rather than the uncomfortable truth.

❖ Poor time management. The meeting doesn't start or finish on time. The chairman waits for latecomers to come before starting the meeting showing a total disregard for the value of other people's time.

❖ The minutes are incomplete or biased.

"Meetings are a symptom of bad organisation. The fewer meetings the better."– Peter F. Drucker

---

PERSONAL ATTRIBUTES OF A GOOD CHAIRMAN

These can be recalled by the acronym DISCARD:

❖ **D**ignity. A good chairman will uphold the position with order and decorum by demonstrating and demanding respect for the office at all times.

❖ **I**mpartiality. A good chairman will be firm but fair and should be above politics, personal animosities and group intrigues when conducting the meeting. They will lose the trust and respect of participants if they are seen to have favourites or shows personal animosity to some participants.

❖ **S**toicism. A good chairman will be calm under pressure, always in control and never lose their temper. Talkative people will try to dominate proceedings and others may continually repeat themselves or get off the point testing the patience of the chair. Controversial matters will engender heated debate. All of these can annoy and irritate. The chairman must exercise self-control and not only control the meeting but also the inappropriate behaviour of participants.

❖ **C**ourtesy. A good chairman maintains harmony and achieves results by being even-tempered, mannerly and friendly. This will help the meeting do its business smoothly and pleasantly.

❖ **A**wareness. The chairman must be able to sense the feeling of the meeting to pick an appropriate time to call a vote. They must know when to cut short pointless repetition of arguments that are illogical, tiresome, unproductive and time-consuming.

❖ **R**espect. The chairman should show respect for the opinions and views of participants. Diplomacy and tact needs to be exercised when curtailing a debate. Few speakers welcome an interruption and may feel they have lost face in front of their colleagues.

❖ **D**ecisiveness. The chairman should exercise problem solving and decision making skills. The chairman should analyse the thinking leading to any decision, and once satisfied that the decision is correct should stick to it.

ESSENTIALS OF A GOOD MEETING

These can be summarised and recalled by the acronym CASTS:

❖ **C**lear objectives.

❖ **A**ppropriate venue

❖ **S**tart promptly and end on time.

❖ **T**imetable (written agenda) should be distributed in advance. The chairman should stick to the agenda and stay on track.

❖ **S**ummary. A summary of the meeting should be sent to participants immediately afterwards. There should be follow up action to ensure that proposed actions have been taken.

Advantages of Meetings

❖ Communicates with many people at the same time and achieves consensus.

❖ Face to face interaction so that you get to know people on a personal basis and develop relationships.

❖ Better decisions because of the synergy effect – the shared skill, knowledge and expertise of the participants.

❖ Problem solving. More heads are better than one leading to better problem solving.

Disadvantages of Meetings

❖ Meetings are time consuming and people at the meeting could have used their time more productively doing something else.

❖ They are a platform for talkative people who just like the sound of their own voice and waste time. Some meetings are out of control with participants talking at cross-purposes and at tangents.

❖ May slow things down. Sometimes meetings are used as a tactical device to slow down or postpone decision-making.

❖ Some meetings take too long. Meetings naturally require more time to consider everybody's point of view and arrive at a decision than the time it would take one person to do so.

❖ Some meetings have no real purpose and the reason for them is not carefully thought through. Meetings are now so prevalent in business that they are a routine part of work life and often called for trivial reasons. Thus meetings may be inefficient, unproductive and inconclusive.

❖ Personality conflicts and fatuous point scoring may hinder the ability of the meeting to come to good decisions.

❖ The participants at the meeting may lack the training, experience, and overall competence to make good decisions.

Meetings are indispensable when you don't want to do anything." — John Kenneth Galbraith

---

Role of Participants

❖ Come prepared. Just like the chairman, participants should do their homework before attending the meeting and consider what their goals are and what they are going to say.

❖ Ask for and give feedback and be prepared to accept constructive criticism.

❖ Maintain good interpersonal relationships by raising difficult subjects diplomatically. Seek different views and look for evidence to support those views.

❖ Build on each other's contributions rather than negatively shooting down other people's opinions and viewpoints.

❖ Actively participate in the business of the meeting by being heard and making their viewpoints known.

❖ Stick to the agenda and the rules and the goals of the meeting.

SUMMARY

Before the meeting you should plan, prepare and circulate an agenda. Meetings are useful when a manager wants to make something widely known. The three elements of a meeting are task, maintenance and process. During the meeting start promptly, finish on time, and in-between encourage debate. After the meeting write up the minutes and circulate action plans. Some of the pitfalls of meetings include allowing interruptions, tolerating talkative people to dominate proceedings, and allowing people to get off the point. The chairman should ensure that the rules of the meeting are adhered to and give participants an equal chance of contributing to the proceedings.

An effective meeting will have clear objectives and stick to the agenda. The main advantage of a meeting is it facilitates face to face communication and better decisions. The main drawbacks are that they may be inefficient, unproductive and inconclusive. The main role of participants at a meeting is to come prepared, obey the rules and make a contribution.

CHECK YOUR PEOPLE SKILLS QUOTIENT – 13

	Circle the appropriate response	
1. Preparation is the key to effective meetings	True	False
2. It's not necessary to prepare an agenda	True	False
3. Before starting you should wait for late comers to arrive	True	False
4. A quorum is the minimum number that must be present to start	True	False
5. Everybody should be invited to attend a meeting	True	False
6. The chair should ensure procedural rules are observed	True	False
7. There is no opportunity cost in running meetings	True	False
8. The participant's role is to come prepared	True	False
9. The task element of meetings takes up half the time	True	False
10. The process element of meetings takes up 5 per cent of the time	True	False

Total the number of true and false responses and check Appendix I at the back of the book for the answers and to determine your score.

FIVE STEPS TO IMPROVE YOUR MEETING SKILLS

1. If it's your first time chairing a meeting attend a course on meeting skills. Before you decide on having a meeting consider if alternatives such as phone calls or emails might do the job just as well. Decide on the purpose, prepare an agenda and give participants adequate notice. Choose an appropriate venue and only invite those people who need to be there.

2. Always start promptly and finish on time. Make sure the procedural rules of the meeting are observed. Encourage open debate by inviting contributions from all those present. Prioritise items on the agenda and stick to the time allocated for each item. Frequently summarise in writing decisions agreed during the meeting.

3. After the meeting fine-tune the minutes and circulate the action minutes. Reflect and review how the meeting went and learn from your mistakes so that you improve the next time. Follow up to ensure that the actions agreed have been done.

4. Avoid the common pitfalls of meetings such as allowing interruptions, letting talkative people dominate proceedings and wander off the topic, and letting the meeting continue beyond the planned time. Make sure the appropriate people are invited and present.

5. Know about the significance of the three elements of a meeting – task, maintenance and process. Even though the maintenance only takes 10 per cent of the time if handled badly it may hinder the task. Similarly, the process, taking up only 5 per cent of the time, if done badly will have a very significant effect on the outcome of the meeting.

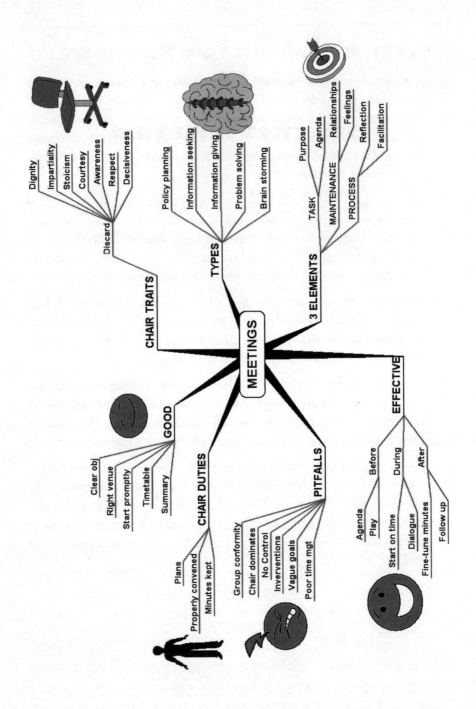

MEETINGS

CHAIR TRAITS
Discard
- Dignity
- Impartiality
- Stoicism
- Courtesy
- Awareness
- Respect
- Decisiveness

TYPES
- Policy planning
- Information seeking
- Information giving
- Problem solving
- Brain storming

3 ELEMENTS
- TASK
  - Purpose
  - Agenda
- MAINTENANCE
  - Relationships
  - Feelings
- PROCESS
  - Reflection
  - Facilitation

GOOD
- Clear obj
- Right venue
- Start promptly
- Timetable
- Summary

CHAIR DUTIES
- Plans
- Properly convened
- Minutes kept

PITFALLS
- Group conformity
- Chair dominates
- No Control
- Inverventions
- Vague goals
- Poor time mgt

EFFECTIVE
- Before
  - Agenda
  - Play
- During
  - Start on time
  - Dialogue
- After
  - Fine-tune minutes
  - Follow up

14

SELECTION INTERVIEW

☑ How can you organise an effective selection interview?

☑ What are the disadvantages of a selection interview?

☑ How do errors of judgement arise?

☑ What are the approaches adopted when interviewing?

☑ What are the skills of good interviewing?

INTRODUCTION

A selection interview is held to assess the suitability of a candidate for a particular job. In addition to interviewing it may involve IQ, aptitude and psychometric testing. Before the interview it's important to prepare a checklist of questions to ask. During the interview you should put the candidate at ease and let the candidate do most of the talking. When closing the interview inform the candidate when they will hear from you. After the interview select the best candidate and make a verbal offer by phone and then confirm it in writing.

There are advantages and disadvantages to selection interviewing. A face to face encounter enables both parties to exchange information, assess each other and build up rapport. Interviews lack validity in predicting on-the-job performance. The main approaches to interviewing are biographical, situational and psychometric. The skills of interviewing include asking questions, listening, building rapport and maintaining control of the interview. Common mistakes of interviewing include talking too much, not identifying the key success factors for the job and relying on hunch rather than objective judgement.

"There are few, if any, jobs in which ability alone is sufficient. Needed, also, are loyalty, sincerity, enthusiasm and team play." — William B. Given, Jr.

Definition

A selection interview is held to assess candidates for a vacant job and to pick the best person for it. The candidate also assesses the company to see if it meets their job and career aspirations. In an interview information is exchanged between the candidate and the interviewers. The selection process may also involve testing such as IQ, aptitude and psychometric. IQ tests verbal, abstract and numerical reasoning. Aptitude tests gauge numerical ability, reading, writing and verbal reasoning. Psychometric tests ascertain personality characteristics. Other tests may include:

❖ Situational. Testing candidates in simulated work situations to see how they would handle a particular task or situation. This may involve dealing with relevant correspondence or completing company forms.

❖ Technical. Testing candidates' technical knowledge, for example, in engineering, finance or computing. If the candidate has a professional qualification it's assumed that this requirement is met.

❖ Graphology. Graphology is the study of the shape, size and style of a person's handwriting. It includes closure of letters, position of words and slope of lines to predict personality characteristics such as attention to detail, persistence, intelligence and so on. Graphology is widely used in France but is treated with suspicion in most other European countries. Its scientific validity has not been established, however it might be useful as a complementary technique with other selection methods.

CONDUCTING EFFECTIVE INTERVIEWS

It's important that the selection is performed thoroughly and accurately and that the right person with the right competencies is picked for the vacant position, as this will save the company future rehiring and retraining costs. It costs money to advertise, review job applicants, interview them and check references. There is also the cost of induction, normally lasting up to six months. All of these costs can be wasted if the new employee does not stay with the company or proves to be unsatisfactory. Conducting effective interviews will be considered under four headings: before, during, closing and after.

Before

❖ Make sure there is an absolute need for the position. Could the job be eliminated or divided up between other jobs? Ideally, a job analysis will have been done defining the job's duties and responsibilities and the key success factors identified.

❖ Allow one hour for each selection interview. If there are more than one interviewer, they should meet in advance to agree roles, common standards, approaches and evaluation criteria.

❖ Study the candidate's CV and look for gaps and inconsistencies in the information provided for probing during the interview.

❖ Study the job specification for the key responsibilities, knowledge, skills, experience and attributions required. Also study the person specification for the type of person needed for the job. A well-written job description gives the necessary information to see what criteria are needed to do the work.

❖ Study the candidate's application form to see how they match up to the job requirements. Then prepare a short list eliminating those who do not meet them.

❖ Prepare a checklist of questions on key issues to ask the candidates. These should be the same for each candidate so that consistency is maintained and comparisons can be made.

❖ Develop an evaluation sheet to assess each candidate against agreed criteria. Some of the areas included are education, job experience, characteristics (appearance, personality, interpersonal relationship and communication skills), technical skills and experience.

"Plenty of men do good work for a spurt and with immediate promotion in mind, but for promotion you want a man in whom good work has become a habit." — Henry L. Doherty

---

During

❖ Define the purpose of the interview and work from notes prepared in advance.

❖ Put candidates at ease. Open the interview with polite small talk, and look for something you have in common to break the ice. Quickly establish a pleasant, relaxed atmosphere to build up rapport and encourage the applicant to talk. Use positive body language such as smiling and encouraging head nods to help the conversation along. Privacy is vital, so take steps to ensure that interruptions such as phone calls and unexpected callers will not happen. Follow the planned structure throughout the interview. For example, ask questions in the proper sequence.

❖ Avoid multiple, closed and leading questions. Multiple questions should be avoided as they create information overload and confuse the listener. Use open questions to encourage the candidate to speak in some detail about their background. Use closed questions when seeking specific information. Don't be afraid to use silence as appropriate to prompt the candidate to elaborate. Use "about" questions, "hypothetical" questions and "reflective" questions. Use the CV and application form as prompts for questions to ask.

❖ Remember the acronym MANIA standing for **M**otivation, **A**cquired qualification and experience, **N**atural aptitudes, **I**nterpersonal relationships, and **A**djustment or disposition. This will remind you of the essential topics to cover during the selection interview.

❖ Appearance, oral communication and self-presentation skills can also be assessed at an interview. In addition, a person's attitudes, personality and work ethic can be gauged. Assess whether or not the candidate is likely to fit in with the culture of the company and the rest of the team.

❖ The body language of a candidate is just as important as what they say. Eye contact, voice inflexion, sincerity, enthusiasm and confidence should be noticed when determining suitability. While most people can tell you what you want to hear, few can hide the nonverbal cues that may belie the words spoken.

❖ Stick to the 30/70 rule, which says that the interviewer should speak 30 per cent of the time and the candidate 70 per cent. Listen for the meaning behind the words. If you don't understand something ask the candidate to clarify the issue to your satisfaction.

❖ If the candidate pauses don't rush in with another question. This is the natural thing to do but should be avoided. Give the candidate plenty of time to think through issues and respond before asking another question.

❖ Springbett (1958) found that interviewers make their decisions during the first few minutes of the interview. "The appearance of the applicant and the application form provide information in the first two or three minutes of the interview which decisively affects the final outcome in 85 per cent of the cases."

❖ Past performance is still the best indicator of future performance. Find out what the candidate has accomplished in the past and the skills and behaviour they have demonstrated in previous jobs. Pay particular attention to how the candidate got on with former supervisors or managers and why they left the previous employment.

Closing

❖ Ask the candidate if have they any additional questions or would like to add something that they didn't get a chance to say.

❖ Inform them when they will hear from you and stick to your word.

❖ Stand up, shake their hand and thank them for attending the interview.

After

❖ Review notes. Prepare a report as soon as possible after the interview to evaluate the candidate and make a recommendation.

❖ Records should be kept giving the reason why the other candidates were unsuitable and held for six months, as they may be needed to protect the company against charges of discrimination.

❖ Select the candidate with the competencies that meet the needs of the job and the organisation. Make a verbal offer by phone and then confirm it in writing.

❖ Check out references. This is essential as some candidates may lie or exaggerate about their qualifications and experience. Former employers may provide information over the phone but are unlikely to give information in writing. Employers have become fearful of potential litigation against them for libel by former employees and so they are extremely careful what they put in writing. Check out qualifications of the candidate chosen with the relevant colleges and professional institutes.

❖ Write promptly to all candidates and tell the unsuccessful ones why they have not been successful in this instance and wish them luck in their future careers.

"In order that people may be happy in their work, these three things are needed: They must be fit for it. They must not do too much of it. And they must have a sense of success in it." – John Ruskin

---

Advantages of Interviews

❖ Enables you to ask questions and compare competencies with job requirements.

❖ Provides an opportunity to build rapport with the candidate. The interviewer can explore the candidate's attitudes, beliefs, values and views to see that they are congruent with the culture of the company.

❖ Gives you the opportunity to describe the job, the organisation and the psychological contract. The employer can use the occasion to create a positive image for the company.

❖ Provides the candidate with an opportunity to ask questions about the job and the company and to find out about the terms of employment.

❖ A face to face encounter is preferred to determine the suitability of the candidate and their preferences for the type of experience they want.

Disadvantages of Interviews

❖ The interviewee's presentation skills may unduly influence the outcome. The candidate may be all style but no substance.

❖ The interview is unreliable as a selection method. It's limited solely to those skills that can be observed at interview. It's difficult to measure the same things for different candidates and to measure on-the-job competencies and predict on-the-job performance and behaviour. It's almost impossible to know whether or not candidates are being truthful.

❖ Relies on interviewer's judgement, intuition and skill rather than scientific criteria. Different interviewers will have different opinions and judgements about the candidate's suitability for the job. There is subjective bias involved. "Gut feeling" may replace objective judgement based on the candidate's strengths and competencies, and may result in hiring mistakes.

❖ The interviewer may lack the skills of interviewing although this can be remedied by appropriate training.

"In a hierarchy every employee tends to rise to his level of incompetence. Work is accomplished by those employees who have not yet reached their level of incompetence. Competence, like truth, beauty and contact lenses, is in the eye of the beholder." — Dr. Laurence J. Peter

---

ERRORS DURING INTERVIEWS

Psychologists have discovered the following causes for errors of judgement in interviews (see also bias in relation to Performance Appraisal in Chapter 5):

❖ Halo effect. When you like, admire or respect a person you are normally going to be very well disposed towards them. In standard psychological tests, if the person doing the testing likes the person being tested they are likely to give them higher scores than otherwise. In a selection interview a manager might be influenced by a person who is well dressed, pleasant, attractive, self-confident and enthusiastic, and also mark them up on traits such as honesty, loyalty, courtesy and efficiency even though there is no link between the first set of traits and the second.

❖ The horn effect is the opposite of the halo effect. The presence in an individual of one bad trait, like selfishness, can lower people's opinion of all their other good traits and they may be seen as less honest or intelligent than they really are. In an interview you should not allow the "halo" or "horn" effect to bias your selection.

❖ Contagious bias. This is where the interviewer's bias influences candidate's replies through the use of leading questions. Leading questions try to direct and control the discussion in line with the interviewer's biases and may produce misleading answers. It's important that the interviewer be impartial and objective and avoids the use of such questions.

❖ Stereotyping. Stereotypes are collections of prejudices. We may consider people with a lower class accent to be common and vulgar, and all men to be macho and all women to be emotional. We may believe that women are intellectually inferior to men. We may believe that all red haired people are fiery. Stereotypes can become self-fulfilling prophecies as when we act towards red haired people in a provocative way. Like any category scheme stereotyping can be dangerous and blind us to individual differences. Our view of people may be based as much on our own ignorance, biases and prejudices as on the person's actual behaviour and personality. In a selection interview managers should be aware of the human tendency to stereotype and try to avoid it. Stereotyping can also lead to accusations of sexual and racial discrimination.

❖ Rating scales. Rating scales tend to be unreliable. Different managers using the same rating scales are liable to come up with different results. When rating scales are used for selection interviews there is a tendency for managers to rate candidates as average. For example, if a one–to–five scale is used, one being the worst and five being the best, managers will rate a majority of candidates at three.

❖ Primacy effect. The primacy effect states that you remember better what you do first rather than what came subsequently. Interviews have been shown to be subject to the primacy effect and to the contrast effect. If an intelligent-sounding candidate impresses the manager, they are likely to underestimate the next one interviewed. The effect also works in reverse. When a poor performing candidate is followed by someone above average, the interviewer will think the second candidate is much better than they really are. As a manager be aware of these potential sources of bias and allow for them when making your assessment.

APPROACHES TO SELECTION INTERVIEWS

❖ Biographical. This is the traditional organised and systematic approach to selection interviewing using the CV as the basis to ask questions. It's better to start with the most recent experience and work backwards.

❖ Planned. Using assessment headings as in the acronym MANIA previously covered in this chapter. This ensures that the main criteria such as motivation, aptitudes, qualifications and interpersonal relationship skills are covered during the interview.

❖ Situational. These are tests to gauge the practical experience of the candidate to perform the job offered using hypothetical but typical work-based situations and may test creativity and personal values. Situational tests may be based on critical incidents.

❖ Competency-based. They are the key success factors needed to do a good job as defined by job analysis. The candidate should show evidence of past use of skills, capabilities and aptitudes pertinent to the job on offer. Questions should be structured around these competencies seeking real-life applications of the skills required. The acronym STAR can be used to cover the points: situation or task demanding certain skills and abilities, actions taken to resolve the situation, results whether satisfactory or not, and if not, how can we learn from the experience?

❖ Psychometric. These are standard tests used for large numbers of candidates and may be used to screen candidates for interview. Those with unsuitable personality characteristics are eliminated.

❖ Stress tests. Tests might be used to determine if the candidate has the right personality needed for a stressful job such as an air traffic controller.

❖ Telephone. Telephone interviews can be used for preliminary screening of candidates.

"When you hire people who are smarter than you are, you prove you are smarter than they are." — Richard Grant

---

INTERVIEWING SKILLS

The following are essential interviewing skills:

❖ Rapport. Put the candidate at their ease by the appropriate use of body language such as smiling and encouraging words and nods. This may be a natural or acquired ability.

❖ Listening. Use reflective listening. Encourage the candidate to talk and summarise periodically what has been said.

❖ Control. Use closed questions when necessary to focus on specifics.

❖ Note-taking. Take notes discreetly, for example, to put marks on the evaluation sheet. It is best practice to write up the notes immediately afterwards.

Asking Questions at Interviews

❖ Self-appraisal questions ascertain how they think other people perceive them. Compare this with actual feedback from their manager or supervisor.

❖ Continuum questions. These try to see how they respond to something on a continuum from low to high. For example, finding out to what degree they love or hate information technology.

❖ Open questions are used to encourage the candidate to talk and explore issues. A "yes" or a "no" answer would not be sufficient.

❖ Probing questions are used to explore issues further by getting additional information from the candidate.

❖ Closed questions are used to focus in on particular issues and to get specific information.

❖ Hypothetical questions try to ascertain how candidates would respond to particular work situations that may arise. They are useful to see how a candidate might address a specific problem.

❖ Capability questions seek to find out the skills, competencies and knowledge of the candidate.

❖ Motivational questions are used to find out what motivates people at work.

❖ Reflective. These are playback questions to check that the interviewer's understanding is correct.

❖ Behavioural. Newton et al. (1999) report that behavioural questions produce behavioural reports, or stories. The interviewer asks the applicant to think of, and describe, actions they took in particular situations. These questions require the applicant to describe past actions and prevent them from offering theoretical answers, feelings or opinions.

❖ Avoid multiply, leading, stressful and illegal questions.

You should also refer to Chapter 2 for more discussion on questions used in a different context.

Common Mistakes of Interviewing

These can be recalled by the acronym SCRIPT:

❖ **S**uccess factors. The interviewer fails to identify the key success factors for the job.

❖ **C**ontrol. The interviewer surrenders control of the interview to the candidate by not using the appropriate mix of open and closed questions.

❖ **R**elying on hunch and gut feeling rather than objective judgement. The interviewer allows subjectivity and bias to dominate their approach to the interview.

❖ **I**nterview questions are not planned. A structured interview is the best. There is a lack of follow up using probing questions during the interview.

❖ **P**lanning. The interviewer fails to prepare adequately. An analysis of job function and necessary personality skill profile is not done.

❖ **T**raining. Poor interviewing techniques. The interviewer has undertaken no formal training in interviewing skills.

SUMMARY

A selection interview is held to assess the suitability of a candidate for a particular job. In addition it may involve IQ, aptitude and psychometric testing. Before the interview it's important to prepare thoroughly and to draw up a checklist of questions to ask. Study the CV, application form, job description and job and person specification. During the interview put the candidate at ease and let them do most of the talking. When closing the interview inform the candidate when they will hear from you. After the interview select the best candidate and make a verbal offer by phone and then confirm it in writing. As a matter of courtesy you should inform the unsuccessful candidates of the outcome as soon as possible.

There are advantages and disadvantages to selection interviewing. A face to face encounter enables both parties to exchange information and build up rapport. Interviews lack validity in predicting on-the-job performance. The main approaches to interviewing are biographical, situational and psychometric. The skills of interviewing include asking questions, listening, building rapport and maintaining control of the interview. Common mistakes of interviewing include talking too much, not identifying the key success factors needed for the job and relying on hunch rather than objective judgement.

CHECK YOUR PEOPLE SKILLS QUOTIENT – 14

	Circle the appropriate response	
1. A job description is the same as a person specification	True	False
2. The interviewer should prepare a checklist of questions to ask	True	False
3. IQ tests gauge verbal, abstract and numerical reasoning	True	False
4. Psychometric tests are similar to personality tests	True	False
5. The interviewer should mostly use closed questions	True	False
6. There is no need to check out references and qualifications	True	False
7. Interviews lack predictability regarding job performance	True	False
8. The interviewer should avoid multiply and leading questions	True	False
9. The interviewer should spend 50 per cent of the time talking	True	False
10. A competency-based interview tests knowledge	True	False

Total the number of true and false responses and check Appendix 1 at the back of the book for the answers and to determine your score.

FIVE STEPS TO IMPROVE
YOUR INTERVIEWING SKILLS

1. Attend a course on interviewing skills. Even if you are an experienced interviewer it is surprising how much you will learn on such a course. You will practise good interviewing technique and get feedback on your performance. Some of your bad habits will be brought to your attention.

2. Before the interview analyse the CV for gaps and inconsistencies. Use these as part of your checklist of questions. Compare the CV with the job description and job and person specification. Eliminate those candidates who do not match the requirements for the job. Then prepare a shortlist of people to be called for interview.

3. During the interview put the candidate at ease. Use positive body language such as smiling and encouraging nods. Use a mixture of mostly open and less frequently closed questions. Stick to the 30/70 rule, i.e. you should spend 30 per cent of the time talking while the candidate should spend 70 per cent.

4. After the interview review your notes and select the best candidate. Make a verbal offer by phone and then confirm it in writing. Check that references and qualifications are genuine. Write to the unsuccessful candidates as soon as possible.

5. Avoid the common mistakes of interviewing such as failing to plan, not identifying the key success factors needed for the job, relying on hunch rather than objective judgement and not preparing a checklist of interview questions in advance.

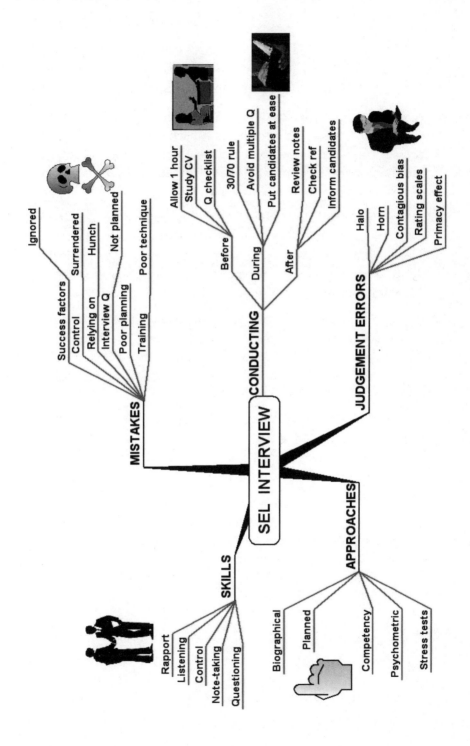

SEL INTERVIEW

MISTAKES

Success factors
- Ignored
- Control — Surrendered
- Relying on — Hunch
- Interview Q
- Poor planning — Not planned
- Training
- Poor technique

CONDUCTING

Before
- Allow 1 hour
- Study CV
- Q checklist

During
- 30/70 rule
- Avoid multiple Q
- Put candidates at ease

After
- Review notes
- Check ref
- Inform candidates

JUDGEMENT ERRORS
- Halo
- Horn
- Contagious bias
- Rating scales
- Primacy effect

SKILLS
- Rapport
- Listening
- Control
- Note-taking
- Questioning

APPROACHES
- Biographical
- Planned
- Competency
- Psychometric
- Stress tests

Appendix

CHECK YOUR PEOPLE SKILLS QUOTIENT

Chapter 1

1. T   2. F   3. T   4. F   5. T   6. T   7. F   8. T   9. T   10. F

Chapter 2

1. T   2. F   3. F   4. F   5. T   6. T   7. T   8. F   9. F   10. T

Chapter 3

1. T   2. F   3. T   4. T   5. F   6. F   7. T   8. F   9. T   10. F

Chapter 4

1. T   2. F   3. T   4. T   5. F   6. T   7. T   8. F   9. F   10. T

Chapter 5

1. T.   2. F   3. T   4. F   5. F   6. T   7. T   8. T   9. T   10. F

Chapter 6

1. F   2. T   3. F   4. T   5. F   6. T   7. F   8. T   9. T   10. T

Chapter 7

1. F   2. F   3. T   4. T   5. T   6. T   7. T   8. F   9. T   10. T

Chapter 8

1. T   2. F   3. T   4. F   5. F   6. T   7. F   8. T   9. T   10. T

1. F 2. T 3. F 4. T 5. T 6. F 7. T 8. F 9. F 10. T

Chapter 10

1. T 2. T 3. F 4. T 5. F 6. T 7. T 8. F 9. T 10. T

Chapter 11

1. T 2. T 3. F 4. F 5. T 6. T 7. F 8. F 9. T 10. F

Chapter 12

1. F 2. T 3. T 4. F 5. F 6. T 7. F 8. T 9. T 10. F

Chapter 13

1. T 2. F 3. F 4. T 5. F 6. T 7. F 8. T 9. F 10. T

Chapter 14

1. F 2. T 3. T 4. T 5. F 6. F 7. T 8. T 9. F 10. F

Give yourself 1 mark for each correct answer. An incorrect answer gets no marks.

140 correct responses	=	100%	Excellent
112 correct responses	=	80%	Very good
84 correct responses	=	60%	Mediocre (needs revision)

An overall score of 90% to 100% is considered excellent. An overall score of 80% to 90% is considered very good. Below this the reader should examine the result for each chapter and revise those chapters where the individual score is below 80%. A score of 60% or lower suggests that the reader needs to revise extensively.

References and Bibliography

Alexandar, Amy (2004). *Greater Baton Rouge Business Report*, March 16, 2004.

Armstrong, Michael (1993). *A Handbook of Personnel Management Practice*, Kogan Page, London.

Belbin, R.M. (1981). *Management Teams: Why They Succeed or Fail*, Butterworth-Heinemann, London.

Blake, R. and Mouton, J. (1962). "The managerial grid", *Advanced Management Office Executive*, 1/9.

Boice, Deborah F. and Kleiner, Brian H. (1997). "Designing effective performance appraisal systems," *Work Study*, Vol. 46, No. 6, pp. 197-201

Buckingham, Marcus (2005). "What Great Managers Do." *Harvard Business Review*. Vol. 83, Issue 3.

Coutu, Diane L. (2004). "Putting Leaders on the Couch." *Harvard Business Review*, Vol. 82, Issue 1.

Crane, J. G. (1991). "Getting the performance you want," *The American Society of Association Executives*, February.

Curtice, Joan (2005). "Want to motivate your employees? Keep your company safe and you will." *Handbook of Business Strategy*, Vol. 6, No. 1, pp. 205-208.

Darling, John R. and Walker, Earl W. (2001). "Effective conflict management: Use of the behavioural style model," *Leadership & Organisational Development Journal*, Vol. 22, No. 5, pp. 230-242.

Fenley, Anthony (1998). "Models, styles and metaphors: Understanding the management of discipline," *Employee Relations*, Vol. 20, No. 4, pp. 349-364.

Galanes, G., Adams, K. and Brilhart, J. (2000). *Communicating in groups: Applications and skills* (4th edition), McGraw-Hill, Boston.

George, J. (1986). "Appraisal in the public sector," *Personnel Management*, May pp. 32-5.

Gibbons, Francis X. and Kleiner, Brian H. (1994). "Factors that Bias Employee Performance Appraisals," *Work Study*, Vol. 43, No. 3, pp. 10-13.

Handy, C. B. (1985). *Understanding Organisations*, 3rd edition, Penguin, London, pp. 327-8.

MacRae, Don (2002). "A Better Person Makes a Better Exec." *Business Week Online*, 3/8/2002.

McGrane, Fodhla & Wilson, John & Cammock, Tommy (2005). "Leading employees in one-to-one dispute resolution," *Leadership & Organisation Development Journal*, Vol. 26, No. 4, pp. 203-279.

Mehrabian, A. (1971). *Silent Messages*, Wadsworth, Belmont, Calfornia.

Moon, P. (1993). *Appraising Your Staff*, Kogan Page, London, p. 7.

Newton, Donald E. and Kleiner, Brian, H. (1999). "How to Hire Employees Effectively," *Management Research News*, Vol. 22, No. 5, pp. 15-20.

Nurse, Lawrence and Devonish, Dwayne (2007). "Grievance management and its links to workplace justice," *Employee Relations*, Vol. 29, No. 1, pp. 89-109.

Phillips, Richard (1995). "Coaching for higher performance." *Executive Development*, Vol. 08, No. 7, pp. 5-7.

Rees, David W. (1997). "The Disciplinary Pyramid and Its Importance", *Industrial and Commercial Training*, Vol. 29, No. 1, pp. 4-9.

Spreier, Scott W., Fontaine, Mary H. and Malloy, Ruth L. (2006). "Leadership Run Amok." *Harvard Business Review*, Vol. 84, Issue 6, pp. 72-82.

Springbett, B. M. (1958). "Factors affecting the final decision in the employment interview," *Canadian Journal of Psychology*, Vol. 45, pp. 393-401.

Thomas, K. W. and Kilman, R. H. (1974) Thomas–Kilman Conflict Mode Instrument, Xicom.

Tuckman, B. (1965). "Development sequence in small groups", *Psychological Bulletin*, LXI I I, (1965), pp. 384-99, 419-27.

Wells, Barron and Spinks, Nelda (1997). "Counselling Employees: An Applied Communication Skill, Career Development International, Vol. 2, No. 2, pp. 93-98

Zack, J. G. (1995). "The Negotiation of Settlements: A Team Sport," *Cost Engineering*, Vol. 38, No. 8, August 1995.

Index